SPEAKING
OF
FOURTH GRADE

ALSO BY INDA SCHAENEN

SPEAKING
OF
FOURTH GRADE

WHAT LISTENING TO KIDS
TELLS US ABOUT SCHOOL
IN AMERICA

INDA SCHAENEN

THE NEW PRESS

NEW YORK
LONDON

Requests for permission to reproduce selections from this book should be mailed to: Permissions Department, The New Press, 120 Wall Street, 31st floor, New York, NY 10005.

Published in the United States by The New Press, New York, 2014
Distributed by Perseus Distribution

LIBRARY OF CONGRESS CATALOGING-IN-PUBLICATION DATA

Schaenen, Inda.
  Speaking of fourth grade : what listening to kids tells us about school in America / Inda Schaenen.
     pages cm
  Includes bibliographical references.
  ISBN 978-1-59558-906-4 (hardback) -- ISBN 978-1-59558-981-1 (e-book) 1. Fourth grade (Education)--Missouri. 2. School children--Missouri--Interviews. I. Title.
  LB15714th .S33 2014
  372.24'209778--dc23

                                        2014003796

The New Press publishes books that promote and enrich public discussion and understanding of the issues vital to our democracy and to a more equitable world. These books are made possible by the enthusiasm of our readers; the support of a committed group of donors, large and small; the collaboration of our many partners in the independent media and the not-for-profit sector; booksellers, who often hand-sell New Press books; librarians; and above all by our authors.

www.thenewpress.com

Book design and composition by Bookbright Media
This book was set in Goudy Oldstyle Std

Printed in the United States of America

10 9 8 7 6 5 4 3 2 1

When the parent or teacher has provided the conditions which stimulate thinking and has taken a sympathetic attitude toward the activities of the learner by entering into a common or conjoint experience, all has been done which a second party can do to instigate learning.

Education is that reconstruction or reorganization of experience which adds to the meaning of experience, and which increases ability to direct the course of subsequent experience.

—*John Dewey, American philosopher and teacher,*
Democracy and Education, *1916*

Sometimes I get bored but I know it's all going to pay off.

—*Lindsay, American fourth grader, metropolitan public school, 2011*

CONTENTS

INTRODUCTION

I spent a year on the road in Missouri to find out what fourth graders say about school. I interviewed ninety-three girls and seventy-three boys from different types of schools—public, charter, independent, Catholic, Protestant, Islamic, and Jewish—located in communities of varying incomes and geographic regions. My face-to-face conversations with students between 2011 and 2012 generated 130 hours of interviews.

You learn a lot when you ask a fourth grader to tell you about a typical day at school. After a minute of informal chitchat while getting settled, I began every interview with the same question: *What's it like here?* Responses to this simple question give you a sense of what children notice, as well as a deep sense of how place shapes experience—children's words and how they are spoken express a social, cultural, and economic landscape, the meaningful context in which they do what they do. As you read the following selections, note the kids' whereabouts.

> I get here and then in about two hours it's lunch and then in about three or two hours it's second recess, and then after that, thirty minutes and it's time to go.
>
> —*Gabriel, white, rural, public school, low income*

You come here and eat breakfast, and then you go to your class and do your morning work, and then in the afternoon you do your work and if you don't do your work, you have to finish your work, in fact if you don't finish your work you have to finish your work during recess and if you don't finish your work during recess, you have to finish it during lunch and that's enough time for you to finish your work, and after that, you go back to the classroom and do science and math and stuff and the reading, like review, and then we do our double dip, our double dip is like finish your work that you didn't have time to do, and then if you have time, you can go outside for an extra recess.

—*Farid, African American, urban, charter school, low income*

So before school starts we go outside and we can play stuff and then the bell rings and then we line up. And then we, like, wait for the classes to come in. And then we go upstairs, get our stuff done. Then we have this thing called the assignment notebook. And you write down all your assignments and your homework and then we do morning prayer on the intercom. And then we do like a subject, mostly English, and then we do, like, math or social studies and then it goes to morning recess and that's, like, ten-fifteen to ten-thirty and then that goes into reading or something and then we go to lunch at twelve. Then after lunch we have a recess. Then if it's Tuesday or Thursday we go to PE. Before lunch some days we go to music on Wednesday and Friday and then PE's on Tuesday/Thursday at one. And two or so is when we do art.

—*Sean, white, urban, Catholic school, middle income*

Typical day I come in, I sign in, they usually have something written on the board and then you don't really have a seating chart so I sit down and if they say, "Read a book or hang out but you can talk quietly," or there's an activity or we gotta go to something extracurricular . . . and then we start our morning classes, well right now the schedule's all messed up because we have Grandparents' Day. And then we had a play, a fifth-grade play on the American Revolution. And then I have classes. My homeroom is social studies and reading, and then we go to PE, which isn't just the bus driver's cousin getting together playing kickball, because it's usually Capture the Cone. Sometimes we do units, like, we did a volleyball unit and then we did a flag football unit, and then we go to lunch, and it's not assigned seating. . . . And then after lunch is recess, which is twenty-five minutes, twenty-five to thirty minutes depending. Then we read aloud for about fifteen minutes, and then we go to math and writing, and then it's specialists which are drama, music, arts. Arts we have trimester in arts, we just finished our drama trimester then we'll go on to our visual art trimester and we'll go to our language art, Latin, our extra language, or French or Spanish, and then occasionally in the middle of your first class, they'll have French and Spanish. You can choose French or Spanish. Most people choose Spanish now because, you know all these explanations, like it originates more to the language than French does and, you know, just there's more demand for it, I don't know, I'm not an expert I'm just a kid [*laughs*]. And then, I take French and I like that, and then after specialists it's come back, oh yeah, I forgot: PM break is in between afternoon classes and specialists, which is a short, ten-minute break, which you can, if you missed homework, I mean if it's big, like a paper, and you need thirty minutes to write it, then you're taking recess and PM break, but if it's just something small like a worksheet they hand out in class . . . and then at the end of the day we come out and they have a big assignment board [*whispers*] do they have it here? [*regular voice*] yes this, so it'll say, you know: spelling packet. . . . I have a planner and we write down and it's designed exactly like this [*pointing to the board*]. Then we fill out our planner, and then I go to aftercare, I sign in at aftercare and then I play soccer.

—*Robert, white, urban, private school, high income*

Gabriel, Farid, Sean, Robert, and 55 million other American kids all go to school, but what they make of school is complicated by who they are, where they are, and what their schools are like. This book confronts these complications. In quantity and quality, Gabriel's 33-word summary says something very different from Robert's 443-word description. The curricular richness of Robert's school stands in stark contrast to the monotony Farid recounts: Farid repeats the word *work* nine times.

Broad categorical differences between public, independent, and charter schools are not state specific; in significant ways, the demographics of Missouri mirror social and economic patterns of the continental United States as a whole. So how *do* children's ideas compare with what older people say and do about schooling? What is consistent with our collective assumptions? What is counterintuitive? What meshes beautifully with findings in sound education research and what indicates that adults running schools are not keeping up with best practices or are misaligned by design? As a person who spends a lot of time in schools, I had reasonable hunches.

WHERE WE ARE

Loud and powerful voices surround, mandate, and evaluate what educators in public schools do—policy makers, journalists, boards of education, families, and those who constitute, educationally speaking, the lay community. The lives of American children are contested fields on which the notions and interests of adults compete over how best to educate, train, nurture, and otherwise acculturate young people. Depending on your ideas, the verbs matter. Whether the national conversation is about phonics, reading, test scores, STEM programming, global competitiveness, having less homework, assigning more homework, school uniforms, minutes of daily recess, gym, art, music, or the effect of grades and rewards on learning, at stake are adult values, adult desires, adult needs, and adult power.

At the same time, cutting-edge research in the social and hard sciences—including the sociology of schooling, sociology of childhood, critical discourse analysis, cognitive neuroscience, developmental psychology, character education, digital and other open-sourced models of learning, human biology, and more—suggest practices, initiatives, and innovations that would, if brought to scale, make for deeply meaningful learning for all children. Mindful of the sticky and politically loaded assumptions in circulation about what should be happening in schools, this book slips under the relationships among adults in order to listen to the younger people who have to be in schools from eight to three every day. My aim was to infuse what they say into what's being said about them. Specifically, what are kids learning in the context of:

- our federally mandated diptych: No Child Left Behind (unfunded) and Race to the Top (funded);
- the deepening and expanding stake of private business interests in schools and the turn to curricular materials as profit generators;
- ongoing attempts to strip teachers of autonomy and classroom power;
- an aggressive push for English-only schools and classrooms during the most expansive period of immigration since the early twentieth century;
- elaborate forms of surveillance, behavior-management policies, and punishment in some schools, all of which can push children into the criminal justice system;
- standards, measurements, metrics, summative tests, and other bureaucratically driven systems of high-pressure accounting in education;
- increasingly inequitable and regressive distribution of wages and wealth in the United States since the early 1970s.

As should be obvious, these policies and practices have affected students and schools differently. Kids who come from communities of higher social status and greater access to goods and services go to private and public schools that do things quite differently from schools that serve "other people's children," to borrow a phrase from educator and researcher Lisa Delpit. The pedagogical and curricular distinctions among public, charter, and rural schools hundreds of miles apart are likely to be far fewer than those between an elite private and poor public school only a mile from each other.

From the cozy neighborhood parish school to the rigidly controlled charter, the best practices are simply not evident to a degree that matters to enough children. Emphasis on "enough." In education, the lag between research and practice at scale is notorious and unconscionable.

If there were such a lag in medicine or consumer product development . . . well, there never *would* be such a lag in those fields.

WHAT IS SCHOOL?

Schools are institutions designed and controlled by grown people. Any
one school represents only one way that human beings can learn how
to be in the world. Whether they are walked, bused, or carpooled into
school, kids assemble all kinds of theories trying to make sense of what
they're doing and why.

> There's boundaries and stuff in school but at home there's not really
> stuff you can and can't do. Like if you have a computer you have
> to do math games at school or whatever the teacher says you have
> to do, but at home if you have a computer you can do any game
> really. Kids go to school just to prepare them for life ahead of them.
> Some kids say that school is just like a waste of time but in other
> countries, like India and stuff, kids don't even go to school. The girls
> don't go to school. The boys mostly do. They're really lucky if they
> ever move to the U.S.A. 'cause everyone gets school. Well, most
> everyone gets school. But in India not a lot of people do. And other
> countries. And I read in a book that you have to be in eleventh
> grade till you even get a desk. They just worked on the floor. Yeah,
> we studied India last year in third grade.
>
> —*Jessica, white, outer-ring suburb, public school, middle income*

For Jessica, school has boundaries; home does not. School pre-
pares you for life and in the U.S.A., "everyone gets school. Well, most
everyone . . ."

In the last one hundred years the notion of school has ossified into
a set of taken-for-granted assumptions: school is a place that mostly
isolates young people from the work and lives of older people (except
for bus drivers, teachers, administrators, and custodians), sorts them
according to age, ranks them according to achievement, and divides
knowledge into ruled disciplines that make claims about what is
known, what there is to know, and why it's important to know.

There are social, historical, and political reasons for schools evolving this way, for knowledge being carved into disciplines and forced into hierarchies, for people valuing certain kinds of knowing over others. One consequence of schools being this way is that there are those whose temperaments, intellects, and gifts are well suited to school-as-practiced, and those whose temperaments, intellects, and gifts are less adaptive to school. Kids are always both growing as individuals and interacting with other people; temperament and intellect are dynamic and fluid, not embossed at birth. A person might be quite comfortable in school in first grade, for example, but miserable by fifth. Or vice versa. The important thing is that all human beings have an innate interest in learning, possess an ability to learn, and tend to have ideal ways in which they can and do learn. These too may change over time.

So people learn no matter what. Where curriculum has been stripped to computation and regurgitation, kids learn that school is for simpleminded people, and critical thinking happens in nonschool settings. And even where curriculum is rich and challenging, individual temperament can obstruct learning in a classroom setting. One student I know was so bored in a middle school math class, he wound up learning pi to the thirty-fifth digit because he spent forty-two minutes every day staring at the number wrapped as decoration around the ceiling molding. Such students are not failing to learn in school. They are simply not learning what the adults in their school are trying to teach. It should go without saying that an inability of a child to learn in school what we say they are *supposed* to learn signals, in most cases, something wrong with content, something wrong with pedagogy, or something wrong about the way content and pedagogy are integrated.

"Tinkering toward utopia" is what David Tyack and Larry Cuban have called attempts to improve public education. We Americans do like to tinker. And yet, given the ever-evolving heterogeneity of our national community, who today constitutes this tinkering *we*? Who are *our* children? In public and public charter schools, 3.7 million teachers teach 50 million American children between the ages of five and seventeen. Another 5 million children attend private schools. The U.S. Department of Education estimates the number of students will grow to 60 million by 2030. By 2100, the pattern of steady increase is expected to result in a total of 94 million school-age children, reflecting an increase of 42 million from 2000. A visit to the DOE website offers a dizzying and captivating amount of data dutifully collected and analyzed for our benefit. Short-term projections by the National Center for Education Statistics say we'll need roughly 4.2 million teachers by 2021. Anthropologically speaking, that's a lot of child rearers.

Inside these numbers are facts about the cultural and ethnic identities of these teachers and children. Public school teachers in kindergarten through twelfth grade classrooms are mostly white (83 percent) and mostly women (76 percent). Until now, these mostly young, white, female teachers have been teaching mostly white students. Now the ratios are changing. The aggregated numbers of African American, Latino, Asian, and kids of multiracial heritage are rising relative to the number of white children. By 2100, about 64 percent of all American children are expected to be from nonwhite families, reflecting a long-term rise from 35 percent in 2000. Schools of education are responding to demographic change by revising educator preparation programs; coursework and preservice practicums are in transition around the country. Bottom line: the we's are changing and public schools will need to respect increasingly complex student identities.

My own formal education straddled different domains. In elementary school I attended P.S. 6 in New York City. As a consequence of political turmoil in the late 1960s, I was pulled from there after third grade and sent to private school. Following high school, I was an English major at a liberal arts college in New England. Decades later, I studied at a land-grant research university in the Midwest.

Like my path as a student, my role as a teacher has crossed boundaries. In the mid-eighties, I spent time as a substitute teacher in Baltimore City Public Schools while working as a freelance writer. From 2002 to 2008, in addition to writing, I taught in the St. Louis Public Schools, where I worked with students in grades two through five. I've taught high school English in a Catholic all-girls school, and undergraduate and graduate education courses at a public university. In the summer of 2013, I was hired as an instructional coach in the Normandy School District, where I hope to remain. My experience as an itinerant classroom leader dramatizes a truth for all educators: teaching identities can be dynamic and complex, too.

Looking back in time, I am two generations removed from Moses Feldman, a pogrom-fleeing Russian Jew who, upon arriving in Texas, traded in scrap leather, a business that failed, and scrap metal, a business that flourished. A hundred years ago, my great-grandfather figured out that unwanted machines were more valuable than cured animal hide. I am likewise into salvage. When it comes to the way we have organized schools, we have to figure out what's scrap, what's worth saving, and what might be transformed into something better.

* * *

This book illuminates what scholars call "the hidden curriculum." The hidden curriculum refers to the lessons conveyed through the processes and products of schooling itself without a single word being spoken. What kinds of *cultural* capital—norms, values, beliefs, and expectations—accrue to which people? The hidden curriculum is never formally assessed. So how can we listen in a way that hears what children have learned tacitly? I suspect that Jessica has learned to feel grateful for school—in contrast to her friend who says it's a waste of time—because she has "learned" that girls in India don't get to go to school at all, boys don't get desks until eleventh grade, and kids from India are lucky to move to the United States. At this moment, Jessica believes that life in the United States is better than life in India. That is a value judgment she has learned tacitly in school.

In 1983, Shirley Brice Heath wrote about how children from different social groups in the Piedmont Carolinas acquired language in their homes and communities. Her foundational book, *Ways with Words*, described how these practices related to what was happening in school. Thirty years later, teachers are still chastising students for speaking something called broken English, as if the ways children tell stories, express love, and get things to happen in the world were something that could break. From a different perspective, Jonathan Kozol has written about schoolchildren's lives. What he calls an apartheid system of education permits the children of wealthy, mostly white families to receive one kind of schooling, and the children of poor, mostly African American families, a worse and separate kind of schooling. Far less studied is what's happening in our exurban regions of sprawl, in rural communities, and in schools where there is a cultural or ethnic mismatch between teachers and the students in their classrooms. In general, as sociologist Sean Reardon has written, kids from wealthy families have better grades, score higher on standardized tests, participate in more extracurricular activities, assume more leadership in school government, and have higher rates of college enrollment and completion than do kids from poor and middle-class families. Of course, high-pressured academic environments like these have their own problems: a lively trade in brain-boosting pharmaceuticals like Adderall, as well as widespread cheating, depressing cynicism, and grade grubbing indicate that all is not well among the elite, either. Writing forty years ago, Jonathan Kozol termed what these kids get from school "the desensitizing education of the victimizer."

Linda Darling-Hammond, an education scholar and activist who was appointed to the U.S. Department of Education's Equity and Excellence Commission, has called for reforms designed to support educational quality and equality of opportunity for all students. Many policy makers are trying to steer the country toward the goals Darling-Hammond has described: protections of civil rights in education; intelligent, reciprocal, and transparent accountability systems; adequate resource distribution; strong professional standards; federally funded grants and awards to support meaningful innovation; and schools organized for student and teacher learning. Were these goals met, we would see an end to what Darling-Hammond has called "educational redlining," a circumstance in which a child's education is a function of social and demographic factors beyond her control.

For decades, researchers and practitioners have been proposing humanist transformations in education. Kris Gutiérrez, Deborah Meier, Michael Cole, Gloria Ladson-Billings, Henry Giroux, Peter McLaren, Carol Lee, Elaine Richardson, and so many others inspire multiple ways forward. But any and all ways forward have to respond to kids where they are. Anyone who understands what learning means understands that learning happens in social and psychological places impossible to monitor from a distance. This book represents what children say when they're three feet away.

***

I selected fourth grade for this project for several reasons. First, as a writing teacher in an urban public school, I spent three years with the same group of children through their second-, third-, and fourth-grade years. Those years enabled me to see individual and group development in a nontraditional classroom setting. Second, many fourth-grade children are capable of expressing complex abstract thoughts in words. Some can even induce general theories from personal observations. Susan, whom I interviewed for this study, said:

> Even though we're a little bit older it still doesn't mean that we can take certain things. And that just because we're a little bit older we can do higher stuff, because there are some kids, kind of like me—I'm really, really good with some things, but I'm also really bad at other things. And so you can't do perfect, but I always try my best and sometimes my parent—my mom, just pushes me a little bit too much, and it gets me really, really upset because it's just like, sometimes I just want to scream at her, "I'm not perfect, Mother!" And that gets me really, really upset. Also, I have ADD which is Attention Disorder. Sometimes I really can't pay attention. That makes it harder for me to do certain stuff. There's a special pill that I take. It doesn't make me feel any different, and I kind of feel the same every single day, but yeah, it makes a difference and it helps me concentrate better on what I'm doing, or it helps me go to the teacher for a long period of time, but at night it wears down by eight o'clock maybe? Six, seven, five, it starts wearing down and that's when I get really, really cranky and it's kind of harder for me to pay attention to my mom or dad if they're trying to help me on something. I don't take it on the weekend. I can still concentrate because my body has gotten used to it, and it acts as if I have taken it. But I still need to take it every single day. It would be better if I took it on the weekends, but I mostly do not.
>
> —Susan, Jewish, suburban, middle income

Susan begins with a general statement, then supports and develops her idea with concrete examples. This rhetorical move represents a huge leap. Younger children are more likely to represent and store experience in action and image. Beginning around seven, children will use oral language (in addition to action and image) to think abstractly. And by the time they are classified into a social group we call fourth graders, children in the United States can range from highly literal (action- and image-based thinkers) to remarkably capable of comprehending and speaking in abstractions. By nine, most children are capable of reading and writing. Cognitively able to assemble concepts into clumps of similar concepts, they can compare and contrast. At least, that's what we expect. Most of the children I interviewed were capable of abstract reasoning to some extent; developmentally, a few were either extremely literal or extremely likely to generalize.

A third reason I focused on fourth grade is because American children are by then generally expected to have developed an ability to identify and comprehend multiple genres of printed text. The Common Core State Standards for fourth grade expect that students will:

> Explain major differences between poems, drama, and prose, and refer to the structural elements of poems (e.g., verse, rhythm, meter) and drama (e.g., casts of characters, settings, descriptions, dialogue, stage directions) when writing or speaking about a text. By the end of year, read and comprehend informational texts, including history/social studies, science, and technical texts. Interpret information presented visually, orally, or quantitatively (e.g., in charts, graphs, diagrams, time lines, animations, or interactive elements on Web pages) and explain how the information contributes to an understanding of the text in which it appears.

Missouri has shifted to the Common Core, but we have not yet created or adopted a testing instrument aligned to these standards. As of this writing, we still test to the less rigorous Show-Me standards, which date from 1996. In any case, most Missouri fourth graders do not meet even these standards. Only 34 percent of our state's fourth graders were designated as proficient readers in 2011, roughly the same fraction as the national percentage, according to the Annie E. Casey Foundation. If students have not sufficiently, adequately, or meaningfully mastered school-based literacy practices by the age of ten, policy makers fear that they will not reach their full potential all across the curriculum, not merely in language arts.

Finally, I chose fourth grade because of its political edge. Fourth grade marks the moment when kids begin to churn out data—through the medium of high-stakes tests—taken up by the people who make and enforce education policy. Education scholars Richard Allington and Peter Johnston write:

> Fourth grade achievement has been a popular political target perhaps because the national achievement assessments and state-by-state comparisons begin in fourth grade. Thus we see state policies such as the "fourth grade guarantee"— all fourth graders required to attain a specified level of reading proficiency on some new state-sponsored assessment to be promoted to the fifth grade. Considerable media attention is devoted to publicly ranking schools based on fourth grade assessment results. Some states even reward teachers whose students perform well on chosen assessments, increasing the stakes considerably.[*]

When children are in fourth grade, the state begins to pay attention.

Teachers have been paying attention all along. Learning happens in and through personal relationships, in particular places at particular times. Our most important and lasting learning is frequently messy, confusing, complicated, and difficult to assess. The seeds of learning sprout in the soil of failure. As a teacher, I often feel I am making progress when I am not; and I think I am failing when something big is happening that I cannot see or later account for. Motivation to learn can take time to locate and ignite. People learn in highly individual ways for highly specific purposes. And yet, any adult who set out to design a complex place that embraced the value of failure would probably not be given millions of dollars by hedge-fund billionaires eager to dabble in education.

*Richard Allington and Peter Johnston, *Reading to Learn: Lessons from Exemplary Fourth-Grade Classrooms* (New York: The Guilford Press, 2002), 15.

***

This project was inspired by specific methodologic and philosophic traditions. In method, it springs from Studs Terkel's oral histories and aspires to be an interpretive collage of personal testimonies about school—a collection of impressions indexed by independent variables of place. Philosophically, I positioned the children not as whistle-blowers but as perceivers. Through abstract and concrete questions, I was essentially seeking phenomenological insight into the nature of a student's experience from the student's perspective. Irving Seidman's careful methods of interviewing helped me learn how to listen to children describe complex activities.

Children play a strange role in the context of schooling: while older people are forever claiming to be serving children's best interests, children themselves have, for the most part, very little authority or power with regard to the structures of school writ large. In this sense, as scholar Jeff Frank writes, "If we can see that others might be better able to speak the truth of our shared experience than we are, then we are in a better position to start doing the difficult work of learning what is true, even if this means coming to terms with the privileged-induced vision we use to filter experience through."*

This book explicitly privileges children's insights and children's truths. I do this so that those of us with power and authority cannot pretend that we do not see or hear the disturbing effects of our current systems. Any adjustments we make ought to be made with children's voices in our ears.

I am also aligned with scholars who have understood and explained education as entailing much more than what is said and done by teachers, including Bensen Snyder, Joel Spring, Michael Apple, bell hooks, and Mary Ann Dzuback. As a writer working closely with words about and in education, I have relied heavily on the support and know-how of Jane Zeni, Rebecca Rogers, and Wendy Saul. Cherishing this great tradition of strong voices, it is my hope that, as

*Jeff Frank, "Mitigating Against Epistemic Injustice in Educational Research," *Educational Researcher* 42, no. 7 (2013), 363–370.

a nation, we might lower our adult voices to a whisper, if only for a moment.

The model of inquiry and interpretation I present in these pages constructs a window into classrooms and student development that is far cheaper to construct than the metrics-driven, increasingly unreliable and invalid high-stakes borehole we have drilled into schools for the last century. In Missouri we spend about $8.4 million to administer, score, and report test results. And for what? As Alfie Kohn has written, standardized tests measure the least important knowledge. Yet plenty of people still do care about the most important knowledge. Any ethical humanist with ethnographic skills could do what I did in forty-nine other states or fan out more thickly right here in Missouri—anyone, that is, who is truly interested in understanding what kids think and feel about what's actually going on *as a step toward* designing richer, denser, more meaningful learning environments. Classroom teachers interested in student engagement and improved pedagogy could do this, too. Whether our unit of analysis is a child, a class, a grade level, a school, a district, a state, or a nation, meaningful assessment of teaching and learning must account for the complex qualities of student perceptions and experience. Careful conversations can help get us there.

STRUCTURE

I begin each chapter with a 360-degree view of its topic. Within each chapter I have organized the children's responses into themes. Within each theme, I have organized their voices by geographic region—urban, metropolitan, suburban, outer-ring suburban, small city, and rural. Before and after the direct quotations, I sometimes interlace my interpretations. Other times I leave the kids' words alone, the better for a reader to see and hear clearly whose children are saying what where. Within interview excerpts, my own voice appears in italics.

Across nearly all social indicators—health, mortality, teen birth rate, education, graduation rates, income, broadband access, and housing—as is true in the United States as a whole, Missourians living in the south, and southeast corner specifically, are significantly worse off than those in the northern half of the state. Missouri and U.S. southerners generally are more highly dependent on Social Security, Medicare, Medicaid, veterans' benefits, or some other form of federal support. Many are also convinced that what they call big government is their enemy.

Communities with wealth and well-being are most highly concentrated in the major metropolitan regions of St. Louis and Kansas City. Thirty-seven percent of Missourians live in rural counties. In general, pushing against a mainstream tendency to ignore the places unseen and unvisited by those with the power to come and go wherever they want, I wanted rural voices heard loud and clear. In addition to region, I have linked every child to a school type and, when germane, and to the best of my ability, an economic status. I have also marked racial and ethnic identity, something I'll elaborate on in the next section. Readers who would like to begin with a more detailed description of Missouri are invited to read appendix A before plunging into chapter 1.

Chapter 1 begins with the big picture: Why do kids go to school, anyway? This isn't as obvious or dumb a question as you might imagine. If you think about how you would answer, think about what school was like for you, and then think about what your own kid is up to all day every day, you will see that this question is the only place to begin. Everyone's got ideas about the meaning and purpose of school. People in schools are responding to the force of these ideas at all times. Social and political pressures on principals, teachers, and students shape personal decisions. Inside schools under pressure, what are the relationships among teachers, curriculum, and students? What is the relationship between what is supposed to happen and what *is* happening? Beyond the classroom, how do schools fit into communities? Given all of these questions, what do kids think school is for?

Chapters 2 through 5 are about teachers and curriculum—what's getting done and how it's getting done. Chapter 2 considers what teachers are like. Educational entrepreneurs such as the people behind Teach for America, KIPP, StudentsFirst, and other "turnaround models" premise initiatives on ideas about how much teachers matter to kids. Schools of education are under scrutiny precisely because of a concern with the quality of teachers they send into classrooms.

Articles in mainstream journals and reports across the political spectrum (*Slate*, the *New York Times*, the *Atlantic*, the *Hechinger Report*, the Hoover Institution, and *Mother Jones*) suggest that if we just get the right components on the teacher-making assembly line, a good teacher would pop out at the end like a shiny new Prius: "Building a Better Teacher," an actual title of an article, is one case in point. One of the more serious and legitimate questions we ought to be asking is this: how should content mastery relate to pedagogical know-how? In other words, how are teachers negotiating the balance between teaching math, history, PE, biology, and so on, and teaching kids? And so I asked children: "How would you describe a good teacher?" and listened closely to their talk about teachers in general.

Chapter 3 is about words and how we inscribe and interpret them: literacy content and instruction. Reading is a complex social activity that involves making meaning out of words, images, diagrams, graphs, charts, numbers, abbreviations, and many other forms of inscribed symbol systems. As a content area, English language arts is the lifeblood of the entire curriculum—it is the vital medium for all school-based instruction. Beyond books alone, the technology of reading includes digital formats and platforms; text appears on pages, on screens, in spaces private and public. People in two or more different parts of the world can simultaneously read and compose shared virtual texts. So how are kids talking and thinking about reading? What are they reading and why? And how did commercial, digital interventions and materials such as those produced by Renaissance Learning get into so many classrooms?

Chapter 4 is about learning how the world works: science, technology, engineering, and math. The people who are children today will be making do with highly unstable fossil fuel resources in a far less predictable climate. Given our urgent need to respond to the real world with wisdom and prudence, as well as competence in the hard sciences, we need all interested hands on deck with conceptual clarity regarding how the world works. How do children today talk about math and science? Who's learning how to conduct inquiry and who's learning how to feed back answers that are already known?

Chapter 5 explores how we obtain trustworthy accounts of what students have learned. As things are now, a handful of crucial tests determine the academic track and project an educational future for most young Americans. What are the real effects of high-stakes tests on kids? Scholars continue to marshal evidence that when it comes to school achievement as measured by grades and test scores, the gap between kids from rich families and every other kid has widened and is projected to widen further. Colleges say that grades are far better indicators of postsecondary success than are standardized test scores. This chapter looks at how children experience the standardized tests they take. Whose children take which tests, how are they prepared, and what does our testing policy do to day-to-day curriculum? How do children speak about the testing that outsiders (not teachers) subject them to?

Chapter 6 shows how kids experience being with other kids in school. Children's friendships can provide companionship, intimacy, and affection. Learning among peers is probably the most salient feature of schools throughout all time and all over the world. What do children have to say about how they relate to other kids? What does social life in school entail? What are the patterns in talk about friendship?

Finally, chapter 7 zeros in on the primary subject and object of education: student identity and transformation. We tell ourselves that we want students to be critical thinkers, innovative, "good in a fix," collaborative, competitive, high-achieving members of a global citizenry. And yet most children—certainly those from low-income, rural, inner-city, and even struggling middle-class families—perceive that being a good student means that you are the opposite kind of person: compliant, obedient, rule following, silent; an answerer of other people's questions, ready to perform to standards and benchmarks imposed by others; a good test taker. How and when students choose to comply with or resist adult regulation is complicated. What are some of the relationships between school culture and individual student identity vis-à-vis compliance, critical thinking, and student agency? What really makes a good student and what can we do in schools to help nurture more of them?

By way of synthesis, chapter 8 brings the themes and claims from each chapter into one place. In any given school, some aspects of schooling are all right. Other aspects are not all right. How might the voices of children factor into the transformation of schooling where processes need to be transformed? Knowing all of this, how might teachers, researchers, and communities tinker with the integration of schooling, teacher preparation, student identity, and families so that formal education is an equitable experience for all children and not just a relative few? Allied squarely with the classroom teacher, I close this chapter with a few suggested instructional practices, drawn directly from my findings, for those interested in turbocharging student agency and critical thinking.

For readers interested in the path I followed in the design of this project, appendix A fleshes out Missouri's social and historical context and describes my research procedures. Appendix B provides the questions I posed.

IDENTIFYING AND DESCRIBING PEOPLE

All names, including school names, are pseudonyms. The children represented in these pages are Asian, African American, Latino, and white. They are Christian, Muslim, and Jewish. Many come from other countries and have added "American" to whatever their nation of origin happened to be. But how we describe people is a loaded subject. Who gets marked with a label and who doesn't? People who are white tend *not* to call out the racial identity of other whites. People who are white tend to positively mark all nonwhites with adjectives and capital letters. In other words, when white people say, "That guy over there let me borrow his coat," other white people assume that the coat-loaner is white. But if the guy with the coat is African American, most white people will say, "That black guy over there lent me his coat," calling out his skin color. This system only works when a person is in the majority.

My fourth-grade students who are African American followed a different custom. When they talked to me about a white person in a book or TV show, they would say, "There was this white dude and he was trying to find his friend who . . ." Skin color was a highly salient feature of every single person and did not go without saying no matter what color you were. If it was something you could *see*, you named it, and sometimes you got it wrong. Some of them called me mixed. If a student happened to refer to me as white, she usually added a "no offense, Ms. Schaenen," since calling someone white might be interpreted as an insult. In any case, marking customs hold true for religious identity and affiliation as well. Here in the United States, if we don't mark religion, people tend to assume that the person is some kind of—how shall I put this?—*neutral* mainline Protestant Christian, not evangelical, not Catholic, not fundamentalist, either churchgoing or secular.

I have marked every one of the children here to the best of my ability and insight and with this caveat: when speaking about variations among human beings, I understand race as a social, not biological, construct. Unlike lizards, humans are not classifiable below the level of the species. Like a molecular geneticist, I will never speak of a person being this or that race because there are no such biologic boundaries. We can talk about different ethnic or cultural affiliations, racial discourse, and racism, but superficial variations in skin color are a matter of melanin. If a student self-identifies as black, I have marked her or him as African American; none of the children I interviewed were black and from another country. This all said, there is more diversity in the DNA of *all* these kids than meets my eye.

SPEAKING
OF
FOURTH GRADE

1
WHY DO KIDS GO TO SCHOOL?
"To Warm Us Up to Get to College"

Everyone's got ideas about the meaning and purpose of school. Some aspects of these ideas are compatible; some are at odds. Thomas Jefferson argued that in order to be informed voters, citizens of a democratic republic have to be able to read. But people can learn to read within their first twelve or thirteen years of life and might learn to read anywhere. In the nineteenth century, Horace Mann pushed for the popularization of schooling. The common-school movement aimed to smooth out the differences among people and assimilate the masses into accepting a work ethic affirmed by a white, Protestant mainstream culture. After the Civil War came large-scale industrialization and a population shift from farms to factories, countryside to city. This is why, today, the hardboiled reason young children spend the hours from eight to three in school is that adults spend the day at work. Making the best of things, we can say that good things happen because of compulsory schooling: children make friends and get to learn alongside each other; schools create meaningful work for adults who have learned how to teach kids and want to. In any case, here we are with 99,000 American public schools on which we spent more than half a trillion dollars in 2012–13.

So that's how and why kids got into these buildings. Once they were there, adults had to decide what to do with them. Curriculum theorist

Michael Stephen Schiro has described four ideologies informing how schools are designed.*

In various forms, these ideas extend the work of Elliot Eisner, Herbert Kliebard, Joel Spring, and many others, but urgent talk about education, as Lawrence Cremin wrote in 1966, has been going on since Plato wrote *The Republic*. The distinctions are not necessarily clear-cut, and the ideologies share theoretical roots. Still, each one carries assumptions about what teachers should do, who children are, and what, as students, they are expected to do. Relying on Schiro, I (re)present a cheat sheet (see Figure 1).

One look at this range of ideas and you can see why we're in the fix we're in. At any given moment, someone somewhere is positioning a child as one of these not-exactly-overlapping symbols: intellectual sponge, future employee, blossoming flower, or problem solver. Collectively incapable of sensibly jiggering the ratios at the scale we've been aiming for, we get stuck doing things one way or another. And we have never reached a national consensus about why everybody's children need to remain in monitored custody all day long until they are seventeen or eighteen years old, long after the period when they require adult supervision. So how can we ever agree about anything that follows, like what should be taught and how. Math facts? Rhetoric? Personal hygiene? Cake baking? Lap swimming? Ancient Greek? Shop? Computer programming? Always there are conflicting social and political forces on principals, teachers, and students that shape decisions made in classrooms. Usually one vision reigns. Right now school is all about churning out employees, and the kids know it.

> We're basically learning it to warm us up to get to college, and
> when we get to college, and to get us to be able to get a job, because
> the thing I wanna do when I grow up, it involves lots of math
> and math skills, because I'm gonna become an engineer, so that
> involves lots of math skills, of how to build the car and everything,

---

*See Michael Stephen Schiro, *Curriculum Theory: Conflicting Visions and Enduring Concerns*, 2nd edition (Thousand Oaks, CA: Sage, 2013).

so, school's basically helping you learn to get to the job that you want to do, and like be able to get a good job, also.

—*Oliver, white, rural, public school, middle income*

For a generation, as we did a hundred years ago, we have imagined children as human capital, young future workers who will grow up to

	Scholar/ Academic	Social Efficiency	Learner Centered	Social Reconstruction
What Are Schools For?	To produce people who know what we know and will be able to pass it along.	To produce people to do the work that will need doing when they grow up.	To develop fully realized people who can live and act in the world with meaningful purpose.	To develop people who will care enough and know enough to transform the world into a better place.
Children are . . .	Sponges/ Blank Slates/ Brainiacs	Future Employees	All kinds of different plants and flowers	Problem solvers
Child's Role	Master content.	Learn skills for future jobs.	Blossom, grow, and learn in their own, individual way, construct knowledge for themselves.	Think critically, imagine possibilities for change, analyze, synthesize.
Teacher's Role	Convey known facts, aiming for canonical, disciplinary content mastery.	Transmit skills to prepare future workers.	Create supportive environment for children to unfold developmentally and construct meaning (knowledge) for themselves.	Expose kids to the world, help them identify problems and envision ameliorative transformation.

Figure 1

serve the interests of the marketplace. Vocational guidance during the Progressive Era was all about sorting and slotting in order to match jobs with job doers. Today, all the talk of education as key to our global competitiveness reflects the value we continue to assign to people as "products" of education. Who will do the work that needs doing? What are the best practices to make these kids come out right? How will we channel the humanity of a child in order to fit the job she needs to do? Whose kids are worth investing more in?

For the children of well-to-do people, the people now called "the 1 percent," formal education is a process that tends to expand the possibilities of how they will participate in the world. For the children from families who struggle to cope financially day-to-day, formal education limits rather than expands their possibilities for participation. Just as the parts they will play will vary, so the preparation varies. This all seems rather obvious. But here's what is not so obvious: who gets to say which kids are prepared for which parts? And what does it mean in the lives of children that adults they do not know make those decisions? Or that circumstances beyond their control—the social class they are born into, the education of their parents, the nature of the district they live in, the color of their skin and the language that they speak—have nearly everything to do with the education they experience? For some children, school is one kind of process; for others, it's another. How do schools fit into communities? What does this all mean from the perspective of the children themselves? Why do *they* think they go to school?

Here and there, a fourth grader had no idea why she or he went to school, no idea why she was learning what she was learning in school. These kids responded to this question with a long, long silence or said, simply, "I don't know." From most of the others, I heard one of four main ideas, paraphrased below. Kids go to school and learn what they are learning in order to:

- fill up their brains with knowledge;
- progress to the next grade level, one after another, and on into college;
- take the MAP test—Missouri's annual high-stakes examination;
- and be prepared for a job, which can be a good one, a bad one, or just "a job."

In the sections that follow I share a few examples of responses in each of these categories and interpret what they're all about in relation to the variously understood meaning and purpose of school. We'll end with the responses that blur ideological distinctions.

SCHOOL IS FOR FILLING UP BRAINS

These responses are characterized by a feeling that the only place a person can learn anything is school. These kids may also have a sense that they are progressing from grade to grade, or are getting prepared for jobs, but the implicit idea they most clearly express is that they are empty vessels, blank slates, dry sponges.

METROPOLITAN

If you don't go to school and learn, you will basically have an empty brain.

—*Chynna, African American, public school, middle income*

URBAN

I think kids go to school to learn, because if you really didn't have schools you wouldn't be able to learn, and I wouldn't call you dumb, but you just wouldn't learn, 'cause you need teachers to help you learn and stuff and you need people around you to help you, and guide you and things, 'cause sometimes you, well, most of the times you can't always just use yourself 'cause you don't know everything.

—*Henry, African American, independent school, middle income*

Less cut and dried than Chynna in his understanding, Henry is touchingly correct in his opinion that individuals "don't know everything" and that "you need people around you to help you," but he also believes in school as the necessary setting for learning to take place. The most extreme version of this belief suggests that without school, a person would be utterly helpless in the world.

> I think kids go to school because they need to be taught, like if they don't know they can't even count or anything. If we don't get taught then we wouldn't be in this building, we wouldn't know how to talk, we wouldn't know how to walk or any of that. So I think we need this help to be taught.
>
> —*Brigit, white, Catholic school, middle income*

In reasoning back from a fairly acceptable first principle—kids do need to be taught—through a series of if-then propositions, Brigit winds up with the idea that without school, people *wouldn't know how to walk or any of that*. While I am impressed by Brigit's effort to reason deductively, the logic of her argument is a nice example of a slippery-slope fallacy.

On the other side of town, Marley attends a well-resourced school with great curricular freedom, dedicated teachers, and a highly educated parent body. As you can hear, Marley, like Brigit, credits school for teaching practically everything to everyone.

> I think I go to school to learn about … like 'cause later in life, if I wanna get a good job or money and stuff [*laughs*], or a house, then I hafta be able to read and understand things that I won't, I wouldn't know if I didn't go to school, because that's where almost everyone learns all of their learning.
>
> —*Marley, white, private school, high income*

Peter and Vince (below) have an equally strong belief in the value of school as provider of learning, but focus not on accumulating wonderful knowledge that will fill up their brains and lead to good things, but on what might be called a worst-case scenario: the empty brain.

> If we don't learn, then we'll just become dumb.
> *And then what happens?*

And then, well, we won't know anything. Like, if school was never invented then we wouldn't know how to work any machines. Like we wouldn't know how to work a computer. We wouldn't know a math problem.

—Peter, white, Catholic school, middle income

We are learning things so we'll understand it when we're older. Meaning like if you don't know it in college then you're not going to be so smart and you're not gonna pass every test.

And what's the it?

It's like addition and subtraction, multiplication. It's a lot of things. You go to school so you're not stupid, so you don't have a problem with it in school and you don't get kicked out of school because you don't know it. Kids go to school so they're not stupid in school. So that they're not stupid in life.

—Vince, white, suburban, Catholic school, middle income

Pause a moment to hear Vince's words very clearly: "so . . . you don't get kicked out of school because you don't know it." Vince believes schools are responsible for teaching kids, *and* he feels that if he doesn't "know it" or if he "has a problem with it," he will be kicked out. But if a person doesn't know it, shouldn't they feel that school is exactly the place they need to stay? Isn't school where the adults and kids who *do* know it are? The message Vince hears is this: learn this stuff here in school or get out of school and be stupid among other stupid people who can't stay in school either.

OUTER-RING SUBURBAN

If you didn't go [to school], you'd be like, you wouldn't know anything.

—Kyra, white, Catholic school, fragile middle income

Teachers are trying to make you learn a lot of stuff and make you not say "Oh I have nothing in my head that I learned."

—Anna, white, Protestant school, middle income

If I didn't go to school, I wouldn't know as much as I do right now. And probably I wouldn't be in fourth grade, I'd probably just keep growing and I wouldn't have an education at all.

—*Douglas, African American, public school, middle income*

Kyra, Anna, and Douglas show us that the "school is for filling up brains" concept crosses boundaries of school type as well as region. Like Vince, Janelle and Nuri (below) speak of an "it" that is all the stuff that is going into their brains at school. Janelle says that if people just spent all their time relearning this same *it*, then they would not be able to go to higher levels.

If we're learning, if we relearn it every day then it'd be no help to get more, like, stuff in your brain to go to higher levels.

—*Janelle, white, public school, fragile middle income*

Kids go to school so like they can get knowledge and if you don't go to school, you won't know anything. Like if somebody asks you and they need help with something, and they ask you, you won't know it. So you have to go to school to know the questions and everything so when you're an adult, you can know, you could help anybody with it. So, I think you need it, the full works, so you know, you could help your kids work it out.

—*Nuri, Syrian American, Islamic school, high income*

The interesting thing about Nuri's response is the connection he makes between his own receiving of knowledge and his future role as a carrier of this knowledge forward to others—in the outside world and to his own children. This is a fitting understanding from the perspective of the scholar/academic model. With these assumptions in the mix, kids go to school so they can learn what their parents have learned, which is what they will be expected to teach, or at least reproduce, for their own children one day. In this sense, school is the site where the stuff in the bucket of knowledge gets poured into the next generation; it is *not* the site for altering what goes into the bucket, or questioning the epistemology of the bucket—the existence of a knowledge container. For Nuri, all of this stuff is just "the full works," which he'll need to know for his own kids. Intergenerational family values, particularly for kids whose families did not always have access to formal schooling, also play into how children frame their ideas about the meaning and purpose of school:

> I go to school to learn more, to learn stuff, don't be dumb. Like my dad, my mom's dad, my grampa who died. He always wanted to go to college. He got the money but something happened with it. I forget, but he wanted to go to college. He passed high school, that's amazing for people in Poland in those times where he was.
>
> —*Artur, Polish American, public school, middle income*

RURAL

> It's to get me smart so when I grow up I know what to do.
>
> —*Jane, white, public school, low income*

> It gets you knowledge. And it makes you a lot smarter.
>
> —*Blaze, white, public school, low income*

> Because you wouldn't know anything if you didn't go to school, you wouldn't know how to count, you wouldn't know how to add or anything, so that's why.
>
> —*Harold, mixed ethnicity (white–African American), public school, low income*

I find Jane's response telling given who and where she is. Pale and softspoken, Jane has a babyish, powdery voice. She struggles academically and socially. People bully her at school, make her do things she doesn't want to do; she alluded to trouble at home in a way that made me feel I had to tell her teacher that something didn't feel right and warranted exploration. Jane was the only child who told me that nobody anywhere really "got her" as a person. Jane's hero is God, "'cause He helps you and He made you and He tries to do everything he can for you." Asked about the most important thing she had ever learned, in or out of school, she said, "That it's hard sometimes, and you're alive because of the things that happen and you just have to kinda deal with it if you can't fix it." Still, for Jane, the purpose of school is clear: *it's to get me smart so when I grow up I know what to do.* Jane says she wants to be a veterinarian, a model, and a singer, and her faith that school will get her smart so she can do those things must be heard in the context of the bare-bones schooling she gets.

The empty-vessel idea is compatible with an antiquated notion of knowledge as a "thing," something external and decontextualized that can be transmitted and received with minimal interference or static, the bucket of knowledge getting passed along through time. An indication that children are viewing knowledge this way is their insistence on speaking of "getting it" or "not getting it." As we have heard, this *it* can be anything at all—a skill, a concept—but it is understood as some form of measurable knowledge. The reasons smart teachers go crazy when students whine "but I still don't get it" are, first, there is never zero static; teaching and learning happen in a noisy place characterized by interaction and transaction. Second, education science has shown over and over again that people actively construct new knowledge, hooking what's new onto what's already known. "I don't get it" suggests that students play a passive role with respect to learning. But knowledge is not scooped from a teacher's brain into a student's; kids in the process of learning are engaged in a dynamic interaction alongside a teacher or a more expert peer or guide.

SCHOOL IS FOR PROGRESSING THROUGH GRADES

This group of responses focuses on the way school is sorted into grades through which children move over time. In essence, the perception here is that kids go to school and learn the "it" *because* they went to school last year and learned something and *so* they can be ready to learn what they need to learn in school next year. My sense is that the children who respond like this are those who are still thinking very literally about the world. The concrete connection of schooling with graded progression was made obvious by a fourth grader with autism spectrum disorder. Max attends a private school for kids with ASD:

> I think that us children must learn to get education. So first of
> all, if you do this, you get to go to high school, you get to get good
> college, you get a lot of money, you can buy a car, you can get a job,
> and … then you retire, and then you're old, and then you retire for
> as many years as you can, and then you go back to a job, and then
> you retire again, and then heaven brings you to his world. I gotta
> have education. If you wanna good job, if you wanna get a car, if
> you wanna retire, you gotta go to school first.
>
> —Max, white, private school, middle income

Talk about backwards design! And it's true. If a person wants to retire, they will have to have had a job to retire from. Jobs entail education, and education, Max believes, entails schooling. Understood in the context of what was voiced by many of his peers, Max's drumbeat logic is extreme, but not extraordinary.

URBAN

Daisy goes to an intimate parish school less than a mile from Max's:

> I'm learning what I'm learning because, like, if you're in
> third grade—I mean second grade—you would need to know
> handwriting. But I already know handwriting really good, like
> cursive handwriting. So we don't have, well, we do sometimes
> have handwriting, but I think that what I'm learning now is that,
> because I'm getting older and I need to know a lotta stuff because
> I'm going to be in fifth grade, and then when that's on a worksheet
> or something then I'll know it right away. Like if a kindergartener
> was trying to do my work I don't think they would get it.
>
> —Daisy, white, Catholic school, middle income

> I kinda think we're learning what we're learning right now
> because when you get older you kinda get harder things and more

homework. But since we're kinda in, like, the middle-ish grades, we have, like, hard-easy-medium homework. So she wants us to just learn that for right now instead-a learning the harder stuff.

—Joanna, white, Catholic school, middle income

I think we're learning that so for next year, you can know the stuff they teach you last year because at the beginning of the year that we are in, they're gonna do some stuff that we did in the past year.

—Guadalupe, Mexican American, charter school, low income

I think I'm learning at school so I can get knowledge and when I go to fifth grade I can remember that stuff from fourth grade and finish it. Because if I don't learn it, I might get confused and, like, I'm gonna need too much help and too much attention. The other kids might raise their hands and they might not get that much attention.

—Azra, Bosnian American, public school, low income

Azra's concern with possibly requiring *too much help and too much attention* is troubling. Azra feels that if she is occupying the teacher's time because she is confused, other kids who have their hands raised are not getting sufficient attention. In her mind, a teacher's attention and learning is a zero sum balance. She had better learn and not get confused, because otherwise someone else might not learn. On one hand, I admire Azra's empathy; on the other hand, uh-oh. Like the fill-up-your-brain responses, it suggests that a teacher is like a cook going around the classroom ladling facts into everyone from a pot. Not learning is like spilling your serving, which in effect harms others, because the teacher has to spend time mopping it up and runs out of time to pass out the rest.

OUTER-RING SUBURB

Because it's in the fourth-grade level, and it's just fourth grade.

—Kamar, Moroccan American, Islamic private school,
middle income

Because it's good to know when you get up in the older grades and when you're a grade ahead in math, you have to know what to expect in the next grade so, in sixth-grade math . . .

—*Julie, white, Protestant school, middle income*

Thinking about school as a steady progression from one year to the next can be associated with pleasure. Paolo was the most exuberant, energetic, positively gung-ho participant in this whole project. He loves school, loves learning, and is in his school's gifted program. He speaks German, Spanish, and English. His mom is from South America; the family moved here from abroad a few years ago.

I know that people think "ugh school is boring" but if you think about it my way, I always do chain reactions: if you get good extra education then you get a better job when you're older and a better job means more salary, more salary means more things better for your life and you're not a just poor hobo on the streets. So then it makes me want to go to school.

—*Paolo, German/South American, public school, middle income*

This is an extraordinary example of a child's ability to defer gratification and imagine possibilities for his future. Paolo is foreseeing a possible life as "a poor hobo on the streets" as well as "more things better for your life." He has crafted a mental image of two different chain reactions, one with a good outcome, and one with a bad one. Aiming for the good one keeps him motivated in school. Paolo loves school so much it doesn't seem all that hard to do.

RURAL

Because at fourth grade you have to be at a fourth-grade reading level to pass and if you don't have a fourth-grade reading level, it's a state law that they have to hold you back. If you aren't at a fourth-grade reading level, if even you have all As, they will force you to go back and take that grade over. They will take, you will go over that grade until you are, until you do that. My uncle Miles says if you're stuck in fourth grade until you are sixteen you can drop out.

—Blaze, white, public school, low income

Blaze is a smart, verbal boy whose family are farmers. Compare his notion of school with Paolo's and you begin to get a sense of who's getting what messages about the purpose and meaning of school. Like Vince, who says kids have to learn so "you don't get kicked out of school because you don't know," Blaze understands very clearly that if you don't learn according to their plan, bad things will happen. In Blaze's world, "they force you back" to repeat the year. And the concluding image here provided by Uncle Miles—"you can drop out"—suggests that dropping out is a release from being stuck. Blaze has no intention of doing this, he said later. He also told me that school "makes you a lot smarter." But the way Blaze frames available trajectories tells us how his family imagines resistance to "state law" and the *they* who make all the rules. Eventually, if you're stuck in fourth grade in spite of your As, you can always drop out. We should be asking ourselves what kind of sixteen-year-old person in that situation would not?

SCHOOL IS FOR TEST PREP

High-stakes testing imposes political, economic, social, and real-estate pressure on district superintendents, who transfer the pressure onto principals, who put the squeeze on teachers, whose worries are finally absorbed by kids. Many kids therefore come to think that the very purpose and meaning of school is, strictly speaking, to take the MAP test. This happens to be the Missouri Assessment Program, but every state has one. The children who expressed this idea were primarily from rural schools or urban and metropolitan public and charter schools—the poorest districts in the state. In cities, these are the kids who have the most to lose when schools are shuttered or targeted for "turnaround" on account of low scores.

RURAL

Asked why he's learning what he's leaning, Nathan, who lives in a gorgeous region of southwest Missouri, began to talk about progressing through grades, then diverted to school-as-test-prep:

> So we can be ready for middle school, and maybe we learn a little
> bit extra, because in middle school, if we don't have, like, your
> MAP test up to Proficient, instead of doing PE and music and stuff,
> you spend that time on extra reading and math lessons, but I've
> already got that covered.

> —*Nathan, white, public school, middle income*

According to Nathan, a person can be chugging along, learning what's necessary for his next year in school when—*bam!*—if you haven't got your scores where they need to be, you are pulled out of the noncore classes and drilled on more reading and math. Luckily, like a dutiful employee who's completed his quota, Nathan's "already got that covered." The *that*, in this case, is being Proficient or Advanced in reading and math. Here's another person growing up in rural Missouri:

> I think we're learning this because the MAP test and like 'cause
> when you get to be an adult you needa get these things. And like
> we learned our numbers in kindergarten and that—and that turned
> out to be a big thing.

> —*Carolyn, white, public school, fragile middle income*

Yes, exactly as Carolyn says, numbers do turn out to be a big thing. The best and most important thing about numbers is that they help us understand and communicate qualities and quantities in the world around us. But another big thing about numbers is that they have turned out to be instrumental in how the state and federal government monitors teachers.

METROPOLITAN

Why are you learning what you learn in school?
   To take the MAP test.
And why do you take the MAP test?
   To see how well the teachers teach.

—Maria, Mexican American, bilingual, public school, low income

I do not want to give the impression that these kids and others who responded in similar ways are unhappy. Nathan sighed a lot throughout our interview, and I do think he intuits that school could be a more humane place, more intellectual, more stimulating, more trusting and caring. But Nathan has a safe, economically secure family life. He's mostly OK. At least he's playing the cards he's dealt. The two girls seemed OK, too. Carolyn lives up in the northern center of Missouri, not too far from one of our state prisons. Bright eyed and game, she likes school, does well, has fun. She has friends and says people can "learn everywhere." It's *we* who have to decide if it's all right that young children feel that this is what they are doing when they get off the school bus in the morning—learning in order to score Proficient or Advanced on a test we make them take in April. To me it sounds like factory work.

SCHOOL IS FOR JOB PREPARATION

I would need a whole separate book to share all of the examples of the ways in which kids from all regions and all kinds of schools connected learning and school with jobs. Being ready for jobs. Getting jobs. Doing jobs. The kids spoke of good jobs and bad jobs, and offered their opinions on which was which. Before we get to the responses organized by region, I want to offer a sense of how in all communities, in one way or another, the overwhelming majority of the children I spoke with said something that boiled down to exactly what Kyra says:

They want you to know certain things so you can get a good job. So

I think they go to school, so you get actually a job and be smart so
if you need to figure out something, like you'll know that for a job.

—Kyra, white, outer-ring suburb, Catholic school, fragile middle income

Recall Oliver, whom I introduced at the beginning of this chapter:

School's basically helping you learn to get to the job that you want
to do, and like be able to get a good job, also.

—Oliver, white, rural, public school, middle income

Interestingly, Oliver distinguishes between "the job that you want
to do" and "a good job." In his case, as a person who wants to be an
engineer, these two jobs are likely the same. But we ought to be listening to how children feed back to us the ways they have internalized the
meaning of the phrases "good jobs" and "bad jobs."

I think we learn what we do to build skills for high school and
college and jobs. I think teachers would be probably disappointed
if like they went to a McDonald's and found one of their students
flippin' burgers back there for a career. You know, if you're workin'
there for college it's understandable, but I don't think that's a
career. I think they do that so you'll be successful in life.

—Hunter, white, rural, public, low income

A well-spoken and thoughtful boy, Hunter has not only associated
schooling with job getting, he has also projected his teacher's feelings
into the range of employment outcomes students might achieve.
Concisely, he conjures a scene: a teacher entering a McDonald's and
encountering a student at work there, "for a career." Hunter has un-
apologetically understood the difference between what we mean when
we say good jobs and bad jobs. Lorraine is another thoughtful child
who, like Hunter, reads a great deal for pleasure:

We're learning in school so we're not, so we can be successful in
life and we're not just . . . they want us to succeed and not just be
sitting at home and have a really bad job. A job that like doesn't

pay that much or if you had to work at McDonald's when you
could've, like, learned stuff and went to college and you could've
like majored in something that you wanted to do and it could've
been something that you wanted to do, too. Like if you didn't, if
you got a bad job it probably was one you didn't want. But if it was
one you *did* want, then I guess it's just your choice.

—*Lorraine, white, outer-ring suburb, Catholic school, middle income*

Lorraine is struggling to reconcile the messages in social circulation. By the end of her response, it's almost as if she feels bad to
have lumped all the jobs and people in the world into two categories:
educated people who have good jobs and uneducated people who have
bad ones. A job isn't bad, she reasons, if a person actually likes doing
it—has *chosen* to do it. According to Lorraine, a bad job is only bad
if you didn't want it. But anyone who has read Barbara Ehrenreich's
Nickel and Dimed knows that there are plenty of low-wage workers
who "choose" to do certain jobs but would never mistake this arrange-
ment as optimal, or even a matter of real choice. They would certainly
not call these jobs, even ones they were grateful to get, "good jobs."
Hunter wouldn't.

Some children focus on jobs that will address needs specific to their
own family or community. Malik attends a chaotic urban public school.
He is a lively, respectful kid from a large, loving family. Listen for the
connections among schooling, reading books, good jobs, a fulfilling
future, and his attachment to the people he cares for:

I'm gonna be in college for two years, get my education, be an
engineer for cars, and if anybody in my family car broke down, I
will know how. I think I'm gonna have two jobs. I think I'm gonna
be a firefighter from when I turn forty. I'm gonna be a firefighter
and when I turn forty before I turn twenty, I'm gonna be an
engineer . . . and then when I turn like an old person, no offense,
I'm gonna have to take care of my kids . . . when they turn into
adults. They need me when I get married. We already going to have
a house. It's going to be in Colorado, it's near Utah and California,
it's the Rocky Mountains. I seen the Smoky Mountains, they

were huge, real big, like 8,000 feet, 18,000 feet. I got a book of all monuments. My sister, she bought it with her gift card.

—Malik, African American, urban, public school, low income

Malik's altruism is evidenced in his vocational ambition: he wants to learn to be an engineer in order to repair his family's car and also a firefighter (presumably to save people and property).

On the other side of town, in the same school district, a shy girl in a head scarf says this:

So I could get smart, and learn how to speak English. So I could grow up and get a job. I want to be a surgeon or a doctor.

—Bahar, Iraqi refugee, urban, public school, low income

While there are a lot of jobs out there, and many ways schools might develop the people who will be able to do these jobs, the main piece of the all-important "it" kids are learning in school that bridges them to their future jobs is . . . math. I will return to the math/jobs connection in another chapter, but here's a small sample of this kind of talk.

Like negative numbers and banking, and like temperature, and if you become a weatherperson and you need to know the temperature and it says "negative two" and you don't know what that means, then you can't be a weatherperson.

—Cole, white, outer-ring suburb, Catholic school, middle income

You need to, like, when you have a job, you can use those techniques. When you're in architecture, you will need to do math.

—Troy, white, outer-ring suburb, Protestant school, middle income

So we could get better like if I become an architect, and I needa know how many spaces there are and, like, how long the building needs to be and I needa do some plusses or times or whatever fraction you do, I needa learn it and it helps with your job when you get older.

—Stella, white, Catholic school, middle income

Turning to regional patterns, we can hear who is talking about schooling-for-jobs where.

RURAL

As you listen to the rural public school kids talk about the purpose of school, know that in rural Missouri, the unemployment rate in 2011 was significantly higher than the state rate. In the worst-off rural counties, the rate was around 12 percent compared to 8.6 percent statewide. More than one in four rural children under eighteen were living in poverty, compared to one in five statewide. The urban poverty rate was 18 percent. According to the Missouri Rural Health Biennial Report, where these data are assembled, the worst-off rural county had an extraordinary child poverty rate of 45 percent. In other words, the economic context in which these kids feel that school is for preparing them for jobs is characterized by poverty and joblessness.

Deep in the southeast region of the state, not too far from the Arkansas border, where the economy has taken an extreme toll on family stability, the statewide methamphetamine epidemic is at its worst, and teachers and principals are under excessive pressure to improve student test scores lickety-split or else, Gabriel said this:

> Just to help us get smarter so we'll know what to do like if we get a
> job or something and we have to do something that the boss tells
> us to do, and like just hurry up and do it.

> —*Gabriel, white, rural, public school, low income*

Gabriel is fully expecting to have a boss, and not just any kind of boss, but the whip-cracking kind who will tell him to *just hurry up and do it.* An hour away, Julian and his family—mom, stepdad, and younger siblings—live in what he calls a "nice trailer park."

> So you can get, so when you're older, you have a job, you can get
> a better job than like a cashier or something, so when you go to

high school or college, you learn more, and then you can get like, a bigger, like a better, work at a bank or become a manager at some store or someplace.

—Julian, white, rural, public school, low income

Other rural kids affirm the power of the school-for-jobs message. All of the following children are white, attend public schools, and, with the exception of Nathan, live in families earning low wages.

I think we're learning it so we can get good jobs and help the community. They just go [to school] because if they don't go to school then they're probably not going to get a very good job.

—Gavin, white, rural, public school, low income

Education, like, if you want to have a big career, you have to have, you don't have to be really really smart, but you have ta, you have ta know stuff, you have to know what you've learned, passed all the school years, an' like if you wanna be like a scientist or sumpin, just for example, you have ta work an' you have to learn stuff from school. Part of the education is from school.

—Casey, white, rural, public school, low income

In school you've gotta follow directions, and if you don't do that in the real world then, outside, then you're gonna be not a successful person, not much anyways. You've gotta have knowledge to get a good job and so, like, you're not gonna get the good job if you drop out of school when you're young.

—Nathan, white, rural, public school, middle income

We go to school to learn about more things and to get a better job when you get, when you grow up and at school sometimes, I like . . . this lady came in today about banks, she teached us about banks and if we didn't get jobs we get like candy, like money candy and if you saved twenty dollars and then you made eighty dollars and

you spent like fifteen of it . . . [laughs]. Sometimes some people are
not built for schools, like how they need to act, but some are, but
they need to go to school anyways, because they need to learn and
get a good job. Like, they are just not very good at it. But they need
to keep on trying to do the best at it and hopefully when they get
older, they get a good job and have a good life.

—Frannie, white, rural, public, low income

All teachers are tellin' me stuff I didn't know before. So I'll have
a good job when I'm older. Well, a lot of times you hafta do a lot
of math, like, an' if you're a carpenter or sumpin. I think everyone
should [go to school] because then they'll get a good job and they'll
be smarter.

—Brody, white, rural public, low income

Lots and lots of people say, you can't get a job if you don't go to
college, and you have to know all that stuff to pass and be able
to go to college, and if you don't make good grades, 'cause like in
math, if you wanna be a cashier, you're gonna hafta know how to
count money, and if you wanna be a nurse you're gonna hafta know
how ta read a bunch of papers so you could sign them.

—Kayla, white, rural, public, low income

Hope's parents are in the food business. She has learned to connect
spelling and math with future work:

To like learn stuff and write, to learn how to write and how to
spell. 'Cause whenever we get older and we are able to get a job
or whenever, or gonna get a job, we needa know how to write and
stuff, and we needa know how to spell things, and just, sometimes
like if you're gonna be someone who works at a restaurant, like
a waitress, and you didn't know how to add and subtract and
stuff. . . school is to learn so that when whenever we get older we
can get a job.

—Hope, white, public school, fragile middle income

OUTER-RING SUBURBAN

As you get closer to population centers, the school-for-jobs talk gets a little less vague and a little more evaluative. There's more candid talk about good jobs and bad ones.

> So that you can get a job, like my two brothers have jobs right now. One has a job at Dirt Cheap and one has a job at the Y.
>
> —*Joseph, white, Protestant school, fragile middle income*

> To learn different things. And, and, and so when they grow up, then, then they won't get stuck in their job, and . . . and they would know everything for their job.
>
> —*Adam, white, Protestant school, middle income*

> I think we're learning for the future, because like if you want to get a certain job, like my mom. She's an accountant. You have to learn how to do multiplication, division. You have to learn to do all those numbers, so I think it's to help us get a good job maybe. Like, I have a good future.
>
> —*Jennifer, white, public school, middle income*

> Well, you can get in a good college so you can, like if you want, you can become a doctor if you wanna become a doctor, otherwise if you drop out of high school you'll just become a custodian or a secretary.
>
> —*Neelish, South Asian–Ugandan, public school, middle income*

> It helps you to know if you want to be, like, a teacher or, like, a banker or something.
>
> —*Mallory, Jewish, public school, middle income*

Like Nathan out in the country, Gracie (below) expresses a rich, complex set of hypotheticals that evoke school as a place where you learn things in order to get jobs, which will help you avoid all kinds of trouble out there in the real world:

> Because later on in life, then something might happen and we have to know that, and if we didn't know that, something bad might happen. Like, if someone got hurt and you didn't know how to help them, you could have science that could help you out with how to treat it. It can really be a challenge when you grow up, when you have to do it all by yourself, and so, that's pretty much why they have schools, to teach you all these things and skills that you can learn. From what I've seen, like, when people grow up and move out of the house, sometimes they can't find a job, sometimes that happens, and school really helps with that, cuz, then you know a bunch of other stuff that can get you a good job. My friends, sometimes they tell me about this stuff, and out on the street sometimes people have signs.

> —Gracie, white, Protestant school, middle income

Gracie is talking about the people with signs who stand out on the street looking for work or handouts. Observing them, Gracie has constructed an understanding of what the alternative to finding "a good job" (or any job) is: begging for work or money.

URBAN

From the poorest communities to the most privileged, urban kids associated schooling with job preparation. Children in families with wealth think about professional occupations—they understand learning in the context of becoming doctors, lawyers, engineers, architects, and so on. By contrast, among urban students in low-income parts of the city, kids tend to talk of more generic "jobs." As in rural Missouri, this generic job talk must be heard in the context of a 2010 unemployment rate of 17.3 percent among African Americans in St. Louis, more than double the unemployment rate among whites. Especially in the hyper-regulated and excessively constrained environments of some charter schools, how students relate schooling and jobs sounds rehearsed and lacking in affect:

I don't know. Cuz if we didn't know how to read, and we didn't read in school, we couldn't—if we wanted a job, we couldn't, if we didn't know how to read, couldn't have a job.

—Darrion, African American, charter school, low income

So we can do something with our life. Like in math, and if you can't read you can't do nothing for real like drive or get like a job.

—Trey, African American, charter school, low income

Small, intimate parish schools can have a more personal feel to them. The children's individuality seems respected. Still, there was a consistent message there, too, about the connection between school and employment.

Cuz you'll learn more and you'll get into a better school and you'll learn more and you'll get a better job and you could make a little bit more money if you do go to school.

—Lucy, white, Catholic school, middle income

I think we're learning this so like, say we want to be a teacher or an accountant or a shoe salesman, when we grow up, we'll know everything we want and if we want to get into a good college, we can get an education and we make sure that we get those jobs and just not end up like, no job.

—Joanna, white, Catholic school, midde income

In urban private schools designed for the children of the elite, the school-to-job story is complicated by richer, more complex curricula. Their paths to future employment opportunities are open-ended and lead to multiple destinations that will hinge on personal interest and aptitude. With regard to job readiness, David expressed a deep familiarity with the processes and outcomes. He knows, for instance, that a person applying for a job, even a job he will be good at, needs to be interviewed. David speaks Italian and English and comes from a highly educated, professional family, which makes his illustrative job applicant—the prospective factory worker heading in for an interview—even more interesting:

> We are learning in school mostly to prepare you for life [*laughs*]
> really. Yeah. So when you grow up and all that, well, when
> you get a job you need experience because you can't just walk
> into—I don't know—a factory and say "give me a job" and just
> get rejected on the first few questions on the interview. You need
> to get interviewed, you need to be good at it, and, well, you need
> to like it because if you have a job it's good but if you don't like
> it, well, you should find another job probably because, going to
> work should be fun. I mean it can be stressful but it should be fun.
> I know that some kids do homeschool and some kids do online
> school so, besides school and online schools and home schools
> and all of that, you can't just like eat a pill and magically be
> completely smart and prepared because [*pauses, smiles*] you just
> can't do that.
>
> —David, Jewish, bilingual, private school, high income

One sign of David's privilege is his judgment that *going to work should be fun*. I never heard this thought expressed among children growing up in low-income communities. Where money is tight and jobs are scarce, work is work; the concept of work does not overlap with the concept of fun. Another sign of his sophistication is how David understands school as a time-consuming process—preparation and experience that takes place over time. *You can't just eat a pill and magically be completely smart and prepared.* David knows there is no quick fix when it comes to important learning.

While David is interested in pursuing a life in science or engineering, his classmate Robert is quite clear about one day becoming a lawyer. Verbally precocious, Robert understands his aptitude for arguing. Why does Robert think he goes to school?

> To prepare us for middle school and beyond, to give us an
> advantage over other people later in life? I think, you know, it's
> also kind of fun when you're forty and then it's like, you know, your

kid's Trivia Night and you get that answer no one knew and you're like, "Yes! I'm glad I went to Pershing School!" I'm sure there are people who have said [*impersonating the deep voice of an adult*], "No, this has to be better than school," you know, and schools can be different, a private academy versus a, little tiny . . . a large private academy versus a tiny little, whatchamacallit.

—*Robert, white, private school, high income*

Clearly, Robert understands how school leads to occupational and other forms of success in later life. Smooth, humorous, and unflustered with adults, Robert speaks of the knowledge he gains in school as preparing him to compete not only in the workplace, but also, one day, in his own child's school's fund-raising social event, the Trivia Night.

Now remember Malik, who attends an urban public school less than three miles from Robert. Malik, too, expressed a sure expectation. He intends to become an engineer and a firefighter. Like Robert, he plans to have children. He plans on being successful. Both boys have dreams, plans, and expectations. But now ask yourself this: how do their respective social, cultural, and economic positions and school environments prepare Malik and Robert to realize their dreams?

Think again of the curricular cheat sheet. This chapter has shown how it sounds when children are absorbing ideas that position them as knowledge sponges and future employees. Because most of the children understood their accumulated knowledge to be in the service of future work, we are really most aligned with the practices, curricula, expectations, and assumptions that underlie the ideology of schooling as precursor to paid employment. But what's so bad about kids learning for the sake of adult occupations?

Problem one: what occupations? The parents of many black kids from the city and white kids from rural Missouri are underemployed. If parents do have jobs, there is no guarantee that these jobs will still be available a decade from now, or that they are the sorts of jobs parents want their children to have.

Problem two: the jobs many of our kids will be doing do not exist yet because they have not even been imagined. Could my teachers in 1969, when I was in fourth grade, have had any idea that in 1989, my job would be filing stories for a community newspaper via home computer and telephone line, and that my newborn would be sleeping by my side as I worked? The job-related generational leaps have been inconceivable. Moreover, futurists are telling us to prepare children to be able to learn how to do many different kinds of things, not just one.

This schooling-for-job-doing conversation needs to be rethought. The real thing we need to be talking about is developing and expanding the identities and aptitudes of young people so that they will be able to figure out how they will learn what they need to learn and do what they need to do as the world turns. (See chapter 7 for what makes a good student.) There is a huge difference between learning *to* work and learning *about* work. Right now, it's mostly only children from well-to-do families who are doing the latter. Ideally, we will start figuring out how to help more kids learn this way, too.

On the bright side, I did hear talk in every region and school type that indicates possible directions for freshly imagined language about school. Here are some of the outlier meanings kids attribute to school experience that are not all about social utility, or at least do not *primarily* relate to the international marketplace of human job doers. That children can voice these ideas in contrast to the dominant ideologies in their learning worlds is a sign of resistance and hope.

MORE COMPLEX AND NOT ENTIRELY UTILITARIAN REASONS FOR GOING TO SCHOOL

We go to school to learn the importance of life.

—*Zach, white, rural, public school, low income*

You can't get much more humanistic than Zach. It was rare for a person to go this broad when thinking about the purpose of school.

Perhaps Zach was overreaching, or echoing something he has heard, but I was pleased to hear it nonetheless. Life, after all, is important, and it would be wonderful if schools impressed only this on children.

Still, in more concrete ways, many more kids talked about how important friends and friendships were to their experience of school; a few actually thought being with other kids is the whole purpose of school. And some brought the idea of friends into especially sharp focus.

RURAL

So they can learn not on their own. You can learn from a lot of other people like your friends, like helping you study a lot instead of just being at home trying to study by yourself.

—Zoe, white, public school, low income

I just think school's a really good idea because you are around people and you learn how to not really be all shy and stuff and you learn, like, yourself, and you can really, like, if you're having a hard time or something, sometimes you don't wanna tell your mom you just wanna tell your friends and you're around your friends to where you can tell 'em like right then about it and stuff.

—Chelsea, white, public school, fragile middle income

OUTER-RING SUBURBAN

Kids go to school so they can learn the stuff they need to learn to be set for life.

—Drew, white, public school, middle income

To have common sense.

—Joey, white, Protestant school, middle income

SUBURBAN

To learn. It helps with the future and problems.

—*Miranda, white, private school, high income*

METROPOLITAN

To make good decisions.

—*Charles, African American, Protestant school, middle income*

So you can become a great person and you can learn things in a
way that you'll remember them.

—*Walker, white, public school, low income*

URBAN

I think they go school to learn, you know, like about the outside
world, like, like directions, north, south, east, west, for instance.
Like, if someone were looking for help or something, and then
it was north, and then they thought west was north, and they
started going west, they never found help and they, well, got hurt or
something, or injured.

—*Lena, white, private school, middle income*

Lena's response is a reminder that all learning affects a person's experience in "the outside world." In this case, knowledge of the cardinal
directions can prevent getting hurt or injured.

Metaphors abound in education discourse: learning is acquiring
tools, learning is blossoming, learning is transforming, learning is getting filled up with knowledge. Learning is like a lot of things. I am not
a gamer, but in speaking of obstacles and how they relate to schooling,
Eliza, below, seems to be relating a concept she has picked up from

some other context that sounds a little game-y to me. And then she connects the idea of learning-as-passing-obstacles to her ideas about God's role in life and learning.

> I guess they're trying to teach us to be good people and learn and teaching us responsibility. That stuff. I guess it's showing you in life you can have obstacles and you needa know how to defend them. And cuz every day in your life you have math. So you need to use that. Every day you have words to speak. Use that. Every day, of course, you read something. And you use your reading skills. Parents have to work. And in all the generations, parents worked. So it's basically saying parents work, they learn there. Why don't kids—kids should learn, too. . . .
>
> Maybe it's just the physics of what's going on in the world. With obstacles, you need to learn to pass those. Maybe it's that. Maybe somebody seeks the obstacles, they learn how to pass them, they pass them, and then they pass it down to someone, then that person learns how to teach it. I guess that probably makes no sense! I'd say God shows you the obstacles that you need to pass but he doesn't tell you how to pass them. He has you pass 'em by yourself. He teaches you how to learn. Yeah, show them, but you don't give them.
>
> —*Eliza, white, Catholic school, middle income*

Eliza has unwittingly and brilliantly imagined God as a Deweyan constructivist: God presents the obstacles, she figures, but "doesn't tell you how to pass them . . . has you pass 'em by yourself. He teaches you how to learn." If schools did nothing else, they ought to be teaching kids how to be good people and how to figure things out.

For the children of the professional elite, school is where you go to wrestle with big ideas in terms of the content you are learning.

> Because it's probably important stuff, like, the Civil War that was the big impact on America and so if you don't know about that then you don't really know one of the biggest impacts 'cause if that didn't happen, we'd be two countries. Then they miss the big idea and they wouldn't be getting it and they wouldn't really realize that that happened and that that was the biggest, that *could* be one of the most important things that happened in history. And then

if people don't know what one of the biggest important things in history is, what happens, what happens in their life? Then they wouldn't ever get to really realize, like what it's about, and why that stuff *happened.*

—*Sasha, white, private school, high income*

In social studies, Sasha is learning in order to interpret the significance of facts. She understands that a person who doesn't know what's important or the meaning of an historical event like the Civil War would be at a terrible loss—*what happens in their life?* Her classmate, Faye, derives from such learning the difference between right and wrong.

In social studies, because we keep going in time order so it's starting with leading up to the revolution and then the revolution. And then, and then it went to the U.S. Constitution. I think the teachers, they want it to go in time order so you don't get mixed up and forget the dates and so kids can learn what's right from wrong and their history of the past.

—*Faye, white, private school, high income*

Yes, we want our children to know a lot of things; content is important. And we also want them to do work that feels meaningful. But when children can speak at age ten about people learning in school in order to be active in the world in more critical ways—seeing and solving problems, knowing right from wrong, making sure to "get" the big idea—then something is going especially right. If a person can see problems and want to solve them, then they are motivated to learn. As adults, they will find or create for themselves an appropriate form of work. Not all meaningful work is paid employment (i.e., jobs); and not all jobs constitute meaningful work.

I will end this chapter with Yasmin, a Pakistani American who goes to a private Islamic school. Yasmin expressed this crucial idea in a sound bite. This is the kind of thing that many of us want kids to believe school is for. Born in September 2001, Yasmin moved to Missouri in third grade and described her school as "noisy and organized." All the men in Yasmin's family are doctors, and she told me that everyone is encouraging her to be a doctor, too. She always gets As, is best in her class at math and spelling, and loves her friends. Her palms sweat when she's nervous. She wears a snap-on head scarf decorated with sequin hearts. Under her white head scarf and black body sheath are turquoise sweatpants and sneakers with pink trim. She rocks rhythmically as she speaks and avoids eye contact and loves to play silly chase games with her younger brother. For breakfast she eats Honey Nut Cheerios. Why does Yasmin think kids go to school? "So that they can solve problems."

2

WHAT MAKES A GOOD TEACHER?

"Nice, Fun, Not So Mean,
Not So Easy on You"

An especially well-spoken student with a keen sense of justice, Hunter views his teacher as a classroom leader, a person with power.

As a fourth-grade teacher, she has to know what she's teaching and how to teach it, when to teach it, what order they go in. She has to know how to describe something. She's gotta back up her answer. She's gotta have a plan B. She's got to be ready if things go south. Or if there's a fire or something she's got to know where to go if there's an emergency. You just hafta really be prepared.

—*Hunter, white, rural, public school, low income*

Hunter's ideal teacher knows what to teach, how to teach it, and what to do in case instructional disaster strikes and *things go south*. According to Hunter, contingency plans are a must for a teacher. In addition to having plan Bs and answer backups, Hunter's teacher must reckon with actual disasters, too—children know that emergencies are a part of life. But they also recognize other important qualities good teachers share:

Nice, playful, active, and serious.

—*Kamar, Moroccan American, outer-ring suburban, Islamic school, middle income*

OK, a good teacher: nice, fun, not so mean, not so easy on you, cuz when they're harder, it makes you learn better. I'm not very picky about my teachers. And decorates her classroom pretty. I don't know why, I just like pretty classrooms, it makes me in a better mood.

—*Ruth, white, rural, public school, low income*

In every way that matters, children's ideas about good teachers align seamlessly with more global conversations about educator preparation.

Anyone talking seriously about education today is talking about teacher quality. More precisely and respectfully, we are talking about qualities that make for ineffectual, so-so, good, and great teachers. But if the school-as-factory trope is over and done with in a service- and knowledge-based global economy, the model of teacher-prep-as-assembly-line has expired, too. Even now, when razor-smart engineers at MIT are rolling out computer software that they believe can fairly assess essays written by students far, far away, what we know is this: meaningful learning is social; what matters most is who's in the room with the kids.

Back in 1942, writing to boost wartime morale, Margaret Mead examined young American soldiers and interpreted, from an anthropological perspective, what kind of life experience they would bring into battle. To Mead, the American upbringing was highly influenced by school and the role schoolteachers played in families: "In America the teacher is, in fact, never the representative of the parents . . . she is always the representative of the future into which parents are anxious that their children should enter and enter well prepared."*

Teachers as harbingers of a marvelous future flavors the original idea of Teach for America, which was to put idealistic go-getters who had excelled in school into schools nearly swamped by troubles. Who better than the children of the forward-leaning elite to drag those being left behind into the present, if not the future? As the most well-known and influential nontraditional route into teaching, Teach for America warrants special consideration in this chapter.

---

*Margaret Mead, *And Keep Your Powder Dry: An Anthropologist Looks at America* (New York: Morrow and Co, 1942), 98.

Alas, the complex problems concomitant with Teach for America today are familiar:

1. The typical TFA teacher enters the field without sufficient professional knowledge, pedagogical theory, and clinical experience.
2. TFA teachers are too frequently directed to teach curricular content outside their areas of expertise.
3. The salaries of early-career teachers are far less than those of entry-level positions in other fields.
4. The mental and physical exhaustion experienced by most TFA teachers is a consequence of how hard they work in the context of the first problem I enumerated, which also relates to class size and curriculum in underresourced communities.
5. TFA teachers have limited opportunities for meaningful collaboration with mentor colleagues and excellent seasoned teachers.
6. There are significant social and cultural barriers between the TFA cadre and the so-called traditionally trained cohort of teachers; TFA cohorts tend to live far away from where they themselves went to high school. Like missionaries abroad, they tend to be housed as roommates and supported by TFA in ways that set them apart from their more "native" colleagues.
7. Given the average TFA teacher's aspirations and ambitions, the majority of them move out of the classroom too soon, before they have an opportunity to learn from their mistakes as most early-career teachers do.
8. There is a macrocontextual philosophical misalignment between TFA boosters and advocates of longtime teachers.
9. Because TFA teachers are placed in failing schools, institutions at the mercy of a state-mandated testing apparatus, TFA teachers may understand that above all, their mission is to raise test scores. As I will argue in chapter 5, this mission is antithetical to student learning.

For all of these reasons, like an organism contending with an intruding microbe, even one that might be beneficial, schools can turn against the Teach for America teacher prematurely. Should humility, grit, and even a soupçon of talent enable a Teach for America teacher to make it past the third or fourth year in the same school, chances are good that she or he will commit to the profession in one way or another and make a moral U-turn away from the organization that fast-tracked them into the classroom at such high cost to their students that first or second year. Reflecting on her experience with Teach for America colleagues, an excellent, traditionally trained classroom teacher with nearly three decades of experience told me, "When they stick, they can be great." This is true. I can personally vouch for great Teach for America graduates I have been lucky to work with.

This tells me that we are on the right track in trying to inject smart kids from the best universities and colleges into classrooms. As Margaret Mead suggests, teachers *are* the future, and smart college graduates ought to think of K–12 teaching in one form or another as the honorable, meaningful, crucially important profession that it is. I write *one form or another* because no matter who's in charge, and no matter what form school takes, there remains an essential question when it comes to teaching and learning. The sooner all of the nontraditional and traditional preparation programs face it squarely the sooner we can be working together and not at odds with each other.

Setting aside the politically freighted accusations against traditionally trained teachers, one of the more persistent questions sober-minded teacher educators ask is this: how should content mastery relate to pedagogical know-how? In other words, how are teachers negotiating the professional balance between teaching math, history, PE, biology, and other subjects and teaching individual human beings? Insightful kids like Hunter are sensitive to this distinction—*what she's teaching and how to teach it, when to teach it, what order they go in*. People studying in universities to become teachers are quite aware of professional tension on exactly this point.

In the old days it was easy. Teachers knew stuff. They stood up and read aloud what they knew; they lectured. Some of the students who listened to them learned the stuff they heard. Most did not. Today we call this the sage-on-a-stage or talk-and-chalk model, and we know that it only works for a tiny fraction of students. That is, only some people can learn anything by sitting still and listening. And that even for these people, it doesn't work much past the time they are tested on the material. After exams, most things learned that way get forgotten. This way of teaching is an unreliable method for achieving permanent learning. In order to learn things for keeps, most people have to be active and interested. They have to make connections between what they are learning and what they already know. They have to understand new knowledge in a social context. They have to find the knowledge useful to know. This approach and its methods, which in the United States date from the seminal work of John Dewey, is known as *constructivist*. In general, as Gerald Duffy has written, "good instruction is a matter of mixing and matching method to student within an overall constructivist perspective."*

When we speak of pedagogical know-how, we are talking about what it is we know about how processes of teaching and processes of learning are related.

Figuratively speaking, people learning to be teachers straddle campuses all over the country. Arts and sciences faculty on the more traditional end of the spectrum push content at the expense of pedagogical expertise. In colleges of education, where faculty know that when people are motivated and active, learning can and will happen in any content area, professors tend to emphasize pedagogical theory and practice at the expense of content expertise.

Teachers-to-be take math courses, for example, in order to master the concepts and practices they might not have learned well in high school; they also take what are called "math methods" classes designed to teach them how to teach mathematics to younger people. Sometimes these two courses are delivered as one. The same is true for science, literature, art, social studies, physical education, drama, computing, and anything else in the elementary or secondary curriculum: teachers need to know content, and they need to know how to teach the content. Mix in classroom management, general educational psychol-

---

*Richard Allington and Peter Johnston, *Reading to Learn: Lessons from Exemplary Fourth-Grade Classrooms* (New York: The Guilford Press, 2002), 15.

ogy, the neuroscience that undergirds the latest approaches to teaching students with special needs—gifted, those with learning challenges, English-language learners—and all the other meat-and-potatoes curriculum preservice teachers require, and you can begin to see the multiple layers of expertise we expect of teachers. But that is not enough.

For decades, researchers have been calling for educators to design curriculum around individual student identity. Children in their home communities and other child-serving, nonschool settings develop ways of being that good teachers respect and build into their practice. Preservice teachers are increasingly expected to get out in the field and work with children long before they are hired for classroom jobs. And so we are talking about developing in every single teacher intellectual and temperamental qualities, abilities to prioritize, and levels of mastery in multiple domains. This requires time and money. The kind of time and money we invest in, say, our air force pilots and brain surgeons.

A thought experiment: tie your shoe. Now teach a five-year-old how to tie her shoe. Next teach that same child how to tie someone else's shoe. Now make picture instructions for the child who needs to see an image in order to learn. Now teach a child who has one arm how to tie her shoe. Now teach a child who is deaf to tie his shoe. And while you're at it, find some way to challenge that kid in the corner who already knows how to tie his shoe, has tied twelve different shoes in the last ten minutes, and is at the moment cutting construction paper into hundreds of pieces and sprinkling them on the floor in a game he is calling "rain storm." Remember to incorporate technology in your lessons, or else you will lose points. Also, figure out some way to deliver the lesson in Spanish because an English-language learner was just transferred into your room yesterday and the district translator is in another building this morning. Don't neglect depth-of-knowledge (DOK), because we value critical thinking about the universal human need for protection against weather and the history of footwear. Be sure to connect shoe tying to English language arts. Recite a nursery rhyme? Compose a limerick? Remember to be extra patient with the easily frustrated child whose mother just lost her job and has moved the family into a shelter. And hurry up, because your assistant principal is conducting a walk-through in an hour and if she sees that all of the children are not on task tying shoes at grade level, you will lose points for that day's observation, which may reflect poorly on your report, which will have hiring and salary consequences for you. Oh, and also please go ahead and pay out-of-pocket for the extra shoelaces you need because the district is broke, state and federal funding has dried up, and your class's allocation of practice shoelaces has rotted away over the summer on account of the roof that has had a leak since last December having gone unrepaired, also because of budget cuts. And smile.

My twenty-year-old education students tell me they don't feel ready to go out and be teachers. Every single Sunday night for the last thirty years, my fifty-four-year-old husband has told me he doesn't feel adequately prepared for the coming week in his English classroom, and he has pedagogical autonomy, a thousand-and-one best practices in his head, and a highly endowed institution at his back. Still, people want to grow up and be teachers. They want to be good teachers, if not great teachers, like the very best teachers they remember from their own younger days. In important ways, but not *all* ways, great teachers today and tomorrow need to be different from great teachers of the past. So what is the right stuff when it comes to identifying and preparing good and great teachers in the twenty-first century? What can we do to help more teachers be great in the ways we need them to be now?

Here I am deliberately evoking the anger and resistance expressed by Chuck Yeager as played by Sam Shepard in *The Right Stuff*. The postwar fighter pilots who competed to break the sound barrier in jet planes were tough, resilient, physically fit, intelligent, and playful in an edgy way. They were problem solvers. When they got the idea that NASA was trying to turn them into chimps—warm bodies in a windowless space capsule controlled by engineers on the ground in Houston—they rebelled. Of course they did. They felt that they were being stripped of the expertise they had worked so long to acquire.

For now I want you to forget about the system we have for developing teachers, forget about the tension between content and pedagogy, the constraints of insufficient funding, resource inequities, market intrusion into the classroom, the animus between Teach for America and teachers' unions, and all the other discouraging aspects of the here and now. Just think about the people we want around our kids all day long. What should they be like? What are they like now? This is what I wanted to hear kids tell me.

How, I asked them, would *you* describe a good teacher? I heard quite a few negative descriptors. That is, many kids told me what good teachers never or seldom do. According to children, good teachers do not:

Yell at you.

Make fun of people.

Get that mad at you.

Keep bringing up [a wrongdoing].

Give a consequence for nothing.

Interrupt.

Just give you a random answer.

Answer the phone when she's teaching.

Pick favorites.

Always go by the book.

All of this seems quite reasonable. It is fair to say that we would not want anyone who is harsh, humiliating, impatient, careless, distracted, unfair, biased, and robotic responsible for our children in school. But what, according to kids, are the positive characteristics of a good teacher? The clusters of teacher qualities I heard from students centered on three overlapping themes: feelings, curriculum and instruction, and behavior management and discipline.

FEELINGS

From the perspective of children, the most significant quality of teachers by far is the emotional climate they create in the classroom. These comments convey children's sensitivity to how teachers seem to be feeling and how teachers make kids feel. Again and again, I heard kids tell me about the affective climate teachers create in the spaces they design for learning. Ruth, in a rural public school, loved the fact that her teacher "decorated her room pretty." A lamp and a string of colorful bulbs made Ruth feel good. Most often, kids described good teachers as patient, helpful, playful, trusting, respectful, and kind.

URBAN

> Ms. S. tryin' to help us learn. Givin' out simple directions. Ms.
> S. can be mean but if you just test her button that's when she get
> mean, and if you do the right thing, she'll get nice.
>
> —*D'Angelo, African American, charter school, low income*

At first glance, this is an innocuous-seeming idea. But the culture of D'Angelo's school is characterized by militaristic rigidity. Punishment and rewards are used to motivate learning; in the passageways students are instructed to know and follow the mnemonic acronym HALL: Hands together, All eyes forward, Lips zipped, Low speed. Unsurprisingly, D'Angelo understands his relationship with his teacher in similarly behaviorist terms: Ms. S.'s mood can switch from mean to nice at the touch of a button.

Brigit appreciates the seriousness of her teachers; she feels their concern for her:

> So I think my teacher kinda knows what we need and what we
> don't need to do. I think teachers are more mature than your
> parents sometimes. Like the teachers are more serious about you
> learning than sometimes your parents. Like my parents are kind of
> telling me that I need to do my homework, but with my teachers,
> they're more into me doing well.
>
> —*Brigit, white, Catholic school, middle income*

Brigit's words convey her impression that, when it comes to student learning, teachers can have more skin in the game than even parents do. Parents might get their kids to school, but it's the teachers who care that they learn something—*they're more into me doing well.* Brigit feels that her teachers feel what's serious about school.

INNER-RING SUBURBAN

Lisa describes a teacher who is in tune with her whole class.

Well, sometimes we have the schedule, but we usually don't follow the schedule, we just do whatever, whatever we feel like. We always do math in the morning, to get it out of the way, cuz we don't like math, and then we get to do writing. And sometimes, we do a little math in the afternoon, and then we do a lot of writing. And we do reading, definitely reading a lot. Sometimes she'll like ask us, "Hey, after math, what do you guys want to do?" And we're all like, "Writing!" So, we usually just write, sometimes she'll take us outside, and once a week, maybe, we go around the school, we just walk around the school, just for a little fresh air.

—*Lisa, Jewish, public school, middle income*

Lisa is aware of her teacher attending to what the class feels like doing. Valuing feeling over "the schedule" and soliciting student input—*what do you guys want to do?*—may be a clever ploy to enact a predesigned plan, but Lisa's teacher has got her class hooked.

OUTER-RING SUBURBAN

She's kind and nice and helps others.

—*Caroline, African American, Protestant school, middle income*

One that helps you learn and one that just makes you feel like she's a private teacher for each person, but not.

—*James, white, Protestant school, middle income*

They feel you, they know that I've had troubles with the past year so like they've been . . . nice [*laughs*], like home troubles and they'll just come up and I'll get really sad. My teachers have always said that if they see that I'm not talking while everybody else is in my learning group, talking and giving each others the answers, and I'm just sitting there and watching, they know I'm either interested in it or they know that I'm like mad at [my friends], or like they've been rude to me, and I'm not talking to them. They know that something's up. And so, after that, they'll ask me what's wrong. But they know that if I'm really focused, I'm not talking.

—Annemarie, white, Catholic school, middle income

RURAL

They kind of push you to do things like your parents do when you're doing your homework, sorta [like your parents] but they [teachers] are a lot nicer [*laughs*].

—Tori, white, public school, middle income

[Mr. W.] knows us well, we say what we think, we don't keep it in, an' he knows how our grades are. When he grades papers, he's not very strict like Miss H., she is really strict. Like if you don't write very neat, she'll be like, "Erase that, do it again." Mr. W., he'll tell you about it, but he won't count it off. He'll just tell you about it and, don't do that again next time.

—Casey, white, public school, middle income

They need to get to know you, to see if you're the kind of person that will never stop until you get the answer, [or] people that just really don't care at all. Then they can look at the scores on your test, and see if you talk to other people in class when you're not supposed to. That'll determine if you don't care. Stuff like that.

—Nathan, white, public school, middle income

Students realize that it's important how people in classrooms feel, that a huge piece of any teacher's job is to make sure that students feel OK, and that good teachers are open and available to help students who do not feel OK. Current research in learning and brain-body science says this, too. Children learn better in environments that are caring and warm. Places that feel right, that make people feel all right, will engage students and motivate them to learn. People concerned with achievement and the metrics of learning outcomes—especially those who may scorn or dismiss classroom climate as a soft topic—should be paying attention to teacher and student emotionality. Ignoring, bypassing, or dismissing emotional factors in classroom settings results in real, measurable consequences for all students, but especially for the students who absolutely require caring teachers.

Note to the cranky old folks: good feeling should not be confused with the degree of frustration and challenge attendant to learning. People can feel OK even when they are in the process of learning something new. Good teachers cope patiently with students during the often frustrating, nonlinear journey toward understanding. Given the overwhelming alignment of trustworthy empirical research and children's own perspectives, it seems to me that the question we ought to be asking through every effort to reform teacher preparation and professional development is this: in what ways does this proposed change empower teachers to create a more sensitive, respectful, emotionally responsive classroom climate?

CURRICULUM AND INSTRUCTION

The second most frequent set of qualities that came up when children spoke of good teachers related to the content, delivery, and assessment of lessons. Here, even filtered through the children's limited perspectives, is where it will be most obvious that there is an enormous range in the quality of teachers, curricula, and assessment. Like fish incapable of talking about water, most kids cannot really talk directly about the intersection of teachers, curriculum, and pedagogy; they swim in this intersection daily. They can talk about *their* teachers and *their* schoolwork, period.

Extrapolating from what kids said, all good teachers know what individual students really need to learn so that their work will be challenging but not too challenging. Good teachers, according to kids, also give students some choices about what and how to learn. Good teachers spend extra time with them if necessary. Good teachers explain things in ways kids can understand. To do this they come up with just the right metaphors and analogies. Good teachers translate hard-to-grasp concepts into concrete imagery until students understand the concept for themselves, for real. Then teachers develop individual ways of figuring out how to tell what students are learning. Mainly what children express are abundant and ingenuous images of teachers moving, watching, listening, joking, interacting, researching, planning, and correcting as they check for understanding.

URBAN

He usually pays attention to everyone.

—Azra, Bosnian American, public school, low income

Teacher figure outs because she looks at us an' she makes sure nobody's like . . . she got her own things she says, like if somebody's in outer space, just not looking at nothing, she's says, "You're acting like y'all are counting purple ponies in the air." And then if they not doin' it, they get a warning. It's like this: warning, buddy room, teacher consequence, teacher consequences and detention, and then you get a referral.

—Kashena, African American, charter school, low income

Miss S. is really funny in classes. Like science. She used someone to, like, be a science experiment. Like she pulled a person out and pretended they were a tree, and started acting like they were a science experiment. And like folded us and used us as trees and put leafs on us. 'Cause we were talking about pollination and a flower tree. And she started cracking up. And she always sings a lot, which is funny.

—Cassidy, white, Catholic school, middle income

She can tell if you're paying attention or not, or she's at—well, sometimes we get our notebooks out and she asks a question. If you're just like sitting there thinking, she can tell you don't get it. If you write down the answer really fast she can tell you get it.

—Maia, Asian American, Catholic school, middle income

If you're paying attention she would usually ask you a question like, "What is this," can you help me with this, and she knows that sometimes a lot of us are not really paying attention and the people who are paying attention, she gives us candy and stuff, when everyone raises their hand, and whoever's not listening doesn't know the answer, usually she gives us candy or erasers or something. That's how she gets us to pay attention and stuff.

—Stella, white, Catholic school, middle income

[They can tell how we're learning] probably from behavior in class, or the ERBs that we do, like the big test packet. And then we have little tests during the year to see how well you're doing in certain stuff. Probably if you're acting crazy and kind of distracted, they won't think you're listening very well. Usually people are quiet and listen and get their focused attention, and like they always say, "Eyes on the teacher."

—Faye, white, private school, high income

At times they just pull us in the room and then they say, "What do you think you know," like, "Do you think you know a lot about this subject or do you wanna know more?"

—Sasha, white, private school, high income

INNER-RING SUBURBAN

Well, we were doing geometry, we were figuring out shapes, because some kids, like, me, I wasn't really good at shapes, but I got it, and I wasn't really good at angles, but I got it, cuz she just explained it really well. And most people didn't get long division. No one could do it really, after Ms. M. explained it, so it actually really helped when she explained it really well, like, she went up to the board, and she did two whole worksheets with us. And, then, if someone still didn't get it, she would go to their desk and help them. I still didn't get it for some reason, so she came to my desk, and after about five minutes, I really got it, and now I like long division.

—Lisa, Jewish, public school, middle income

OUTER-RING SUBURBAN

She goes and just stays with one person and helps them. And then after she thinks that he gets it then she goes to someone else who doesn't get it, and if I get it and someone else is having trouble and I finish, then I will go over and start helping them until Ms. R. my teacher comes and helps him or her.

—June, white, public school, middle income

In the description of the following science lesson, Jennifer recounts precisely what she and her classmates were up to. Remember that it was her teacher who facilitated the activity and her teacher who established the "figuring-things-out" atmosphere that research shows is most conducive to learning. When people talk about teachers as guides on the side developing hands-on, minds-on learning environments, this is what they mean.

Science we're doing right now, we made these little cars out of connectors and like we have different obstacles. We have different obstacles that we can try, like we decide which one we want to do. And the one my group is doing right now is . . . our car . . . we have a certain money budget and all the different groups have a different one and ours is three thousand eight hundred dollars. And different pieces cost a certain amount of money and so we have to build this car that goes ten feet in four seconds and then back in seven seconds and it has to carry one pizza which is one block hopefully. Well, we have test trials and then on a certain day, Mrs. R., she will run the car. And you could do it in front of a fan or you could do it with a rubber band that you wrap around, or you can do the pulley system. And if it doesn't work that time, you can try to fix your car but it has to stay in the money budget. We have three people or four people in each group. We tried the rubber band, then we tried the pulley system, now we're doing the fan, and we're sticking with the fan 'cause that's what had our best progress.

—Jennifer, white, public school, middle income

The teachers can find basically anything on their computers, so they can teach us almost every—anything that they want, it's like they have special lessons planned out for the day first. Like in computer lab, Mr. S. the computer teacher, he would say like five or ten minutes and then we can do any kind of math game, and then we could do any math game we want, and in reading time Mrs. G. sometimes'll just say, "Work on your own story," like when she has to get to us, this week we're doing publishing, so while we work, while the other students are working on publishing with Mrs. G, she had us working on any story we wanted or we could read. So we could do like any kind of story, it could be nonfiction, fiction, realistic fiction, and like it could be a fable. Most of the time they're not strict at all but if we get in trouble they're strict just like adults and parents.

—Jason, white, public school, middle income

Echoing the blank-slate ideological model from the previous chapter, Gracie describes her teacher as the person who gets the *it* (knowledge) into the brain that lacks *it*, kind of like a friendly baker squirting jelly into a donut.

A good teacher is one that knows how to teach really well, and how to stick it in your brain, and that's nice to you. Well, our teacher has, every once in a while, we watch little videos, cuz we think that helps us stick it in our brain better, and it does really work.

—Gracie, white, Protestant school, fragile middle income

She goes around the room, she hardly ever sits down, so she's walkin', weavin' through the lines. She's observing, not talking to us.

—Joey, white, Protestant school, middle income

When I get good grades she gives me a pat on the back and stuff like that.

—*Laurence, white, Protestant school, middle income*

RURAL

Whenever she's over there grading she looks up and looks over and see who's doin' their work and see who's like thinkin' or starin' off into space. That's what she said.

—*Gabriel, white, public school, low income*

A lot of times we will sit in circles and discuss things where we have to raise our hands and just work together. And they're always telling us to show your work and if we're grading something they always tell us to X it out so they know what we're doin' wrong.

—*Hunter, white, public school, low income*

Elementary school children will respect their teachers' competence as long as the other adults in their lives do, too. If the emotional connection is there, students will defend their teachers even when other adults don't. One of the last interviews I conducted took place in the first few days of the student's summer vacation in 2012. I sat in the living room with Lisa, her dog, and her mother, who was a high school teacher. Lisa had been expressing unmitigated love and respect for her fourth-grade teacher. She cited example after example of the ways in which her teacher seemed just plain perfect. Toward the end of the hour, the mother could no longer contain herself.

LISA'S MOM: [*To me*] Can I interject something? It's kinda interesting, because my perception of her teacher is that her teacher is disorganized, her teacher—

LISA: —No, she wasn't.

LISA'S MOM: Hold on, honey, I'm gonna say something really positive about her. [*To me*] Academically, she wasn't the best teacher in the world. There weren't a lot of cool projects going on, I didn't see anything really in-depth going on, but, she had such a sparkle and she created this sense of community that was so deep, and Lisa would do anything for her. And it kinda made up for the fact that . . . and then this other teacher, her gifted teacher, had some very cool and very strong academic programs. Yet Lisa doesn't have a connection with her, doesn't like her personality, and it doesn't seem to matter that much to her. So, that connection is so important to Lisa, much more important than the academics. I mean, it'd be nice if the teacher had both [laughs].

LISA: You can't have both, Mom.

LISA'S MOM: Sure, you can.

LISA: No.

Powerful relationships come into being in classrooms. Teachers spend far more time with children than children's parents do. For some parents this is the blessing of school. For other parents, this fact alone can make them miserable and guilty, and anything less than a perfect teacher delivering a perfect curriculum can trigger remarks that are not in the best interest of the teacher-child relationship. But young children thrive when their home and school worlds are aligned, when belonging to one community does not make them feel totally alienated from the other. The cultures of the two places can be different, and good things can happen when there is some difference, particularly with regard to critical thinking. Bearing these tensions and conflicts in mind is essential when preparing educators for the responsibility they assume, particularly in preschool through sixth grade. The most current empirical and theoretical research tells us that most children learn best when school learning respects and draws upon home values and cultural competencies. By the same token, families who collaborate with teachers, who do not undermine the positive relationships formed by their children with adults in school, will help lay the foundation for successful school careers. Here the question we ought to be asking through every effort to reform teacher preparation is this: will the proposed change empower teachers to more thoroughly respect, know, understand, and communicate with the home worlds of students? And will the changes empower families to collaborate in a living curriculum that is responsive to students' own worlds?

BEHAVIOR MANAGEMENT AND DISCIPLINE

The third set of qualities students identified in good teachers have to do with how teachers establish, nurture, and sustain the physical, emotional, and intellectual peace and safety of the classroom, how they develop disciplinary practices that strike kids as fair and respectful, neither draconian nor overly permissive. Frannie, below, is translating impressions of her school's implementation of PBIS—Positive Behavioral Interventions and Support. In Missouri, it's called Schoolwide Positive Behavior Support (MO-PBS), an initiative launched in 2005 to help ameliorate school climate. PBIS involves a lot of rewards, consequences, and data collection, all of which take up considerable teacher time.

> Well, usually, they just watch us, see how well we're doing, and they usually go by our desks to see what we're doing. And then if you do the right thing and you're responsible or respectful, you get a horseshoe—it's blue. And then, if you get enough, like five to one hundred or two hundred, there's a little special trip we getta go on. Or like we could spend it at the Pinto Pushcart market over there [another room in the school].
>
> —*Frannie, white, public school, low income*

Students say that good teachers are on top of things and do not let kids get away with wrongdoing.

> A good teacher is someone who's nice, like not very strict, but not too nice to where like you don't get consequences for when you do something wrong, and someone like when you don't get something, they just help you through it and they'll even take out of their time to help you. They bring you up.
>
> —*Dahlia, white, outer-ring suburb, Protestant school,*
> *middle income*

Children like Dahlia do not like to feel that nobody's paying proper attention, or that classmates can get away with wrongdoing. Deion told the most extreme story of teacher inattention:

> I be like [*to a classmate*], "No, man, don't do that cause, that's just gonna get you in trouble". . . then he'll just be playing with it [*a gun brought into school*], he'll be all like this [*pretending to play with a small object in his lap*]. 'Cause the teacher'll be lookin' at her computer or givin' him some math or something . . . and they be like [*voices the kid with the gun*], "Oh, I got me a gun in my desk."
>
> —*Deion, African American, urban, public school, low income*

Good teachers are fair in their approach to discipline and consequences. They don't punish the whole class if only one person did something wrong. Interestingly, students did not bring up all that much about discipline and classroom management when I asked them to describe good teachers.

Most conversation about management and discipline emerged out of questions directly posed about getting in trouble. Punishing infractions is one side of discipline, the stick; getting kids to behave in the first place is the other, the carrot. With a few exceptions, all kinds of extrinsic, reward-based incentives are firmly in place to manage and control the behavior and decision making of children. In most of the schools I visited, kids are instructed to work and behave "nicely" in exchange for stickers, treats, candy, and parties, as well as abstract rewards—keys and "numbers" that are traded in for concrete prizes. School policies encourage teachers to tap the most immature quality of children in order to "get them" to do what is desired. This is a classic Pavlovian or behaviorist approach. It was state of the art in 1913, a time when students in rural Missouri were still drinking from a common cup dipped in an open bucket of well-drawn water.

Children are human: they mess up and make mistakes. How do we guide them to self-regulate? And when they err, what do we do? I heard all of the following consequences: get sent to in-school suspension (ISS). Attend lunch detention. Flip your card. Move your clip. Write your name in The Book. Write your name on the board. Write several copies of scripted sentences on the board. Go to the principal. Suffer a call home. Receive a talking-to. Be banished to something called "a buddy room," which is another teacher's classroom. Be banished further to out-of-school suspension (OSS).

Teachers and administrators have many ways to punish kids. By far, the most routine and common disciplinary action is to strip minutes of free play from recess, the time of the day many children love most. "Five on the line" is one school's shorthand phrase for having to spend five minutes standing on a painted yellow stripe in a parking lot while everyone else plays. Fourth-grade students are remarkably clear about teachers' roles in the cause and effect of behavior management.

Well, there's only a couple kids that get their work done and do all the extra sheets. And I'm one of them. Yeah, I get to do puzzles and stuff. We get to do like crafts. But we don't usually get to do anything fun because we have to earn class keys, your class has to work together. And they get something but my teacher never gives out keys so it's really hard to get sumpin special. She'll only let us watch a movie if we've learned something. Like in third grade, at the end of the day you get to watch a movie. It's usually about multiplying. It's like eddicational. If you forget your homework or something, you'll have to get a number and that means like. . . it's hard to explain. You don't want numbers. If you get three reds, you have to go to the principal and some kids in my class they're not, like they have like work from all the way to last week. So sometimes if they don't get it finished, they make them go sit with the principal so they can get it finished.

I think the littler classes get them because my brother gets them cuz he's in kindergarten and I think the older you get, it's kinda harder to get things. If you get ten keys you get a prize. But the only bad part about it is that you have to wait for [the prize drawer] to open up. We went to it like a couple days ago but then you have to wait for the principal to set it up again. She gets to decide when to have it so people say if you tell her that you forgot your homework and you tell the truth, she'll just give you a key [giggles]. I don't know if that's true. And I don't think that was fair 'cause our teacher doesn't really give us things. The other class gets a lot of big keys. We've only got one set of ten one time, and some people don't get to play their electronics, because they have to get everything finished, like if they're almost caught up, she'll let you play it. But you have to get that stuff to play it.

—*Kyra, white, outer-ring suburb, Catholic school, fragile middle income*

Kyra thinks and talks a lot about behavior management. It actually seemed to me that this talk represents the most impressive aspect of her teacher's curriculum: behavior management as curriculum. It's what Kyra had the most to say about. And in all schools, there are moments when rules are taken up by the students themselves, who then police each other, eventually more as a joke than anything else.

We have a rule that you can't yell "no talking" at the person that's talking, and then they can't yell "no talking" back. So, a lot of people, are just like, doing that for fun, they were yelling, "No talking. No talking." So whoever was talking even if they were saying "no talking" they had to go put their name in the book, [*whispers*] luckily I wasn't talking. But then the teacher punishes everyone, and I think teachers do that because they don't know exactly who it was. Like they might know if they were really paying attention, but the teacher wasn't in the room at that moment. So, she doesn't know exactly who it was.

—*Jennifer, white, outer-ring suburb, public school, middle income*

Mainly, I heard students tell me about the various ways they saw teachers getting kids to do what was expected of them. I suspect that Kashena is paraphrasing how her teacher prepared her for our interview.

URBAN

Once they get to know us, like, some people in our class are very intelligent, they think a lot, but they choose to do bad things. They [the teachers] either have a talk with 'em before they get in trouble like, they sit down, they tell 'em why they shouldn't behave that way when certain people come in so, so we can represent our school.

—Kashena, African American, charter school, low income

Teacher get on you when you playful. They give you a consequence.

Like no recess, stand up in a corner, write "gum," like if you chew gum, you gotta write gum two hundred times. The spirit is to help you learn, get a job, education.

And what makes a bad day?

Like, dropping your pin down. Like, if you on yellow, it start off from green, blue, yellow, orange, and red, if it on the orange or red, you have a bad day. But we start on yellow, though, and gotta work our way up. I did that before. I've worked my way all the way up to blue.

—D'Angelo, African American, charter school, low income

Certain teachers have different punishment strategies, "OK, when could you make up that time," and then somebody would just say [claps], "Minute!" like he just says [clapping on each word], "Minute Minute Minute Minute." He'll give you a number, he just says, "Minute." You know, that's for like something tiny, but if you do something like, I don't know, if you get in some trouble, they'll say, "Break for the next week, break for the next week." P.M. break you miss . . . so P.M. break is another version of recess, it's shorter and in the afternoon, you'll sit in the classrooms, sometimes, or sometimes they'll say it's just about homework, sometimes they say, "OK, bring it in tomorrow," but that's just gonna stack up your work.

—Robert, white, private school, high income

SUBURBAN

There's occasions when it's fair and sometimes not because sometimes it's only one person that ruins it for the whole class, but sometimes it's just individuals. And like there's this teacher that's sometimes mean, but also nice. Everybody doesn't really like her because she made these winning and losing games in gym, so people got mad and they don't really like her that much? But I think she's kinda nice, and so they were like really disrespectful to her, so my class made a consequence that we had to like sit away from each other at lunch? So that was kind of our punishment once. Because we'd rather put our heads down for like half an hour than to have recess taken away. So I would sit with the fifth graders, somebody with the third, somebody with the second. . . .We talk a lot in the line, especially the girls, and the boys are just, they can NOT listen to orders, they just don't stop. [Teachers] usually say maybe if we're having a field trip, "You're not gonna go to this field trip if you don't start acting nice," but there's this new kid that, he doesn't really listen to the teacher? so it's really hard for him? and so since he just came back from another school and now he's back in fourth but so he has these slips if he shouts out or something like that, if he does something she takes a slip away, and if after a week or a month if he has twenty slips, we get to have an extra thirty minutes of something, so like, he had twenty of those slips and so we got thirty minutes of recess. We added thirty minutes, because he was being good.

—*Naomi, Jewish, religious day school, high income*

RURAL

It's really neat, because of the PBS, which is Positive Behavioral System, I'm pretty sure. And if you do something good, you're responsible, respectful or safe, and a teacher catches you doing that, then you'll get a lucky horseshoe, and then there's prizes.

—*Oliver, white, public school, middle income*

A good teacher, she would probably let us be in partners, which Mrs. R. is doing that, and sometimes not and that's OK because sometime we need to study on our own, not let the other person do it. And trying to do one or two activities in like a month. Or just the teacher's trying to get everything done and having us have a little more fun in the day. Like recess, if we do really good

sometime, if we do really bad sometimes [it's] like five minutes. But
if we were really good it's just probably thirty.

—*Frannie, white, public school, low income*

Children like Ruth, below, are incredibly attentive to which teachers are monitoring which infractions. Ruth is not only keeping track of
who's adjudicating, she can detail the various and specific consequences
depending on who's in charge of you. "Recess running" is accounted for
in minutes, and relates to the offense. When I heard granular accounts
of the relationships among behavior, recess, teacher identity, and consequences, I couldn't help but imagine how such reasoning and memorization might be applied to, say, constitutional and case law.

Like, OK, so we have this sign, it says, "Warning," "10 Minute,"
and "Home Contact," and if you get to home contact, it's twenty
minutes. And if you have to move, like, another two times, then it's
alternate recess running. And I usually move my clip once a day,
because, like, our planners, if we spell something wrong, we have
to move our clip. Easy. But, don't move it again or else you have
to owe ten minutes at recess. It depends on who's teaching. I like
when Ms. R. is Recess 3 because she makes us stay out longer. But
now that Ms. R. is a teacher, she actually does it a bunch, Mr. C.
does it once or twice a week, and she makes us [do] forty-five. Ms.
B. makes us maybe fifty minutes, and Ms. R. makes us stay out for
a whole hour. And at lunch, if you're, like, way too loud, and Ms.
M. can hear you, sometimes it's Ms. R., too, sometimes Ms. R. does
both, but sometimes she does lunch and sometimes she does recess,
but when Ms. M. or Ms. R. can hear you, they'll make you go sit all
by yourself, and you have to owe five minutes of recess. And we run
a daily lap, and when Ms. F.'s here, she always runs with us. It's not
really fun, because, if she passes us, and she's done with her lap, you
have to run an extra one.

—*Ruth, white, public school, low income*

Sometimes the watchful eye of the teacher is supplemented by technology. At Nathan's school, surveillance is also performed by recording
devices strategically placed.

There are cameras outside, they're longer range, they're way back there, and barely anybody can see them, and they blend into the school, not like the ones out in the hall, but that one out there, and it sticks out, and it's got long range, so it can look at the playground, at least it only looks at a certain part. There's two outside cameras, one of 'em's looking at the playground, and I think the other one is looking at the sidewalk where we walk in and out to get to recess. It kinda, you know, *looks* at you, and it just kinda creeps ya out a little bit, and it seems like they actually want to make ya do something so they can punish you or somethin', cuz why else would they stare at the playground, there's already monitors out there, like, teachers. Two teachers out there, already watching you, and you have cameras, too.

—*Nathan, white, public school, middle income*

Nathan approaches a genuinely critical stance but always pulls back a bit. Of course, his instincts are absolutely accurate. Why do school officials need cameras when adult eyes are on the playground at all times? Reflecting on what these kids have to say about systems, policies, surveillance, and punishments, I imagine moans from researchers who work in the field of character education and citizenship. They moan because we know that there are far better ways to develop morally grounded children in school, and that all children deserve school environments that will promote their development as individuals in caring relationships among peers and adults. Moreover, even if children themselves believe that these carrot-and-stick systems are fair, or good enough, this paradigm is not where we ought to be in 2014. Operant conditioning is fit for circus lions, not children.

At scale, there are sobering correlations with the prevailing behaviorist disciplinary policies designed to maintain order in classrooms. In a 2009–10 study of 72,000 schools representing 85 percent of all U.S. students, researchers found that while 18 percent of the student sample were African American, African American students were 35 percent of those who were suspended at least once, 46 percent of those who were suspended more than once, and 39 percent of all expulsions. African American students were three and a half times more likely to be suspended or expelled than white students generally.

And among the group of students who were involved in school-related arrests or referred to law enforcement, more than 70 percent were either African American or Hispanic. In such a context, the gallows humor of the "offense" known as *driving while black*, extends to another we might call *going to school while black*, since the very experience of school seems to likewise set up students of color for negative engagement with the criminal justice system. In some charter schools, the alternative to resistance and "trouble" seems to be the zombification resulting from total compliance.

Great teachers nurture every single student's personal agency, sense of belonging, and competence. These are the basics of sound character education programs. State-of-the art, research-based practices can help schools develop a pedagogic culture so that student classroom behavior stops being something to be managed by teachers, and recess behavior by cameras, and instead becomes part and parcel of the student's intellectual, moral, physical, and imaginative growth. With regard to student behavior, the question we ought to be asking through every effort to reform teacher preparation and professional development is this: in what ways does this proposed change empower teachers to create more just, trusting, caring, ethical, collaborative, democratic, interactive classroom environments?

THE GROWN-UP IN THE ROOM

According to students, good teachers are caring, intelligent, fair, and authoritative. I would not disagree with this. So, returning to the question from the beginning of this chapter, what is the right stuff when it comes to identifying, recognizing, and preparing great teachers in the twenty-first century? What can we do now to help more teachers be great in the ways students need them to be? First, because the most important work teachers do is model roles, we need to be sure that teachers are educated to be the kinds of people we want our students to be. They cannot be all alike, but they should—by professional design—demonstrate qualities of self-efficacy, intellectual and critical agency, compassion, courage, flexibility, grit, resilience, persistence, optimism, and all the other traits we hope to cultivate in our children. The more we train and treat teachers like script-following automatons at the mercy of carrot-and-stick incentives and punishments, the more likely students will turn out like that, too, or resist and get thrown out for resisting. If we want students to be adaptive innovators, problem solvers, and critical thinkers; if we want them to be able to observe, question, experiment, network, work collaboratively, and make connections across domains—transfer learning from one content area to another—then we had better figure out how to bring to scale the processes that will develop all teachers into people who can and do show the way.

Here's where the subject gets touchy, because at the same time we have to speak candidly about social class, cultural identities, individual disposition and temperament, and the complex intersections of these qualities in educator preparation. Teachers who enter the profession from communities of wealth and privilege tend to have empowered dispositions, at least at first. Teachers who enter the profession from communities with relatively less status and privilege can also demonstrate the right stuff. In both cases, a spirit of curiosity and a know-how about recruiting resources in learning—from other people, from intergenerational family pride, from books and global digital platforms—powers such a teacher's energy, and sets the example of "the active inquiring mind" in the classroom. Learning is a lifelong stance. Receiving a diploma does not put an end to learning. If you are human, you are always learning something. Indeed, in terms of content, we all learn the most and the best in the five years after we are born, before we ever *start* going to school: Gravity. Object permanence. How people treat us. Language. Teachers who think of themselves as people with agency and show self-efficacy with regard to their own learning and professional growth will conduct themselves in the classroom in ways that set this example for students. By virtue of their own responsiveness to an ever-changing world they will upload a living curriculum fresh every single morning. Alas, public school hierarchies, hubristic expectations, institutional bureaucracies, intellectual mediocrity among administrators, and lack of pedagogical know-how can cause even excellent novice teachers to wither on the vine and drop out of the profession.

And here is a twist: teachers who enter the profession from communities of relatively less status and privilege who demonstrate intellectual and temperamental aptitude can, with support, develop an empowered stance of confidence, competence, and inquiry, even if it's not there at first. I see this happening at my university and in my work as an instructional coach. Such transformations are well documented in education scholarship.

And equally important but hard to talk about: there are educators who enter the profession from communities of less status and privilege relative to the mainstream middle class. At the beginning of their careers they are absorbed into—and promoted within—an oppressively hierarchical, bureaucratic system that uses rewards and punishments to control behavior and values administrative compliance over intellectual engagement. These teachers are *set up* to be obedient, sullen, compliant, frustrated, helpless cogs in a system. When they teach in underresourced districts, these sorts of teachers and administrators—well meaning though they are—come to think that highly monitored, unquestioning obedience is "what these kids need in order to learn" in school. Kylene Beers, president of the National Council of Teachers of English, has referred to this as "the genteel unteaching of America's poor."*

Averaged nationally, 25 percent of all children are not graduating from high school. More kids stay in school in the Northeast and Upper Midwest and Great Plains; in the Southeast the graduation rate drops to around 70 percent—nearly one in three drop out. Given these statistics, I do not think we can make a case that school *is* serving children at scale—or that militaristic drill-and-kill, highly policed schooling is somehow "what these kids need in order to learn" because "their lives outside of school are so chaotic." If a teenager values what they are learning in school, they tend to do everything they can to stick around, and will drop out only if what's happening in their lives outside or inside school makes school absolutely unmanageable.

Given the vital influence and power of teachers in classrooms, we have to start candidly taking into account the culture and background

---

*Kylene Beers, "The Genteel Unteaching of America's Poor," National Council of Teachers of English (March 2009).

of teachers in our professional development within the context of the schools where they teach. Not doing so ill serves students, particularly students from low-income communities, communities of color, students who are learning English, and students with learning disabilities.

Let's revisit the goals threaded through this chapter.

We want classrooms to be just, trusting, caring, ethical, collaborative, democratic, and interactive environments. We want teachers empowered to create sensitive, respectful, emotionally responsive classroom climates. We want teachers to respect, know, understand, and communicate with the home worlds of students. We want families to collaborate in a living curriculum that is responsive to students' own worlds.

Therefore, educator preparation and professional development initiatives need to be addressing this question: given a teacher's identity and background, and given the students she or he will be serving, what can we do to empower this teacher to identify problems, imagine solutions, be creatively resourceful, model cognitive plasticity, set an example as a intellectual engaged in learning, take risks, experience the failure necessary for learning and growth, persist, and weather setbacks with resilience?

We want to cultivate these qualities in teachers because it is the right thing to do. But we also want to do this because then, and only then, will teachers be the role models our children need in order to be global citizens of the mid-twenty-first century.

3

CRASHING THE A.R. PARTY

"I Read Because We Have This Thing Called A.R."

R eading is a complex social activity that involves making meaning out of words, images, graphs, charts, numbers, abbreviations, and many other inscribed symbol systems. The texts we read are the fabric of our interactions with billboards, pages, screens, fliers, shopping lists, owner's manuals, receipts, invoices, and other materials. If we imagine Big Data and the online world in general as a communally cared for ocean of interconnected knowledge, we want as many people as possible able to contribute to and learn from it. In the last thirty years, literacy researchers all over the world have explored and explained how a student's background, culture, and home language practices contribute to reading identities and performance. Given the massive expansion in the range and depth of understanding we now have regarding kids and texts, how are different kids talking and thinking about reading? Who's reading what where?

I found five different kinds of reading happening among fourth graders: reading for rewards; reading as oasis; reading for information and enlightenment; reading related to religious practice; reading for pure pleasure.

READING FOR REWARDS

In a public school a few weeks ago, I watched a fourth grader examine books on the classroom rack looking for what he called "a good-fit book," which he described as one that was somewhere between a 3.4 and a 3.6, a number he searched for inside the front cover. According to a digitally administered diagnostic test, these numbers signified this child's reading level and correspond to a grade level. This student did not consult the text on the front or back, nor any of the words in the book itself; his eyes scanned for the good-fit code: a book algorithmically aligned with a person between the fourth and sixth month of third grade.

In a shaky middle-class, public school setting, Janelle wanted to show me the book she was reading "for Six Flags," as she put it. As a reward for directing her eyes across lines on pages for a certain number of minutes, Janelle would earn a field trip to an amusement park: "So I'm reading for that and I have to git three hundred and sixty minutes, right now I'm like at ninety-five minutes."

Kyra participates in a summertime reading-for-reward system that has her list the number of pages read:

> I read a lot. We had a Raging Readers for this waterpark in the
> summer. And I already read a lot then but that made me even read
> more. So I filled up the whole thing. And some of the back. It was
> like one thousand–something pages.

> —Kyra, white, outer-ring-suburban, Catholic school, fragile middle income

Barack recalls a reading-for-reward program from years past:

> In second grade we used to have a long chart in reading and it said
> how many pages you read, and we all got to a hundred-something,
> we won something, I won a Six Flags ticket to Ragin' Rivers, so I
> read a *lot*, it was like a chart with lines and people's names, and it
> had long lines, like thirty-three thousand pages. We got up to five
> hundred fifty thousand, something like that, and it was three kids
> from our class and I was one of 'em.

> —Barack, African American, urban, private school, middle income

Reading for rewards has been around a long time. Literacy curricula of this sort are typically commercial, point-based, leveled, and mandated; materials are bought by districts and managed by teacher-administrators. The massive standardization and commercialization of reading for rewards is exemplified by the number-one form of reading instruction I heard kids talk about: A.R. In Missouri, reading time mostly means A.R. time, and A.R. stands for Accelerated Reader. I had interviewed several children before I began to piece together the deeper significance of A.R., letters that came up again and again.

RURAL

Isaiah attends a peppy, mindfully led school south of Branson, a twenty-minute drive from the Arkansas state line. Isaiah's got strawberry-colored hair and freckles, and says that his home life and his school life have nothing, really, to do with each other. School is a job; home is for everything that seems to matter most. Isaiah lives on a beautiful lake with his mother, a speech therapist, and father, an accountant. He hunts, fishes, and boats; he observes and questions what he notices out in the woods. He and I had a long sidebar conversation about hunting and identifying plants, trees, and other forms of life in the woods, but this is how he talks about reading in school:

> We have a A.R. goal, and we should read a lot. A.R. goal is where you have a certain goal to get to, by reading and taking A.R. tests, so if you take all those tests and get them all a passing percentage, then you get a point, a half point, whatever, how many the book was worth. And if you make it to that goal, then you throw a party, at the end of the year but if you don't you don't get to.
> *Do you know what A.R. stands for?*
> No. I've just heard A.R. a lot.
>
> *—Isaiah, white, public school, middle income*

Julian lives in a trailer in a rural community in the southeast corner of Missouri, also goes to public school, and also mentioned A.R.

> We have to read A.R. books and take a test on 'em and you get points if you get a certain amount right, but if you get under that certain amount, you get not even one, you get a half a point or less.

Do you know what A.R. stands for?
Um, no.

                    —Julian, white, public school, low income

Talk to enough kids, or spend enough time in schools, and you will
learn that A.R. talk is related to reading, kind of. Mostly it's talk related to points, time, accounting—math of all sorts, really—along
with rewards and punishments.

> If we get all our work done we can read A.R. but that's if you
> haven't met your goal and if you have, then you can just do like
> basically whatever you want, math stations, but you can't be too
> loud otherwise we'll get in trouble for the people that's reading.
> Like, this morning, I said, "Ms. S., I'm bored but I already met my
> A.R. goal and I got all my work done."
>
>   *—Prudence, white, rural, public school, low income*

> Well, I read because we have this thing called A.R.—A.R.
> reading—and we have to get up to this goal to make it to a party.
> And if we don't make it we have to stay in one room and read while
> everybody else is playing.
>
>   *—Gabriel, white, rural, low income*

I read because we have this thing called A.R. I would argue that Gabriel
is not understanding what reading is, and is not reading in a way that
will ever help him understand or enjoy what reading is. Many schools
have set up a system whereby the activity of reading is positioned as the
opposite of having fun at parties and playing outside. Being isolated in
a room while everybody else is playing—and all because you have not
made it to your A.R. goal—sounds like a nightmare. But this is the
way it is:

> BRITTANY: We had to get our A.R. goal up to twenty points. And
>   it stressed you out because you almost didn't make it, and
>   then at the end when you do make it you're like, thank good-
>   ness I did.

KAYLA: 'Cause like today is our last day to get our A.R. points and I was supposed to have twenty and I'm only at, well, I need two and a half more points.

What happens if you don't get those points?

KAYLA: If you don't then you don't get to go to a party called an A.R. party where we get ta bring snacks, DSs, not phones, so we're not allowed to bring our phones, and we can go in different rooms, one room is music room, one room is reading for the people that didn't make their goal. They have to read while the other people are doin' a party and there's one room for board games and sometimes you get to go outside.

DAKOTA: And if you get to be in those four parties—there's four quarters so every quarter we get a party and if you meet all those quarters then you get to go bowling at the fourth quarter, if you make that quarter, too. I've met all three quarters already.

Not only associated with stress, discipline, and rewards, A.R. came up in conversations about engagement and achievement. Here is how Ruth, a thoughtful, chatty, vivacious student from a rural public school, connected her A.R. reading with fluctuations in personal interest. I asked her whether she was ever bored in school.

Depends, like, sometimes, I'll have books that I don't really care for, and I kinda don't want to exchange 'em, cuz I want to know what's the end, and sometimes I don't feel like reading, but, I don't think I should work on my bare book [a commodified blank book template for kids to create], because she might want us to read. Just depends, because sometimes, there's some books I really like to read, and sometimes there's ones that are just ehh, I'll read it just in case. Like last year, there was this book that I really wanted to read, and it was called *Cat in the Kitchen*, and it was a long Animal Ark book [a specific series on the A.R. list], and I was like, "I don't know, I guess I'll try it," and I got halfway, and I just started being bored a bunch, and then, next few days, I started reading it, and I got finished, and I actually got a ten out of ten.

Ruth narrates a consciousness of her own reading engagement and decision making. And yet the story concludes with the points Ruth earned on the A.R. quiz that wrapped up her reading of *Cat in the Kitchen*. Even though she had slogged through boredom and didn't really like the book—it had been *just ehh*—she still got a ten out of ten. Is this good or bad?

Ruth's response raises questions about what we mean by the phrase "a good reader" in the context of A.R. The *she* in the first sentence is her teacher, and shows that Ruth is making her reading decisions based on hypothetical interpretations of her teacher's desires (*she might want us to read*). When I told Ruth that what she said during our interview was not graded, she was cheerfully relieved.

I'm kinda glad it's not graded cause I would probly fail cause I'm not very good at answering questions.

Oh, what makes you say that?

Because usually when I answer a question, and it's in my own words, I usually get it wrong.

Can you think of an example?

Like one time, when it says "I think" and I write what I think and then I end up getting it wrong.

In A.R.-dominated literacy practices, Ruth and other children whose vivacity is expressed in words have an entirely inaccurate and conceptually muddled sense of their own evident powers with language: if they say or are instructed or prompted to say what they think in their own words, they get it wrong.

OUTER-RING SUBURBAN

A.R. talk is not only in rural communities. Closer to a city, in a well-resourced and growing outer-ring community, a couple of bubbly, confident girls who go to a shiny clean public school situate A.R. in their reading lives:

I read like big thick chapter books over the summer, only over the summer, because we have reading contracts and you have to get a certain amount of A.R. points to be able to meet your score? And so, and I'm a slow reader, and so I can't read the big thick chapter books, like the Harry Potter series or The Hunger Games, so I read those a lot over the summer.

—June, white, public school, middle income

I can read fast so I don't really like thick ones I read probably like that [she indicates thickness of the books with her fingers], like two hundred pages, yeah, because like I already finished my A.R. goal and when you're finished you don't have to read any more but I still do 'cause it's really fun, my favorite subject is reading.

—Alex, white, public school, middle income

For people like June and Alex, A.R. reading is contract work. Figuring out what to read means understanding the overall strategy— earn enough points to meet your contract—as well as the tactics—select short books that will help you accrue enough points. Luckily for both girls, this work has not yet killed their ability to read for pleasure. Alex reads even though she doesn't "have to anymore," and June saves the books she really likes to read for summertime.

Jason, a thoughtful student in an outer-ring community, came close to knowing what the letters stood for:

A.R. is accelerated reading. It's when we read all kinds of books and then we take a test on it and then if we get a special, like if it's a chapter book, we have to get either a ninety or one hundred but if it's a picture book we have to get a one hundred and then we get a little Starburst.

—Jason, white, public school, fragile middle income

I heard A.R. talk in suburban parochial schools, too. Helen, a big strong athletic girl with a twinkle in her eye, shared sly forms of resistance to authority, including passing notes written in code. Helen was the first person who told me exactly what the letters signified and explained the sequence concisely and clearly:

Accelerated reader. Like you read a book and then there is a test on it to make sure that you read it, then you get points for it.

—Helen, white, Protestant school, middle income

Notice how she phrases that explanation: in Helen's view the test is to make sure you read the book, not to make sure you understood it, or, heaven forbid, enjoyed it. There were schools where nobody spoke of A.R., and I will get to these A.R.-free zones, but first, honestly, what is this program and what is it doing in school?

Accelerated Reader is a reading-and-assessment software package produced by Renaissance Learning, a company owned since 2011 by Permira Funds, a U.K.-based global private equity management firm with roughly $20 billion in assets. Nearly half of all schools in the United States—70,000—are using Accelerated Reader. In Missouri, thousands of schools, and by extension the millions of taxpayers who support our schools, as well as the families of independent schools who have bought the Accelerated Reader package, are paying customers of Renaissance Learning. In the context of school-based reading instruction and assessment, not to talk about Renaissance Learning would be like trying to talk about beverage consumption in the United States and not mention Coca-Cola Company.

Renaissance Learning tracks the numbers of books (and words) read based on the online quizzes children have passed with a score of 80 percent or higher. Renaissance Learning advertises on its website (ren learn.com) that it sells "advanced technology for data-driven schools."

The company takes what it considers school-appropriate, commercially published books and assigns points to them. Picture books are given fewer points and texts of higher linguistic, if not multimodal, complexity are given more points. In 2012 there were 150,000 books in what they call their quizzable collection. The company has developed an Advanced TASA Open Standard for Readability (ATOS), which they use to inform an "ATOS readability analyzer," a tool they say helps teachers, who may wonder about the "level" of a classroom text. Renaissance Learning says that their ATOS readability analyzer "makes it easy to get the answers fast."

So children select books that have been determined to be at their level. Their reading is managed and monitored through the software. Quizzes are provided, graded, and made available to classroom teachers immediately, with widgets tracking these numbers at each school. Children are encouraged to earn lots of points, even if it means selecting books they are less interested in, because points translate into stickers, treats, and what kids and teachers call A.R. parties.

If this all sounds behaviorist, Pavlovian, and dystopian, more like *A Clockwork Orange* than like, say, reading books, that's because it is. Industry titans who rely on techno-jargon, psychometrical mania, and transnational capitalism have identified and made profitable use of an ever-growing crop of vulnerable and available customers: other people's children and their teachers. Low down in the corporate hierarchy, well-meaning employees of Renaissance Learning probably think they are serving children's needs. But critics and literacy researchers look at this kind of thing and boil over with rage. Reading specialists know that interest and engagement will always trump "level."

Here's copy from Renaissance Learning's parent company's website (permira.com):

> More than 1.5 million tests are taken every school day on a Renaissance product. . . . With strong market positioning, high recurring revenues and significant growth and transformational potential, the Permira funds will draw upon the expertise of Permira's long-established TMT sector to back an exciting growth strategy opportunity that capitalises on long-term secular trends in education technology.

We have to think about what a TMT sector is and what a TMT sector has to do with Isaiah reading *Because of Winn Dixie* in southwest Missouri. The companies purchased by Permira are divided into sectors: Consumer, Industrials, Healthcare, Financial Services, and TMT. Renaissance Learning falls under TMT, which stands for Technology, Media, and Telecommunications. When Permira bought Renaissance Learning, the Wisconsin-based company had been profitable since its

1985 founding, a period of time characterized by ever-shrinking state, federal, and local budgets allocated to education. Permira, after all, was capitalizing on "long-term secular trends in education technology."

Financially pinched, politically cowed, and historically risk-averse, public school administrators and education policy makers have pushed A.R. into classrooms, believing that this kind of curriculum will save schools time and money. So a kid will read a book and then move to the computer to take a quiz. The results of all A.R. quizzes pour into Renaissance Learning's pool of statistics for tracking. At the local data collection point, namely the classroom, the teacher tracks the accumulation of points for each of her students and her class overall. Sorting, managing, monitoring, and testing the reading done by children has proved to be very profitable.

Renita Schmidt, a former fourth-grade teacher, analyzed in the journal *Language Arts* the effects of A.R. in the classroom. Back in 2008, Schmidt wrote:

> According to the website, schools that already own a "desktop version of A.R." are charged one flat fee for access ($599 in 2007); schools that own a "Renaissance version" are charged no additional fee, but all schools are charged "an annual student fee of $1000 for 250 students or $4 a student" to access "Accelerated Reader Software," (more than 100,000 A.R. quizzes), "9 hours of Web-based Professional Development," and other support materials listed as professional development or technical support systems.

No doubt these numbers have gone up, and I will leave it to others to do the math, but Permira paid close to half a billion dollars to add the company to its TMT roster in 2011.

Linking its program to Common Core Standards, to Missouri's own statewide test, and to various other standards, rubrics, and benchmarks around the country, Renaissance Learning keeps itself an essential part of a seemingly unquenchable thirst for measurements and statistics. Accelerated Reader plays a dominant role in the dehumanization of children and deprofessionalization of the classroom teacher. Accelerated Reader transforms reading into accounting. Children are logging pages that have been preanalyzed for readability in exchange for extrinsic rewards. As hidden curriculum, this teaches kids to view reading as a conditioned response to a corporate process housed and regulated in cyberspace.

Renaissance Learning has designed Accelerated Reader to make money in schools. Lots of money. Meanwhile, as a reward for their screen-based quiz taking, people like Jason get a little Starburst.

READING AS OASIS

The second kind of reading, also established by the teacher, brackets free reading time within the overall structure of the day. This is what I would call the something-to-do-when-you're-done-with-your-work way. Students may turn to books when they complete other work and are waiting for classmates to finish. Or the teacher may simply grant them the privilege to read. Some kids use time like this for building up A.R. points; others turn to books that have attracted them personally when they have completed their worksheets, or gotten done what everyone else is still working on. True, this kind of reading is sort of a time filler, but it's certainly more like real reading than strictly monitored and measured A.R. reading. The activities known as D.E.A.R. time (Drop Everything and Read), S.S.R. (Sustained Silent Reading), and even R.A.D. (Read All Day) are also in this category, although the way teachers put these designs into practice—how much freedom kids have to choose their reading, how long a period of time they read, how much pleasure they take in the activity, what teachers expect to come out of this time—varies widely. When kids talk about how reading fits into the onrushing flow of a day it can sound like this:

> It's usually math and then like A.R. reading in the morning, and then we usually have a special like computer or music and sumpin.

And then something else like a fun activity and then we go out to recess and then we come back in fer lunch and then we have D.E.A.R. and then, the rest of the day, like whatever we have going. And sometimes a second recess.

—Cole, white, outer-ring suburb, Catholic school, middle income

URBAN

Finding pockets of time and place to read and write in peace is what keeps some kids out of trouble in socially volatile schools.

On the bus I read Jiminy Cricket. At the end of the day we usually read a book to our own selves, a different book. What goes on in my school life is we have kids that fight so much. They've been trashin' up the toilets, they've been writing curses. Some kids tried to fight me, it's five kids against me, and then we almost got expelled, they thought I was fightin' but I wasn't. Then my friends came, and then he [my brother] stood up for me . . . Lowell is like crazy, for real . . . Cuz it's real bad. They have too much food fights. They have food fights. Really I don't do that stuff. They just threw a milk carton at me, with the thing open. Oh, me and my friends we were just talking. Then, the kids that was acting bad, they get in ISS [in-school suspension] for five days or ten.

—Malik, African American, public school, low income

I read by myself so nobody won't interrupt me. 'Cause it's too much bullies and . . . and people always bringin' lighters and guns to school. I eat my breakfast, I go to the gym, sit there, pull out a book and read it, or I sit there, pull out my homework and do it. Then I just sit there, write, don't like, people be yellin' and all that, I just want 'em to be listenin', I just be sittin' there writin' and doin' my homework. 'Cause I like sitting by myself.

—Deion, African American, public school, low income

Malik and Deion turn to books to keep themselves safe outside the social drama in their school. Given the zone of solitude that reading can create, it is especially terrible that the classroom libraries in schools attended by children like Malik and Deion tend to lack a variety of interesting and challenging trade books for them to read.

In schools that value free reading time, kids are around books and have space and time to read during the day.

> After lunch we have a book break. It's like twenty minutes where we can just read a book and each—a couple people get a day to sit in the book corner which has, like, pillows and you can check out a book from the library.
>
> —Cassidy, white, Catholic school, middle income

> What kinds of things do you do during your free time?
> I read. I read like the world record books and stuff. We have Ripley's Believe It or Not.
>
> —Sean, white, Catholic school, middle income

> I think Rosedale does a really good job on reading. They don't make you, they don't say, "All right, the whole class is reading this book and you have to finish it by this day." They let you, I mean we have to read for thirty minutes but that's not a problem because they have such good books that everyone is excited to read and so I feel like I have a lot of freedom when we have reading because I can read any book I want! I could read this book and this book and I really like that.
>
> —Marley, white, private school, high income

OUTER-RING SUBURB

> In school, in my free time I like to read. I like reading Captain Underpants books.
> And outside of school, I like to play outside.
>
> —Kamar, Moroccan American, Islamic school, middle income

When you're done with your work you usually just read, go to . . . there's a reading corner, you can go there and read. I like this book called *Diary of a Wimpy Kid* and *Captain Underpants* and I've read the series of Diary of a Wimpy Kid. I've one book left to read for the Captain Underpants.

—*Nuri, Syrian American, Islamic school, high income*

Right now, in D.E.A.R., she lets us read fiction.

—*Cole, white, Catholic school, middle income*

Do you have a favorite time of day?
Probably either after lunch or right in the morning, because it's not usually like too loud and we have time to read then. I really like to read [*laughs*].

—*Lorraine, white, Catholic school, middle income*

RURAL

If you get your work done, then you get free time to read a book.

—*Oliver, white, public school, middle income*

If we get done with our morning work, we can read or get on the computer or sumpin. And when we get done, like if we do a test or sumpin, if he tells us he wants us to read a book, we'll read a book.

—*Casey, white, public school, low income*

READING FOR INFORMATION AND ENLIGHTENMENT

The third type of reading in school is demonstrated by kids who actively and autonomously take up books for learning about something they are genuinely interested in. Often these subjects are related to nature and science, but they can also relate to historical people, places, and events like ancient Egypt, the city of London, sports or sports figures, and other individual interests. More than any other topic, what seizes kids' imaginations are animals. I heard students talk with passion about birds, snakes, zebras, and tigers, among other animals, and how their interest in these animals drove them to books, libraries, digital sources of information, role models, and other adults with expertise. Out of caring for animals, the student wanted to learn more and more about them. Christopher said that the most important thing he ever learned was:

> When we learned about how the animals survive in the wilderness. We learned how in the ocean, how whales, and what kind of whales, and fish, how they would survive, and zebras, how they would hafta live by water and stuff. Cuz I like science a lot. I like animals, I do like zebras, and I like to learn what they do.
>
> —*Christopher, white, rural, public school, low income*

Toby was another kid with a passion. Asked if he had any ideas about future plans, he said he wanted to be an ornithologist.

> I'm super interested in birds. I've read Sibley's a couple times, I've read all of 'em. I've got this binder of different birds and I maybe have half of North America's birds, I have twenty-four pages of birds, North America and the whole world. It's actually done. I do work fast. My heroes are Sibley and Phoebe Snetsinger. She's kinda insane but she was a birder. She went all over the world to see almost every bird in existence. She saw the most birds out of any birder and that was eight thousand seven hundred and forty-six, and the record was eight thousand.
>
> —*Toby, white, small city, public school, middle income*

And Alyssa:

> Right now I'm really reading Christmas books and I usually read the books that are about animals I like, about wolves and stuff.
>
> —*Alyssa, white, urban, Catholic school, middle income*

The only thing Christopher, Toby, and Alyssa require are adults to help them find the books they need to read.

READING RELATED TO RELIGIOUS PRACTICE

Christian, Muslim, and Jewish kids from observant families are reading historical and religious texts in school if they attend parochial schools. If they attend public schools and their families engage in religious practices, they will be exposed to reading these texts outside of school. Catholic and Protestant children read Bible stories, both in church and in weekday religious classes at school. Muslim kids read the Qur'an verse by verse, learning Arabic and memorizing their whole scripture in school and out of school. Jewish kids, whether in Jewish day schools or after-school programs, read stories from the Torah or cultural or history books. Some are learning to read and write Hebrew.

Deep and persistent connections between reading and religion in this country should not be surprising. If we trace the historical roots of literacy learning, we end up with the Puritans in the early seventeenth century: a child raised to have a personal, unmediated relationship with God and God's word needed to be able to read the Bible. In a manner of speaking, this is how the democratizing of literacy can be traced from Massachusetts in 1620 to Missouri in 2013, where 37 percent of the state's population are evangelical Christians, and a boy named Trevor in a rural school told me that the most important thing he has ever learned, in or out of school, is "probably to get saved by God, like, let God go into your heart and know that he is your master and that you'll go to heaven." Trevor's mom worked in the school part-time. She sat in on our interview and nodded her head.

Speaking with his customary maturity, Hunter said:

> I'm at church a lot, so I read a lot there. I read stories from the
> Bible or usually we'll do crossword things in Sunday school. It
> just depends. Sometimes we do activities like we'll make crosses

from Popsicle sticks or sometimes we'll do activities, like, we got to remember who did what and things like that.

—*Hunter, white, rural, public school, low income*

Greta goes to a suburban Protestant school. As I did with all of the kids attending religious schools, I asked how God and faith fit in with her daily life at school. I had not expected a literal response, certainly not one that focused on the books themselves. Using her hands as she spoke to indicate the hugely thick books crowding the interior of her desk, Greta showed me exactly how much space she was talking about that God was fitting into.

When I look in my desk a religion book is like this thick [*she indicates a very big book*] and then we have a giant space for a Bible and then this religion thing in our notebook that's like this thick and then all the other books are this thick or this thick or maybe the biggest book other than my religion book is this thick. If I took my religion book out of my desk it would be so much cleaner in there. And then the Bible is this big and I have to put my three-ring notebook in and then that giant book I'm reading called *The Candymakers*, which is as big as the Bible.

—*Greta, white, Protestant school, middle income*

Setting aside Greta's matter-of-fact spatial considerations about literacy, it seems to me there is a deeper, if unintended, truth in her response. For children who attend schools with only A.R.-type reading going on, religious observance at home or in school that requires engagement with texts and stories in print can provide significant opportunities to integrate reading with meaningful social purpose.

READING FOR PURE PLEASURE

The fifth way of reading is so far from A.R. and also so obvious that it should go without saying, but at this moment in the history of American schooling, it cannot. There still are children who read for pure pleasure and entertainment, in school and out of school. They pick up a book and read because they like to. It makes them feel good. Whether the story is sad, scary, or disturbing—which science fiction and fantasy can be, of course, not to mention "real life" stories and information books— the act of reading is pleasurable and doesn't have to serve any other purpose apart from giving pleasure. Because they read for fun, kids like this develop strong personal tastes about the kind of books they like.

URBAN

I like fiction books. I kinda like fantasy. I've read a lot this year. Mostly I like to read a whole series, like I just finished the sixty-five Nancy Drews, I read all of them, so I like to stick to a series. And then I like the same author usually. So this year I did *Fable Haven*, which is, fantasy [not] with creatures. I don't like fantasy with creatures. I don't like sci-fi or nonfiction, I mean it's OK but I like fantasy better, but I don't like totally misbelief things, like totally, out of the world.

—*Allison, white, private school, high income*

Kashena's reading is like this, too, in a way. Kashena, who is African American, attends a regimented, hyperdisciplined charter school in the city. For fun she reads fashion and celebrity magazines about pop stars like Selena Gomez and Justin Bieber. In an outer-ring suburb far north of the city, Xavier reads Star Wars books on his own time for pleasure. Unfortunately, Xavier's interest in books does not transfer into school-based recognition or academic success. As a student with autism main-streamed in a Catholic school, Xavier, who is white, reports that he "gets bad grades" in reading. In a very different setting, Aini is a native Arabic speaker whose English is still developing. She goes to an Islamic school and loves the Boxcar series. She's read them all.

The *Diary of a Wimpy Kid* series was named by more children than any other as a favorite:

I like diary books. Dork Diaries, Diary of Wimpy Kid, Grandma Stilton, I just like hearing what people have to say for their self, it's funny

for me. In *Diary of Wimpy Kid*, Greg's brother, you know how you have
a hot dog? and the mustard goes on like this? He likes it straight across
[*laughs*] like lines. He likes one line straight across and it has to be in the
middle of the hot dog or he'll have a really big fit. And that's really funny.

—*Lucy, white, Catholic school, middle income*

The more advanced readers in urban and suburban private schools
have mostly outgrown the Wimpy series.

Connecting the books they read with other media—film, video
games, and television—many children build socializing into reading.
Lucy's classmate Georgia says:

There's this show that [*she names three friends*], we watch it together
like every single week, because it comes on once a week. The show
and the book is called *Pretty Little Liars*, and I'm reading it actually
right now, and it's really cool 'cause the show is kinda related to the
book, but I think the book gives more details.

—*Georgia, white, Catholic school, middle income*

Lena goes to a socially diverse school in the city:

I love to read. I want to either be an artist or work at a library, 'cause
those are my two favorite subjects. We read this amazing book, I
loved it, I forget his name, he's a really good author and I should
remember it 'cause I heard it before we read [his book] *Where the Red
Fern Grows*. It was sad but it had amazing details. And I just loved the
determination and the main character Billy. Like with the tree, he
was chasing it, he was chasing a raccoon with his two dogs, he spent
one or two days chopping it down just so he could get that raccoon.

—*Lena, white, private school, middle income*

Her classmate Henry also reads for fun:

I usually like to read just stuff that doesn't make sense. Stuff like,
when people . . . like robots and stuff that doesn't make sense.
There's a whole series about this boy who, a whole bunch of weird

things happens to him while a bunch of, like his great uncle came back as a cat from dead, from the afterlife, and then he came back and told him about how he died, he got hit by a bus, and then, and then it was funny that a cat smoked cigars.

—Henry, African American, private school, middle income

The readers who read routinely for learning and pleasure are the readers we say we want to nurture. They are reading the way we say we want all children to read. Once children are hooked on books, adult interaction and tinkering in formal and informal settings will connect them with the literature, information books, histories, journals, and other forms of print that will support their learning in and out of school. Alas, the bad news: the kids who are reading this way tend to be found less frequently among poor and working-poor families in both city and rural communities. Scarcity of books to take home, emphasis on A.R. and other test-driven ways of reading at school, lack of appreciation for the texts they *are* reading and writing, and preoccupation with screen-centered forms of entertainment have made reading for pure pleasure in these settings less likely. What can we learn from children who are really reading in school?

NURTURING REAL READERS

One thing we know is that reading should not be isolated from thinking, speaking, and writing, and that all aspects of literacy should be part of what happens with books in school. Jake's favorite place to learn is school; he turns to books and newspapers in order to keep abreast of current events, politics, and history, which particularly interests him.

Right now I'm doing a project, like, independently, about the history of my school actually, so I do a lot of projects like that, like history. I [also] write a political newsletter every morning actually. It takes probably an hour, so I wake up really early so like six to seven . . . it's just news.

—Jake, Jewish, inner-ring suburb, public school, middle income

Robert is the son of an attorney (mother) and a physician (father). He goes to a selective and respected urban private school. When the conversation turned to reading, here's what Robert said:

> Reading, is basically, well they really try to mature us in our reading, not "did you read how many pages," they do actual lesson plans and they read teacher books. They don't really assign us reading homework, we're supposed to read thirty minutes every night and then mark it down and look at our minutes and say what we notice and then we reflect on our reading after a month—once again a lot of reflecting in fourth grade—we can say "I read best, by forty-five minutes my page-per-minute has gone way up, but after I get over an hour and a half . . ." If I do some crazy readings like I have no homework for some reason or worked ahead. . . .
>
> We get to read in class, too. You noticed they have a lot of comfy stuff, the ball chairs, the beanbags. We just call it reading, R.A.D., read all day! We have R.A.D. maybe once every month. Reading's encouraged and everybody loves reading. And we get book clubs instead of [*impression of deep adult voice*] "well, I'm just gonna give you this huge test on this book." We get to choose a book with a friend, four to two friends, occasionally five or six, but no usually four because it's too easy to—you know, "oh I was ten pages behind this guy, he was ten pages ahead of me, but he was twenty"—and then you read a little and then you plan, we're gonna read to, we're on 120 now and we're gonna read to 160 tonight. . . .
>
> Currently, well, I'm in a book club, we can also have book clubs about series—have you ever heard of Margaret Haddix? A lot of people are doing that, the Missing books I'm doing. And we get to discuss the books. I just finished up a book club on an English book called *Cosmic* by Frank Kattrell Boyce, and actually one of his books, *Millions*, was made into a movie, and he's a really good author. I think it's my very favorite book ever.

If we are going to speak honestly about whose kids get what kinds of reading experiences in school, and what public policy and the open market have to do with these realities, it is important to pay close attention to what Robert has said and how he has said it. First of all, Robert respects his teachers as professionals making decisions collaboratively—*they really try to mature us in our reading.*

So how does this teaching team design the experience of reading? Robert's teachers make him think about how he reads as well as what he reads. Within the boundaries his teachers establish, Robert and his classmates have considerable choice. The kids choose exactly the right number of members for their book groups, they plan how many pages they will read that night, and then they meet in school to talk about their book. There are books Robert likes, and books he doesn't like. He can ask a stranger, me, if I've read something. If I have, we can compare impressions and critiques.

Robert understands that his ability to practice real reading is a consequence of expert pedagogy jointly designed. He is not at the mercy of a single classroom teacher. His teachers make plans and read "teacher books." At Robert's school there are teams of teachers at every grade level. Kids learn how to relate to different personalities. Still, as Robert pointed out to me in another part of our conversation, he thinks of himself as "just a kid." What he "gets to do" is read books and discuss books because that's what his teachers have planned for him to do. Robert is not uncomfortable complying with his teachers' expectations because he feels that what they are having him do represents the best of all possible pedagogies.

In short, Robert is relating to books in exactly the way a highly educated adult reader relates to books. The reading in Robert's classroom has nothing to do with points. And here's another thing: Robert can even voice what he imagines teachers sound like in other schools— *"well, I'm just gonna give you this* huge *test on this book"*—where, presumably, in Robert's mind, teachers are autocratic and bureaucratic taskmasters.

With energy, poise, and self-consciousness, Robert was in "interview mode" with me. He played the role of interviewee with flair. Although he good-humoredly acknowledged what he could not know because he was *just a kid,* he did know what reading was all about and Accelerated Reader was nowhere to be seen. Families with secure social status, access to social goods, and experience in higher education would not tolerate A.R. for a single second.

While Robert and his classmates discuss the qualities and meanings of books they read in self-selected groups to deepen their understanding and expand the range and power of their critical faculties, kids like Kayla, Dakota, and Jason (with the help of their teachers) are very busy generating data in a data-driven world where data-loving corporate entities can and do make it easy to *get the answers fast.*

If we want children to read books, we have to make space and time for reading books. But space and time don't just materialize. Kids accounting for pages, quizzes, and rewards are not spending time in more personal and social ways of reading that matter much more. Kids who are not ever free to position their own bodies in space—lounging on beanbag chairs, curling up on sofas, reclining in armchairs, and doing so with books (or tablets!) in hand—are not going to experience the kind of reading that the people reading this book, for instance, take for granted.

4

STEMing: SCIENCE, TECHNOLOGY, ENGINEERING, AND MATH

*"Like in science, we're learning, wait—what
are we learning in science? We haven't done
science in a while, so I can't really remember."*

Earth's got problems. People have always been born problem solvers, but now we need to raise a proportionally greater number of people who will solve urgent problems relating to environmental science, engineering, and human behavior. At the very least, we have to start raising people who can comprehend and adapt to changed ecosystems on a hotter, harsher planet. The thing is, we've been here before; evidence suggests that Homo sapiens nearly went extinct around eighty thousand years ago when severe droughts and extreme climate fluctuations reduced our population to ten thousand adults of reproductive age. Better tools, better ways of living with each other, and better systems for working with the environment kept us going. So successful have we been as a species, we have brought ourselves right back to the brink of catastrophe. Lucky for us, we're hardwired for crux moves.

Among the many reality checks Bill McKibben has issued in the last few years, the key idea that connects his influential environmental activism to education is this: if humans are to survive in this habitat, we are going to have to change ourselves. The only way to change ourselves—alter our behavior at scale—is to change what and how we teach children at this moment in history. This is why I believe that raising children to live in a radically different climate means teaching them more holistically about our global environment. Teaching them how people and places interact means viewing education coherently across disciplines. The age of the discipline-specific academic silo is over; people who know and do science, art, math, humanities, and music have to communicate with each other as well as respect all the different ways people pay attention to and in the world.

It is impossible and irresponsible to talk about the current demand for better student outcomes in science, technology, engineering, and mathematics, what everyone now calls STEM, without examining the curricular context of the last decade that has lead to today's push for STEM achievement.

For more than a decade, in response to federally mandated but unfunded No Child Left Behind legislation, schools were—and many remain—stripped to the bare bones of basic reading instruction in order to prepare kids for the mandated testing that allegedly shows a school's annual yearly progress (AYP). For a long while, science and math disappeared, and reading was everything. In the public district where I taught from 2002 to 2008, a teacher once told me that she felt like she was basically shouting math facts at the back of the school bus as it pulled away at 3 P.M. During the day, teachers were expected to perform regular and frequent assessments of emergent and developing reading skills. Stopwatch in hand, they used a trademarked measurement instrument called Dynamic Indicators of Basic Early Literacy Skills, or DIBELS. When a classroom teacher was in the process of what we all called DIBELing, first graders sat on the floor reading aloud from books in their laps while their teacher clicked the stopwatch in order to chart their "indicators of phonemic awareness, alphabetic principle, accuracy, and fluency with connected text, reading comprehension, and vocabulary." DIBELS established "economical and efficient indicators of a student's progress toward achieving a general outcome," according to the Dynamic Measurement Group website (dibels.com). What teachers say is that processes like DIBELS developed word sayers, not readers.

Other literacy programs mandated by district leaders—and over the protests of teachers—included SRA Open Court Reading and Step Up to Writing. Produced and sold by SRA/McGraw Hill, Open Court Reading described itself in its materials, website, and brochures as a program of "systematic instruction" grounded in "40-plus years of research-validated results." Teachers and literacy coaches working in the district's elementary schools all participated in the professional development and training programs, but frequent turnover at the highest levels of district administration, including superintendent, meant that follow-up studies and oversight of curricular implementation from school to school was sporadic or nonexistent. Students deemed at-risk participated in a supplemental SRA literacy intervention called Kaleidoscope. Because these curricula were based on what the U.S. Department of Education called "scientifically-based reading research," schools using Open Court qualified for Reading First funds, money allocated from the federal government. Poor districts needed money. Federal money came tied to programs like these. Reading ruled, which is why science and math went AWOL.

Meanwhile, as education policy makers and school folks busied themselves with DIBELing, phonics, and basal readers, things in the material world were falling apart. Hurricane Katrina and a collapsed chunk of I-35 in Minnesota exposed our nation's rotting infrastructure. In 2013, civil engineers gave Missouri's roads and bridges a grade of C minus. Tap water flowing out of people's faucets near fracking sites started catching fire. Out west, ever more frequent and intense lightning storms sparked uncontrollable fires. Rivers and groundwater sources ran dry. Year in and year out, the prairie states turned crispy in conditions of drought. More recently, in the summer of 2010, BP's catastrophic oil spill in the Gulf of Mexico revealed the risk and difficulty of reaching desperately for hard-to-access pockets of fossil fuel. Hurricane Sandy splintered Jersey-shore homes to matchsticks and inundated office tower basements on Wall Street in 2012. In January 2013, a satellite image showed that 80 percent of the Arctic Sea ice had melted. Himalayan and South American glaciers have melted, too, draining into acidifying oceans, which pummel our most populous coastal regions. In 2013, barges in St. Louis ran aground in the dried-up Mississippi River just weeks before torrential spring flooding surged up under the barges, breaking more than one hundred loose and knocking them into a bridge. By spring of 2013, carbon dioxide in the atmosphere had passed 400 parts per million. Nobody knows the exact threshold beyond which the future is a disaster that only a colossal, planetwide effort will avert. My hunch is that we're already there.

Given the state of the world, and under the leadership of Barack Obama, education policy makers realized that it was kind of stupid to have stopped teaching children science and math. And I have not mentioned China, India, and what everyone keeps calling our global competitiveness. Nor Singapore, nor the amazingly educated children of Finland with whom our children are, presumably, globally competing. Turn in any cardinal direction and someone, somewhere, is saying that American kids aren't learning what they need to know in the overlapping and interrelated subjects of science, technology, engineering, and mathematics. Turning its attention to elementary, secondary, undergraduate, and graduate school science education, the administration's 2014 federal budget calls for $3.1 billion to be directed to STEM programming. Of this amount, $450 million is earmarked specifically for kindergarten through high school education and innovation, to be split between an integrated effort on the part of the National Science Foundation, the Smithsonian Institution, and the Department of Education. Given our track record in reading, however, some people are worried that DIBELing will simply transform—for children from poor and low-income communities—into STEMing, a crudely realized and decontextualized presentation of a bunch of disconnected or misapplied math and science facts. In early elementary education, this means sticking cotton balls on blue paper and calling it a lesson on clouds.

Today we have the opportunity and the need to get literacy and math/science education intelligently integrated. Cutting-edge researchers today cross traditional boundaries of discipline. Insights are emerging out of hybrid endeavors: a neuroscientist works with an anthropologist; an Italian art scholar pokes into a cadaver in a medical school's anatomy class. Even within the sciences, biological and biochemical research is corroborating the predictive models generated by mathematicians and physicists. Regardless of personal faith, everyone will need to be humanist—able to consider why and how human beings function and behave the way they do. Everyone will also need to be scientific—able to carefully construct new knowledge that corrects and extends prior knowledge. Everyone will need to be critical—able to question the status quo and see possibilities for alternatives. In the context of a global human imperative, the trickle-down of science and math into individual districts and schools cannot be as absurdly short-sighted and lopsided as the reading craze was. So how do we do this?

As always, new knowledge needs to hook onto prior knowledge. That goes for curriculum development. Before we try to figure out how to get all these kids to learn what they need to learn when it comes to integrating science and math with the arts and humanities, where are we right now? What do kids say about math and science in school? Spoiler alert: you won't hear anything about greenhouse gases.

MATH

Fourth graders are learning computational skills like multiplication and division at various levels of difficulty using one-, two-, and three-digit numbers. Others are working with fractions and decimals. Some are learning geometrical concepts and the properties of shapes and angles. Some are learning about rotational symmetry. Still others are learning basic algebraic concepts and skills having to do with functions, or how to calculate conversions—feet to yards or inches, dollars into quarters and other change. In one private school kids reported learning about graphing, grids, and coordinates. I heard methodological talk about Kumon, Saxon Math, Chicago Math, and—in two private schools in high-income communities—Singapore Math. This is what they are doing with numbers. But what do they say about what they are doing with numbers? What's math for? I heard three different and overlapping ways of talking and thinking about math: math as school subject; math for money transactions and other activities; and math for jobs.

Math as School Subject

Some fourth graders have their noses to the grindstone. They view curriculum—what happens during the day—as the stuff kids do because taller, older people called teachers tell them to do it. These nine- and ten-year-olds tend to think quite concretely about the world and their place in it. Like the work they do in every other content area, math is just math. It's what you're up to when your teacher starts saying things about numbers. These kids were quite sure of curricular connections from year to year: you learn math in fourth grade because, first, you have already learned your third-grade math, and, second, so you can be ready to learn harder, higher math in fifth grade. You can be good at it or bad at it, but if you work hard enough, eventually you can get good grades in it.

RURAL

The fact that math can be "got right" is what satisfies people like Nathan:

> I like that usually things are exact, even though sometimes you have to estimate, and there's not just one formula to do something, there's like a whole buncha different things that you can do to find just one answer.
>
> —*Nathan, white, public school, middle income*

I hear good math teaching in Nathan's words. Somebody has made it clear why it's important to show your work: because there are many different ways of coming up with "just one answer."

OUTER-RING SUBURB

Unlike Nathan, Greta is not a big fan of math. Nevertheless, she believes that "long division and times tables" are the most important things she has ever learned, in or out of school. Out of 166 children, Greta was perhaps the least self-conscious person I interviewed. Recall from the previous chapter her concrete explanation of how God, in the form of a Bible, literally *fit in* with her life at school.

> Math is boring. Math is very boring and hard. I think math's hard because it's boring. And it's boring because it's hard, but it's mostly hard because it's boring.
> *So if you found something not so boring it might not be so hard?*

Yeah. Like horseback riding. I love horses. But I feel good today because I got an A– on my math test. And my other friend got a C or a D because she didn't check over it. And I check over it five times. It takes five times to get an A–. I don't like math and I am not the sharpest tool in the box at math.

—*Greta, white, Protestant school, middle income*

Greta may outgrow the notion that long division and times tables are the most important things she has ever learned. More interesting is her idea (one which she shares with Nathan) that math is the kind of thing that can be got right—even if a person is "not the sharpest tool in the box at math"—as long as that person checks over her work five times. I suspect that an adult has used this derogatory language around Greta, and that because of what adults say to her face, she has come to think of herself as a dull math tool in spite of all those A-minuses.

Justine, who transferred to Greta's school from a Catholic school not too far away, was very clear about what it means to switch from one math curriculum to another.

I've never done Saxon Math before, and we've always done Chicago Math, which is way easier, and it's harder to understand, though. Here Saxon Math is much, way more fun to do.

I'm not familiar with Saxon Math, how would you describe it?

Well, Saxon Math has like division, cuz in Chicago Math, it's not the funnest of things, it's just stuff with groups, but it's different than division because the division problems are just, like one hundred and twenty divided by three, so then the Chicago Math is just, like problems, solving problems, word problems and stuff. And that's basically what it is. . . . Like, if you can't go to school, how are you supposed to know what is five times four or something?

—*Justine, mixed ethnicity (Cherokee/white), Protestant school,*
middle income

What's going on in the mind of a child who thinks that school is the only place where you can learn what five times four equals? This is reasoning that mistakes correlation for causation: "In school I learn what five times four is; ergo, the only place I *can* learn what five times four is, is school." I spoke with plenty of kids who think the only place a person could learn what they needed to learn is school. However, I also spoke with plenty of kids, kids more capable of abstract reasoning, who know that it's possible to learn outside of school—at the science center, from parents who homeschooled, from tutors, independently outdoors, and so on. In an effort to develop the reasoning skills of younger students, the more sites we can correlate with learning, the better. If kids feel themselves learning in multiple places—not just at school—they will be better equipped to absorb the idea that they can learn anywhere. In the short term, they will be more likely to acquire the concepts that underlie any mathematical computations they practice at school.

But what happens to a student's ideas about "math as school subject" when more and better mathematical learning happens outside of school in a real-world setting? Right before fourth grade, Faten switched from a metropolitan public to an Islamic private school. Faten's father runs a beauty supply shop. She spends Saturdays and Sundays helping him out:

> Oh, I work on the cash register.
> *So you must be pretty good at math if you're working the cash register.*
> No, I'm not really doing good in math. On my tests I usually get, you know, Cs and stuff. I mean, my dad's like, "How is this happening, you work on the cash register, and you give them the right change back and you can't do math?" And I told him I don't really know.

Faten and her father are puzzled by this phenomenon. And, except for division, it's not as though Faten doesn't respect math at school:

> Math, it's a really important skill we get homework every day on. Sometimes it's useful, sometimes I think I'm never gonna use it. Like, multiplication, it's useful, for me. Division, I don't think it's really useful, cuz I could just, you know, one-two-three, or I could just times, or plus, or minus, but I mean, division, I don't think it's needed. Because every day we usually have a multiplication sheet,

and we get timed on one minute to do fifty facts. I'm still on my fours, and everybody's on their divisions now, and I'm like, I need more time to do them. Cuz I really have to think about it, and sometimes I have to go one - two - three - four - five. But, I'm still on my fours.

Faten's out-of-school math competence is not transferring to classroom outcomes. The math tests Faten takes are not assessing what she knows and can do with numbers. They do not provide a valid account of her abilities and aptitude. Most teachers complain that students cannot transfer knowledge—neither from content area to content area, nor from school to nonschool settings. All this time we've been working so hard to hammer home real-world applications of math. Faten's a kid who can't get her aptitude to transfer the other way.

Money Transactions and Other Activities

With the exception of a singularly progressive school I visited, the idea most pervasive in all schools, all communities, and all school types was that the purpose of learning math was in order to understand and manage money. Not just money in general, but money in the specific context of conducting transactions—mostly shopping and ordering food. In response to being repeatedly instructed to connect curriculum to a real-world purpose, teachers have almost universally connected the learning of math to handling money in the context of shopping. Here in the United States, buying stuff, talking about buying stuff, wishing we could buy more stuff, and making stuff people can buy more of is what we do around the clock. We live and breathe marketing and commerce. Retail and wholesale business—grocery stores, car dealers, clothes shops—represents 15.3 percent of all the jobs Americans do. This sector provides only slightly fewer than the number-one source of American jobs: local, state, and federal government, which provides 16.6 percent of all paid employment. In every way that matters, buying and selling things is what kids watch adults do. Which means it's what they associate most with math.

RURAL

Because when you're in the store if you don't know how to count money or something then you might give them too much money or less money and then you can't buy that or then you just waste your money.

—*Jane, white, public school, low income*

OUTER-RING SUBURBAN

Like if they're going shopping, and the cashier says how much money you need and you look in your, whatever you have, and you don't know how much money you have. And you say, "I don't know how much money I have." So you don't know how much money you need to pay or you need to give.

—*Denise, white, public school, fragile middle income*

Let's say you went shopping and it cost three-ninety-nine plus tax, which would be—and the tax is one dollar—you would know that, it would be four dollars one cents? I think? And so you need to know that stuff so that you don't pay the wrong amount of money or you know the right amount of change, if they give you the right amount, or you know when you should get change.

—*Susan, Jewish, public school, middle income*

If you're at a restaurant, and she says, and like the waitress says, "That'll be $6.53," then you have to know, like, how much money you have and what that means.

—*Patrick, white, Protestant school, middle income*

I'm not a big fan of math. I don't think it's really hard, it's just a lot of stuff at one time we need to know in life. Like for instance if you go to the store and you take this, this, and this, you should be able to have a good idea of what you're spending, like just round it off and add it up. So you need to know if someone forgot to give you your change.

—*Dahlia, white, Protestant school, middle income*

INNER-RING SUBURBAN

Sometimes Mrs. C. says, when we're learning money, you kind of have to learn how to know money because when you go to the store when you're older, when you do everything. Kind of like, you kinda have to know it, it's like a life lesson. You have to know how to count money, so sometimes I think it's that, and sometimes they just want us to learn it. Just to know it. And, sometimes, I think they just want to take up time [*laughs*].

—*Martha, white, Catholic school, high income*

URBAN

Maybe school's for . . . like when you need to buy food, almost no one gives out food for free, just gives out food, "here you go, here you go," so learning exactly how much you would need to pay, like in math class, money. Like in the first- through third-grade math that Mrs. T., the old third-grade teacher, teaches, there's like this Tucker Hill School math grocery thing in the back, where they count up a bunch of money and there's this toy cash register.

—*Lena, white, private school, middle income*

Learning math is useful for helping us deal with money, which we all have to do. It should not surprise us that children, in linking the learning of mathematics to conducting market transactions, have perfectly absorbed a cultural and political set of messages so dominant in this decade they have been alive. Curriculum theorist Michael Apple writes:

> For neoliberals, the world in essence is a vast supermarket. "Consumer choice" is the neoliberal guarantor of

democracy. In effect, education is seen as simply one more product like breads, cars, and televisions. By turning it over to the market through voucher and choice plans, education will be largely self-regulating. Thus, democracy is turned into consumption practices. *In these plans, the ideal of the citizen is that of the purchaser, not the worker.* The message of such policies is that of what might best be called "arithmetical particularism," in which the unattached individual—as a consumer—is deraced, declassed, and degendered [italics added].*

I am not suggesting that children ought not to be learning how to calculate change for a dollar. This is a good and useful skill. However, given how dominant, pervasive, and narrow the skill is in relation to what mathematical concepts are all about, and how mathematical concepts connect with science, with reading and writing, with art and music, I do think we are shortchanging kids.

Some children connected math with nonschool activities unrelated to commerce. Generally speaking, these were the more critically minded kids who were more developed as abstract thinkers.

RURAL

In everyday situations you need to know how much gas to put in a lawnmower. Or how much diesel to put in your truck. Or, no, what size of bolt to put on your car and stuff like that. How many coats of paint.

—*Hunter, white, public school, low income*

Hunter's classmate, Oliver, connected geometry content to real-world activities. It's a very good sign when kids take what they're learning in school and bring it to bear on independent, intrinsically motivated ac-

*Michael W. Apple, "Work, Power, and Curriculum Reform: A Response to Theodore Lewis's 'Vocational Education as General Education,'" *Curriculum Inquiry* 28, vol. 3 (1998), 342–343.

tivities. Oliver's mother is an elementary school teacher, and Oliver also has extremely positive feelings about school in general:

> I like using numbers to help solve problems and things, and sometimes, I actually try to use numbers to help me with other things. Sometimes, I try to use angles when I'm, like, say, drawing a picture, I try to use angles a little bit with it, to help with getting, practicing on math, but also practicing with my drawing.
>
> —*Oliver, white, public school, middle income*

We should be teaching math from a stance whose purpose is to explain and understand worlds beyond the wallet. At the very least, we should be teaching kids to use math to help them understand their own personal worlds, like how to track and graph the amount of carbon dioxide released into the atmosphere by factories located x number of miles from the playgrounds of schools.

Math Is for Jobs

Teachers work hard to make real-world connections for their students. And in addition to describing present-day applications, discourse in school also projects children into an imagined future where what they learn in school will be "useful." Visions of the future may vary, but as I showed in chapter 1, kids have absorbed another adult message loud and clear: the future means getting a job, and jobs entail math.

RURAL

Casey is self-consciously candid, aware of herself as a kid from the country, aware that ignorant country people—whom she conjures up for me with an impersonation—are people who cannot do things like multiply single numbers.

> I sometimes have troubles in math, I'm not good at all at story problems. So I have to work really hard on them.

And why?

So that like whenever we get older, fer like a job or sumpin, we know how to do at least basic stuff like math, know how to count money, so that whenever we get older we know how to do stuff, and that we won't be like [*mimicking a "hick" accent*], "Ah, five times three, what is that?" but [*laughing*] it's fifteen. I think it's important to learn all the math things 'cause in most jobs, you have to have math and money and all that.

—Casey, *white, public school, low income*

Like Casey, Brody understands the connection between today's math in school and tomorrow's work in the world:

A lot of times you hafta like do a lot of math, like if you're a carpenter or sumpin.

—Brody, *white, public school, low income*

OUTER-RING SUBURBAN

I'd say adding is the most important thing I've learned because it's like, if you want, for some time, your starting job is like a cashier or something and you don't hafta, adding and subtracting is like really helpful 'cause if the person pays you extra, you have to subtract that by the number, you have to pay and give them that change, so, and number stories also go along with that really well.

—Nuri, *Syrian American, Islamic school, high income*

I feel like, when I want to be an architect when I grow up, I'll really need math.

—Adam, *white, Protestant school, middle income*

An engineer needs to figure out the math to do to fix a car or something like that.

—Patrick, *white, Protestant school, middle income*

SMALL CITY

Like you'll actually know, like, there's probably *no good job*, like even if you're working at McDonald's you have to know math, a little bit of math. Even if you've done no social studies, you've gotta know . . . I don't see how you can't know math with a good job.

—*Toby, white, public school, middle income*

URBAN

Like when I get a job and I have to count money or something, I'll need math.

—*Margaret, white, Catholic school, middle income*

Like later in life, if you work at a bank or something, you're gonna hafta do math. Those jobs need math.

—*Faye, white, private school, high income*

Nearly a hundred years ago, Albert Einstein said that we should not be bothering so much over "the learning of many facts." If that was true in 1921, before calculators and Wikipedia put all facts, not just math facts, at our fingertips, it is more true now. Don't get me wrong; curricular content matters. When teaching an American literature survey course, I insisted that my high school seniors learn the publication dates of all we read. Literary artists speak to each other across time and good readers think about who might be emulating whom, who has probably read what. Emphasizing this point, I tested my students on dates. Honestly, though, what I really aimed to teach was the reason for wanting to know such facts. If any of those dates stuck after the final exam, it's because they meant something to the student. My own storage of facts is personal and a little ridiculous. Off the top of my head I can tell you the date of the signing of the Magna Carta and the formula for solving a quadratic equation. I have retained the home phone number of my best friend in second grade and permanently acquired an understanding of the path of food through the digestive system during tenth grade. I like knowing that the rays of light my cat is basking in left our sun about eight minutes ago. There seems to be no rhyme or reason to my fact retention. I remember facts because somewhere along the line they were so interesting to me they stuck. Besides, Einstein's not telling us not to learn *any* facts; he's saying let's not bother so much about teaching facts. He is saying that facts are not as important as other qualities of mind.

A friend of mine is a research scientist, a cellular biologist who runs a laboratory in an American university. My friend trained in a former Soviet state and says that the most important trait of a scientist is curiosity. She and her husband, who is also a scientist as well as her co-researcher, emphasize the importance of patience, perseverance, open-mindedness, and the imaginative initiative to collaborate with specialists across fields. Good science takes time. "The things that we do," she says, "we cannot get answers fast." Decades of hours spent peering into a microscope have enabled my friend to gather the evidence she and her colleagues need to warrant valid and reliable claims about the behavior of proteins in cells. And the one thing an excellent scientist like this is quite sure about is that content knowledge is not a requirement for being a scientist, except "as a little background."

As we shift from math to science, where and how do the habits of mind of practicing scientists emerge in the perspectives of children?

SCIENCE

All scientists are driven by two related questions: what's going on in the world and how does the world work? These questions emerge from human curiosity, which drives the desire to learn anything at all. Whether or not they called acting on their curiosity "science learning," children expressed a wide range of science understandings in both formal and informal settings. Reflecting across the transcripts, I found six themes. These categories overlap in many ways: general ideas about what science is; science as spectator sport; animals and habitats; exploration and wonder; identifying with scientists; informal and deep engagement with the natural world.

General Ideas About What Science Is

In relatively well-to-do communities, children have fairly clear ideas about what we are talking about when we talk about science. No less curious than anyone else, many children in our poorest communities have extremely limited exposure to an extremely constrained science curriculum. As I mentioned earlier, the Bush-era reading craze of 2000–08 pretty much got rid of science learning among the poor. In these settings, children express patchy or fuzzy understandings of what "science" is and means.

URBAN

In Malik's case, science is great, but it's something he has watched, something his teacher has done. His teacher's boilerplate demonstration of static electricity is, to Malik, "all about doin' physics."

> My favorite subject is science. It's wonderful. My teacher do science.
> *What kinds of science do you do?*
> Physics, earth, water, earth and water, electric and technology.
> *What did you learn?*
> I learned all about doin' physics. If you rub a balloon together to a shirt or some fabric, it sticks, if it's not anything like that, it don't stick. It just way out . . .
> *Why does that happen?*
> Because it, I think the arrangements in the air . . . I forgot, I did got that right but I forgot.
>
> —*Malik, African American, public school, low income*

I like that Malik says that there are people who *do* physics. And I like that he knows that something is making the balloon stick to the shirt. The balloon "sticks" because of something—arrangements?—that Malik "got right" but has now forgotten. Malik expresses a shred of understanding, but based on this exchange, nobody would claim that Malik has mastered the concept of static electricity even though the content has been "covered."

METROPOLITAN

In some places science is lost in curricular wilderness; as a discipline it is consequently associated with posters and famous Missourians. With their ideas about potions, projects, and fun, Dahlia and Maaz, below, seem like they're on the right track. I have borrowed the epigraph for this chapter from Rosie, below.

> We did a poster for science but we never finished it. We don't talk about it anymore because we don't do science as often. We don't do science every day. Sometimes we don't do it at all. And if we do do it, it's for a short amount of time.
> *Do you do experiments and things when you do science?*
>   No, just posters and at one time, we were supposed to do a play, but we had to do posters to see what our play was gonna be like.
>
> —Chynna, African American, public school, fragile middle income

> Science just has me learn about the earth, and how it works, and I get to know more about my home.
>
> —Lindsay, white, public school, fragile middle income

OUTER-RING SUBURB

> When I was little I used to always think I liked science 'cause I used to think we were gonna make potions and stuff. It's really interesting. You learn about the history in social studies and you learn all about your earth and the animals in science.
>
> —Dahlia, white, Protestant school, middle income

Science has more stuff like you put, it's kinda like when, you always do projects. To me, projects are fun. You sometimes go in a group and then you get a group, your teacher gives you a group, you go with boys, and then you have fun together doing the project. Those people who put those, you know the dipping liquid. Those type. And I build houses a lot. Like out of Lego.

—Maaz, Pakistani American, English second language, Islamic school, middle income

RURAL

Like in science, we're learning, wait [*whispers*] what *are* we learning in science, we haven't done science in a while, so I can't really remember. Like science, we're learning about famous Missourians.

—Rosie, white, public school, low income

Plenty of "famous Missourians" were scientists, so maybe that's where the connection is in Rosie's open acknowledgment of confusion. Still, Rosie and her classmates deserve more science clarity than this.

Science as Spectator Sport: Reading, Learning Facts, Watching Others

Very disheartening was the number of students whose experience with science in school was limited to reading in textbooks, completing worksheets, and otherwise learning facts that other people have already figured out.

RURAL

Science is kinda a little hard, just depends on what we're reading.

—Ruth, white, public school, low income

We haven't done science for a while, I don't remember, but I
might be able to tell you some things we were doing on it. I like
science a lot better than all the other subjects because it's easier,
all you usually have to do is read. I like to learn how . . . we learn
the coral reefs, we learned about animals, we've learned about
camouflaged animals, and insects. We've learned about how people
that are disabled have monkeys to help them. And some of 'em
have dogs to help, too.

—*Blaze, white, public school, low income*

The problem here is not that science is totally absent, it's that scientists are scientists because they wonder about the world, read what
other people have figured out so far, and do things themselves. In
thinking about science, Blaze recalls his mother's youthful victory in
a science fair. His knowledge about the relationship between light and
plant growth is rooted in his mother's story:

Probably, I know my mom did something with which she got three
fourth-place science things. One is she did this thing with plants
to see the best, the biggest one. She had a plant, and she had these
different colors of glass and some, and most of them died, but the
red one that was over a flower, the red flower just kept on growing
and growing and growing and growing. And that was actually one,
all she did was put a light over the top of it and it made some type
of sunlight go down in the flower making it grow.

—*Blaze, white, public school, low income*

It is both poignant and outrageous that Blaze has to recount his
mother's childhood science experience in order to access a telling example of scientific content knowledge. What we know about
what Blaze knows is this: Blaze's mom told him her story in such
a way that he has retained an interesting tidbit about the relationship between the light spectrum, the color red, and plant growth.
Mostly we know that she talks to him and that he is proud of her past
accomplishment.

URBAN

Like Blaze, Maida is actively interested in the workings of the world. Curiosity led her to the Internet. Maida's mother tongue is Bosnian, and she goes to a diverse public school in the city.

> I go at my cousin's house and like we go on the computer and we find stuff. Like I wasn't catching up in math that good, well, math and science. And she went on YouTube and found a science experiment and I saw a lot of them that were dangerous. One of them like . . . one wasn't dangerous that much but I saw one that like this guy, he got a pumpkin for Halloween and a lot of soap in water, in something, I don't know in a cup, like a lot of soap. And they just put it in the pumpkin and it was like, the soap was popping out and it was really fun and creative. And the other one I saw, it was dangerous. Because it was this hot, hot water and if you have a soda can you don't have to just crush it and throw it away, you have to like, there's like this really, really hot water or cold. And you just put it in but you have to get the safety glasses and gloves and then you put the can inside and it just like crushes.
>
> —Maida, white, public school, low income

It's great that kids like Blaze and Maida are capturing science information, even partial information, from family members and the Internet. But what we want is for kids not simply to master science facts, or even to be science spectators. The point of knowing and doing science is not to score higher on standardized tests relating to science content. We want more children to adopt the identities of scientists, to be the kinds of people scientists *are*.

Animals and Habitats

When asked about what they were learning in science, many children reported on animals, earth, and human biology. Listen for the science-specific working vocabulary: I hear the most in Charles's talk. Charles's Boy Scout troop had just gone to the science center for a geology class.

URBAN

> My favorite subject is science. Like figuring out about the waste and just that stuff about it. I just started liking science this year, knowing the form of shapes and solids and like . . . just that stuff. And the waste.
>
> —*Selena, white, public school, low income*

INNER-RING SUBURB

> We all wrote a research project on an animal, and then we got to go see the animal. I did the zebra. Well, I wanted to choose something that no one else had, so once everyone had picked theirs, I asked everybody if they had done the zebra, cuz I like the zebras, and none of them had done that, so I just did the zebra. Well, there's three types of zebras: mountain zebra, the Grevy's zebra, and there's another one, but, it has a weird name, so I can't remember it. And they are born alive, which I already knew, and other things I can't just, I can't remember them right now. [At our zoo] we have the mountain zebra, I'm pretty sure. But, the mountain zebra doesn't need water to live on, but the Grevy's zebra really needs water, and the Grevy's zebra are usually much bigger. The Grevy's zebra lives on water, they always need it.
>
> —*Lisa, Jewish, public school, middle income*

> Well, in science we are learning about, like cells and boring stuff [laughs], like chloroplast, all the stuff in, like a plant's body and an animal's body. And now we're working on like, to identify the trees, like to know what tree it is and stuff like that.
>
> —*Martha, white, Catholic school, high income*

OUTER-RING SUBURB

In science, we're doing stuff about lizards, and I don't like lizards
so I'll probably never forget in fourth grade when lizards . . .
good thing, we're not touching 'em, so we're puttin' 'em in a
cage, but I'm still scared. Well, my science teacher does it. But
they're superfast. I don't remember what kind they are, but they're
superfast.

—Janelle, white, public school, fragile middle income

So, like, science. Let's say a bee is on you and it's on your shirt and
it's really, really colorful. Well, bees like to look at the pattern of
different things, so if you didn't know that you'd be like, "It's gonna
sting me it's gonna sting me it's gonna sting me!" And, but in
school you learn they only sting if they're threatened or something
like that. That's probably what you learn.

—Susan, Jewish, public school, middle income

In science we're doing the human body. Like skeletal system,
respiratory and cardiac. I actually like animals, and like, most of
the boys in my class don't like animals, and I like geology, and
rocks. I have geodes and graphite and jades. Yesterday my Boy
Scout troop went to the science center. We took a geology class and
we had, I had a snowflake obsidian and he gave us graphite, I mean,
not graphite, but granite and metal and an' he broke a rock in half
and it had like crystals in it. I like medical stuff and stuff.

—Charles, African American, Protestant school, middle income

Science is my favorite subject. We do different topics, like my
favorite one was electricity. And now we're doing weathering. And,
well, we took the test on it on Friday, and I think I did pretty well,
and some of them were like temperature so we put marbles under a
flame and then we took 'em out really quickly and put 'em in ice-
cold water? And they started cracking.

—Andrew, white, public school, middle income

RURAL

I like it when we get to do the science projects, like when we
had our ecopoem, and ecosystems. You get a cricket and three
fish and we got to raise 'em, and some of the moms, they had
babies and we were supposed to realize what's it's like to be in
an ecosystem. We learned about how the animals survive in
the wilderness. We learned how in the ocean, how whales, and
what kind of whales, and fish, how they would survive, and like
and zebras, how they would hafta live by water and stuff. I like
science a lot. I like animals, I do like zebras, and I like ta learn
what they do.

—*Christopher, white, public school, low income*

Lots of kids love animals. Lots of kids care very much about the
well-being of animals. A fundamental precept in education is that
the interest of the learner—student engagement with the material—
is necessary for meaningful learning to take place. Now factor in a
seminal concept in learning science. It's called the zone of proximal
development, a model of learning cognition that was developed by
Soviet psychologist Lev Vygotsky in the early twentieth century and
has been fleshed out in theory and practice in western Europe and the
United States for the last thirty-five years or so. The zone of proximal
development is the cognitive workspace between what a student can
learn on her own and what she can learn with the help of a more
knowing peer or teacher. Just as interest trumps reading level, a highly
motivated learner, say a little boy living deep in the interior of the
United States, is already primed to learn anything at all about faraway
animals.

Exploration and Wonder

And now for the good news: there are children who get to act like
blood cells! All their senses are open and there's a place in the curriculum for asking questions about the world.

OUTER-RING SUBURB

Right now we're getting into the unit of weather and I think that would be most important because, there's a lot of questions going in my head. Like, how do tornados form, like why hurricanes occur? And, and I'm like well, you know, if my name is Benjamin, I'm kind of like trying to ask a question that Benjamin Franklin asks, and I'm like, "Huh?" Yeah. And he was a printer.

—*Benjamin, white, Protestant school, fragile middle income*

Here is the sound of wonder integrated with empirical investigation of the natural world:

URBAN

I'm really into this because one time we brought in some flowers and stuff, we gotta take 'em apart and really like, we got a magnifying glass and we gotta look really inside of the flowers. We use paper knives for cutting open to see what's actually inside the flowers and stuff and we also, we do a lotta things like that. We getta, we look in our books and for art class, same going along with flowers, this girl—when you just look at a flower you just see a flower—she actually got into, she *really looked closer* to the flower and she drew it on a piece of paper, and we gotta draw those and it was really cool.

—*Stella, white, Catholic school, middle income*

Stella and her classmates are conducting meaningful inquiry into the nature of flowers. Their exploration uses multiple tools: minds, language, hands, art, paper, and magnifying glass. Across town, Brigit also "gets" the idea of observation:

Science I think you can just like watch a flower each day or something and you can learn its life cycles of that.

—*Brigit, white, Catholic school, middle income*

OUTER-RING SUBURB

Like so many of the girls I interviewed, Kamar wants to work in "an animal care place." She sounds very much like a scientist in the making:

> In science I learn lots of stuff and then if I come across something like that outside, I can just remember what I did in science, and do the same thing. Like we could experience by ourself, like if you go out in the wild and then you eat something and you get sick, and then someone can make a medicine for you and then you could live better and you could tell your children that that's poisonous and your children could tell their children that's poisonous and it keeps going on until everyone knows that you're not supposed to eat that.
>
> —*Kamar, Moroccan American, Islamic school, middle income*

In this brief hypothetical narrative, Kamar "comes across something" that she has learned about. She replicates "what she did in science." In her example, she learns from experience that a certain plant might be poisonous, then passes that knowledge down (disseminates it) through the generations until "everyone knows." Slightly off and incomplete as it is, Kamar has described the scientific method. Careful guidance and time will see her directly to full understanding of scientific inquiry.

The most extensive description of a science curriculum I heard was from Jennifer, who lives in an outer-ring, high-middle-income suburban community known for the quality of its public schools. In addition to learning about animals, Jennifer was working with concepts of physics—including energy, motion, and electricity. The car project also touched on the mathematics of budgeting.

> We did a fun crawdad unit, and we got to pick up crawdads. Like each group got two and we named them. Science, we have it everyday in the afternoon. Well, like we do couple units in science and then like one unit in social studies. Like there's not really a pattern.

parts and circles back to the right atrium. Then after it goes to the brain, it goes back to the right atrium.

Wow. I am so impressed. How did you learn that?

They have signs up like at each station, and me and my friend Molly, there's like a little test that's due—next Thursday, and we have to draw a path of the blood cells, so when we are walking around the gym, we try pointing at each station and naming its name. And if there's like a right ventricle, we point to where the left ventricle was. Yeah, we act like the blood cells.

What Jennifer is describing is called embodied learning, and it works. She and her friend have moved themselves through labeled space as if they were blood cells. They point and they name. They recite the process in precise vocabulary. They translate their movements into a drawing. This is memorization, but it's the right kind of memorization. The process through which Jennifer got the circulatory system memorized was meaningful to her. And fun.

Identifying with Scientists

Children really into science start to identify with adult scientists. This can begin at the level of the science fair.

OUTER-RING SUBURB

I gotta tell you something: we're doing this invention, science fair or whatever and my invention, it's like this mailbox, and then there's bolts in it. I made a mailbox thing. It has Velcro, all this stuff on it. Well my dad made it because I couldn't make it—but I came up with the name and stuff. And my invention is Postal Pop-up. That's what I named it. Postal Pop-up. Yeah. Well, I came up with the name Postal Pop, and then my dad said, "How 'bout you make it Postal Pop-up?"

—Joseph, white, Protestant school, middle income

And earlier in science, we were doing electricity and we had like all these wires and batteries and like a little light-bulb and we tried to figure out. And we learned all about circuits and closed circuits and open circuits.

We made like a house and we had to have one light [*laugh*]. One light in every room that works and like the batteries have to be like, like you can't really see the battery so it has to kind of be like a real house but wirings—and then, we had to learn to make a switch with the lightbulb thing. We had piece of paper, card stock, and then we had two brads, yeah. And we had like a paper clip that connected to one. And we had to put the wires some way so when you touched the paper clip to one brad it was already connected to the other and the lightbulb would turn on, so it was kind of like a switch.

In Jennifer's lengthy report we can hear evidence of intellectual engagement, collaboration, problem solving, hands-on learning, critical thinking, autonomy, and curricular structure. In short, we hear the best of the best practices. And that's just in the part of her day she calls "science." Jennifer is learning science content in other curricular areas:

PE might be my favorite time of day, 'cause like we're doing an obstacle course, 'cause we're learning how blood cells flow through the heart and I memorized the whole thing. Do you want me to recite it for you? Okay, so it starts out with the blue blood cells and at the right atrium, then it goes to the tricuspid valve, then the tricuspid valve, 'cause the right ventricle goes to the pulmonary valve. The pulmonary valve goes to the lungs. The lungs goes to the left ventric—atrium. The left atrium goes to the mitral valve. The mitral valve goes to the left ventricle. The left ventricle goes to the aortic valve. The aortic valve goes to the aorta. The aorta, if you take a left, it goes to the brain. And if you go right out of the aorta it goes to all the other body

Like real scientists, Joseph and his partner—his handy dad—have collaborated on the invention from bench to market—the idea, the execution, and the naming. Deeper identification with scientists and engineers can lead the way to vocation. In such ways, reading expansively and widely and exposure to current events can develop future scientists.

URBAN

David comes from a brainy, high-achieving, cosmopolitan family:

> I plan to do something that has to do with math or science. I have a lot of heroes. One of my heroes is obviously Einstein because he discovered something out of nothing but then one of my nonheroes is the person who decides to use Einstein's inventions to make the atomic bomb! So I don't like that, one of my heroes is Nelson Mandela, Gandhi, what's his name, Schindler, and then Steve Jobs is also my hero because he teaches, he teached me a lot about persistence because he tried to make everything perfect because obviously, well, in a business you wanna make your product perfect . . . and he reinvents a lot of things so I think that being a perfectionist, it kind of helped him, people can be really angry at perfectionists because they always want everything perfect and it kind of gets other people desperate to just make them stop coming up with so many ideas, but he was really persistent and in the end, he just made a lot of things kind of perfect.
>
> —David, Jewish–Italian American, bilingual, private school, high income

OUTER-RING SUBURB

Like David, Paolo is exposed to formally educated adults at home. In this case, though, one of his parents is a working physician. Paolo exuberantly connected home, school, science, and the use of technology. Like Jennifer, he is engaging in embodied learning, complete with sound effects, while operating the Lasik machine in a simulated experience of doing eye surgery. Paolo is also trilingual; his favorite subject in school is science.

> Me and my dad, for example, yesterday at dinner we talked our heads off all about the speed of light. And compared to the speed of sound. For example if you go—if you run close to the speed of light but not exactly the speed of light but if you run close to the speed of light and you run for one minute everybody around you is like sixty years older and the people that you know are dead. So yeah. I maneuvered a eye surgery thing and I did a sample with glass in it. It's pretty much like Battleship. Like a computer Battleship. You just like [*here he mimes running the Lasik machine with sound effects*] beep *beep beep* center center center still *boop*. Done. Yeah. It's really fast. And I always see him using PowerPoint and then like I see pictures of his, of eyes getting like eyelids like this [*spread wide open*].

> —Paolo, German–South American, public school, middle income

Informal and Deep Engagement with the Natural World

Finally, there are kids whose lives unfold in close contact with the natural world. In settings that are less formal than labs, medical offices, and schools, kids who live in rural communities and are still connected to the outdoors will come to know and understand things about the world—and acquire the vocabulary that describes the world—in ways that other kids simply do not. This is Frannie, who lives on a farm. Listen to how the geography of her father's land becomes clear as she names the ponds individually. Each repetition of the word "pond" is another site.

> But, at my dad's, I usually have a lot of work to do because I have chores and also if I have a friend spend over, we usually go and play and we have this haystack thing that we climb on and then we jump on each other on the haystacks. I also have a little pond, like three

ponds, one lagoon, another pond and another pond and one pond by our cows' pen that has snakes in it. We saw three snakes in it 'cause we was trying to catch frogs and then one was trying to chase us so we was running home. One was a milk snake, but that's common. And I don't know what the other one is. We looked it up but I forgot. We looked it up on the Internet to make it easier on us, because we have no snakes book. If we couldn't find it on the Internet, I would just probably go here [to school] and see or go to a libary [sic] this summer. Also, at my grandpa's, we usually go check birds.

Like if they're bad birds. My grandpa will throw the eggs so they won't get too populated and kill the good birds. Like bluebirds and martins.

—Frannie, white, rural, public school, low income

Like the children of farmers, students who hunt know things about the natural world—reproductive patterns, animal development, food chain, habitats, trees and other plants—simply from hanging around outside with adults who know more than they do. Remember, kids from hunting families are not out hunting in the woods alone. They have a vested interest in what they are observing and learning because the people who matter to them care about these things, too. Recall Isaiah, who spoke about A.R. reading in the last chapter:

We do a lot of hunting in my house. This year, October deer season, favorite season of all, last year I killed a turkey, so we turkey hunt, dove hunt, deer hunt, and occasionally when I get older my dad's gonna take me moose hunting. But there is elk up in [names a canyon] but you can't hunt 'em there, but . . . up in Arkansas there's elk, but Dad's gonna get me a moose tag when I get a little bit older. I'll be happy for that. To get to go moose hunting. That's what I'm really lookin' forward to. I do a lot of hunting. Whatever's edible, we eat it usually.

Is there anything you hunt that's not edible?

No, not much. Unless there's an armadillo or a raccoon tearing up the trash. Or, where we deer hunt and turkey hunt and dove hunt is up at my dad's cousin, and he's settin up the tree stand 'cause it's deer season's comin up in about a week or two, but up there there's raccoons that, they have a chicken, an old, old chicken house and they have chickens in there and the coon killed the three chickens and ate most of their eggs so we had to kill the coon, we killed the coon, usually if it was just there eatin' the corn out of the little coon trap we would have just let it go but, like pests, sometimes we get rid of . . . they've actually found turkey eggs and got turkeys but the three, it killed two chickens and two of their turkeys, those turkeys they found their eggs on the side of the road. That's why we killed the coon, but . . . yeah, but they were little, they were only about that big [indicates that they were small], they were little jakes, as you'd call 'em. Not yet, not yet old enough to hunt.

My favorite place to learn new things, that would mostly be in the woods. Saturday when I was with my cousin he came over at my house and we found a cocooning caterpillar. We learn a lot in the woods. We find a lot of cool new things and I go and ask my dad, "Dad, what is this?" And once when we were on our way to the deer woods or deer camp I was asking so many questions and the next question I asked was, "Dad, am I getting annoying?" [laughs]. But I learn a lot in the woods. My dad asks me like, "You know what kinda tree that is or you know what that is?" And he'll tell me. Yeah, he knows a lot because he was in the woods a lot with his dad.

—Isaiah, white, rural, public school, middle income

When it comes to understanding the seasons, the habits of animals, the taxonomy of trees, habitats, and various other concepts large and small, the richness of Isaiah's base knowledge is enviable. In sharing with me what he knows he demonstrates narrative proficiency—the words are there for him to express what he needs to express in a way that makes sense to an outsider. Everything he shares about the natural world is grounded in his relationship with his father, which echoes his father's relationship with his father. For better and for worse, Isaiah's science curriculum has just about nothing to do with school. His apprenticeship into understanding the natural world is not through formal education as we have currently designed rural public schools to be. However, were Isaiah explicitly taught the process of knowledge building specific to science (the scientific method), his baseline content would serve him well.

For those who don't get much science in school here in Missouri, we happen to have other extraordinarily good options. Several kids mentioned the St. Louis Science Center as their "favorite place to learn new things." And the Missouri Department of Conservation is exemplary. Dating from 1937, when a citizen-led movement realized that fifty years of unregulated logging, mining, hunting, and fishing had just about ruined this place, the apolitical, science-based MDC has been restoring, conserving, regulating, and educating the people of Missouri about our forests, fish, wildlife, and water systems. The most ingenious thing about the MDC is its funding: since 1976, an eighth of a percent of our sales tax—untouchable by politicians—goes straight to its mission to sustain the health and diversity of Missouri's plants and animals.

STEM and Us

The last time the United States made such a concerted policy push into science was in the 1950s. The successful launch of the Soviet Sputnik satellite in 1957 kicked off the space race during the Cold War. In response to the Soviet accomplishment, the U.S. government spent a billion dollars on science education—mostly in institutions of higher learning but also at the state level. The National Defense Education Act of 1958 was designed "to strengthen the national defense and to encourage and assist in the expansion and improvement of educational programs to meet critical national needs; and for other purposes." There were objections to the mandate—tying funds to national loyalty oaths was a big one—but basically, loads of science was folded into the elementary and secondary curriculum, and plenty of research was funded. Well, here we are at another moment of critical need, only this time the need is global. It would be very nice to get science education right for the masses. We've got more than three times as much money to do it with this time around.

One thing we can do is listen closely to the kids right this minute who are sounding like people who do science: Jennifer (outer-ring, public), Paolo (outer-ring, public), David (urban, private), Isaiah (rural, public), Stella (urban, Catholic), and Frannie (rural, public). Drawing upon what these kids are up to at home and at school and why it's working, we can construct sites of school-based science inquiry of the sort called for by researchers and described by master teachers in a book called *Science Workshop.*[*]

Given what will be their increased need to respond to the real world with wisdom and prudence, as well as competence in the hard sciences, all children should be given meaningful opportunities to: examine the world; pose questions; read and consider existing answers; test existing answers and design new experiments; and develop new and better explanations about how the world works.

Good science education needs to be primarily about developing identities, not cramming facts. In the best of all possible curricular worlds, science, art, language, social studies, math, and technology will come together. Scientists communicate concepts and facts to each other by means of symbols, pictures, charts, diagrams, gestures, formulas, equations, and graphs. Researcher Jay Lemke has written that literacy education "usually begins with an emphasis on language and texts—how they are made and what they mean." On the other hand, Lemke writes, "science education begins with questions about how things happen in the world." (I am quoting from Lemke's contribution to *Crossing Borders in Literacy and Science Instruction: Perspectives on Theory and Practice* published by the International Reading Association in 2004. Edited by Wendy Saul, this volume honors the relationship between the humanities and the sciences in school curricula.) So how do concepts about reading and writing from English language arts transfer over to science?

Some of the questions and answers about what happens in the world—whether understood as scientific or not—can be framed in nat-

---

[*]Wendy Saul, Jeanne Reardon, Charles Pearce, Donna Dieckman, and Donna Neuzte, *Science Workshop: Reading, Writing, and Thinking Like a Scientist* (Portsmouth, NH: Heinemann, 2002).

ural language. For example, *all birds have hollow bones* is a scientific fact expressed in natural language. But some scientific ideas require other forms, or genres, of communication. If we want to show someone what a bird's hollow bone looks like, we might make an annotated image or drawing. Scientific knowledge grows because scientists write to each other; they write in ways specific to their field and these ways rely upon symbol systems that are much larger than those which rely strictly on alphabets. Our ways of communicating are roomy enough for the humanities and the sciences, and as we integrate curricula across disciplines, we will be well served by Einstein's words: "A society's competitive advantage will come not from how well its schools teach the multiplication and periodic table, but from how well they stimulate imagination and creativity."

5

ACCOUNTING FOR HIGH-STAKES TESTS

"To See What We Gonna Be in Life"

The MAP test was kind of scary, cuz if you get two wrong, then you're on Proficient, and then if you get like four wrong, you're on Basic. Basic's bad. MAP helps your college thing, so you can get Advanced, if you get them all right or miss one you get *Advanced*. Basic is the worst. I don't think you'll get in to a really good college, I'm not that sure though. I think I do OK, I usually get Proficient, cuz I don't know all the questions in math, like, we went over miles, but it was really, really hard, so I got it, but it had, like, how many miles are in twenty-five . . . or, how many feet are in twenty-five miles, and I didn't get that, so I just guessed, and I got it right.

—*Lisa, Jewish, inner-ring suburb, public school, middle income*

Actually, Lisa's not quite right. Here in Missouri, Basic is not the worst; Below Basic is the worst. Teachers who work in failing or so-called turnaround schools are not worried about the kids who score Proficient or Advanced; they worry about the children they call "my Below Basics." When the number of Below Basics gets too high, the state dismantles elected school boards and takes over. That's what happened in St. Louis and Kansas City. When the state takes over, the state tells schools to make data the driving force for improvement. "We Are Data Driven" proclaims the giant placard in a teachers' resource room I entered as a researcher in the spring of 2013. Below the poster are bar graphs that chart rising and falling student test scores because, although there are many kinds of trustworthy assessment data teachers might be generating in their classrooms, it's the numbers that are most wanted.

No sensible and responsible person is arguing that nothing should be done in or about dysfunctional schools, or that there is no room for *certain* kinds of standardized tests used in *specific* kinds of ways. I am going to argue, however, that when we speak of children as if they are goods—products we label and sort into lumps we call Advanceds, Proficients, Basics, and Below Basics, as if kids were footwear or some other commodity that comes in a quality determined over the course of two nerve-racking weeks every year—we are already on the wrong track. In one rural Missouri town, the Advanceds and Proficients "get to" walk in the annual town parade behind a banner proclaiming their test score label. Cosmopolitan, educated parents of means do not send their children marching down Fifth Avenue or M Street behind a banner that reads "2200 to 2400 SATs." That would be considered crass and humiliating. But then again, elite students do not have to publicize tip-top performances so explicitly. The scores those kids earn on *their* standardized, high-stakes tests are more subtly disclosed by admission into the world's most exclusive institutions of higher learning.

For more than a century, enough people have decided that sorting-and-stamping is an essential part of education, or at least an education *system*. But this system is neither humane nor optimal. It bears no decent relation to human development or learning. If members of a privileged elite do not believe a way of doing school is OK for their own children, let's not pretend it's OK for the children of those who don't have enough money to buy their way out of it. How can this testing racket be something we, anthropologically speaking, let ourselves get away with in the rearing of our young? In any case, how do children speak about the testing we subject them to?

Students say a lot of interesting things about what they call "normal tests"—all those charged moments, usually once a week or at the end of a particular curricular unit, when they have to produce for their teacher spelling words, math facts, state capitals, types of leaves, and other learned content. While the design and purpose of those kinds of tests are important subjects in and of themselves—summative assessments is what they're called in the field—this chapter is not about regular old tests. This chapter is about the high-stakes tests, the tests that generate the data that people in schools are instructed to be driven by.

First, a few abbreviations and acronyms for the uninitiated since the children use them quite fluently: DRA (Developmental Reading Assessment); NWEA (Northwest Education Evaluation); MAP (Missouri Assessment Program); ITBS (Iowa Test of Basic Skills); DEA (Discovery Education Assessment); RTI (Response to Intervention); ERB (Educational Records Bureau); ESL (English as a Second Language), ELL (English Language Learners). When teachers tell their students they are going to "do a Tungsten" tomorrow, they are referring to Tungsten Learning's Benchmark Assessment System. These tests and test-related products are used for different reasons, and kids talk about them in different contexts. Some are more common in independent schools; others in the public districts. Every state's got one that dominates conversations and classrooms.

Here in Missouri, we talk a lot about the MAP, which is the test "that makes sure we're at the right level," as a Bosnian American girl in an urban public school says. The kids realize that grown-ups really, really care about getting your level right. Some children view the MAP as a measure of their performance as individuals, an indicator of which box they belong in as a student. Other students understand the connection between their performance on the MAP and the fate of their teacher and/or their school. Many students are aware of the way MAP test preparation boots other curricula out of their schedule. The temperament, outlook, and culture of individual schools, teachers, and parents have a lot to do with how students frame the experience in their own minds. I found that kids who understand standardized tests as a measurement of individual achievement can be cheerfully disposed to the process, emotionally neutral about it, or highly critical of the experience. The kids who dislike standardized tests find the process boring, hard, disorienting, redundant, and even unjust. Thus the responses fell into three categories: high-stakes tests express individual academic identity; performances on high-stakes tests reflect on teachers, schools, and the community; and standardized tests are a reasonable part of institutional self-assessment.

TESTS EXPRESS ACADEMIC IDENTITY

These children have internalized high-stakes tests as a legitimate indicator of their own individual learning and development. For this group, performance outcomes are tied up with self-understanding.

URBAN

I'm Proficient in math. And com arts. We take baseline tests at the beginning to see where you are, and at the end to see how much you've learned. I feel it's a long test. And we're timed. But we get peppermints when we're taking the test, and we're like, "Here comes the big test," cuz we have private folders to make sure nobody's cheating. And you're just in a little area on a little desk surrounded by a folder. We have homework to improve our learning, so we can move up to Proficient and Advanced and people won't stay on Below Basic or Basic.

Why do you think you're learning what you're learning in school?

Because on the MAP test, because we're behind. But we're moving up.

So you're learning what you're learning for the MAP test?

Exactly what's on the MAP test. Because even if you're Below Basic, you could move up. I used to be Basic, and I moved up to Proficient. And I know I could take the next step and be Advanced.

—*Kiara, African American, public school, low income*

So we take tests, we take an NWEA and we test how good you are in the beginning of the year. We test and then there's like this machine that gives you a score, your goal for you, when it's the end of the year, and you take it, so I'm in like, in the ending of a fifth grade level. I feel good [taking tests]. I kinda feel like "I hope

I get it, I hope I don't fail," because some, some stuff was hard and I didn't know. Like in the NWEA, they give you in the beginning where you started from that last time you took it, and, and if you get it right, the questions, you go higher to next grade or level, so that's how you know that it's getting harder.

—*Guadalupe, bilingual (Spanish/English), charter school, low income*

We take all the stuff that we've learned at, in the year, and then we, or then they ask questions on stuff, and on the test, and then we write down what we know about it.

How do you do on the MAP test?

Um. I don't know.

So you don't ever see the scores or anything like that?

At the end of the year they give you an award if you are Advanced or Proficient. But I didn't get it.

—*Donald, African American, charter school, low income*

We take the MAP test so we can see what grade level we in, and if we take a reading class, we do, well, if you score Proficient you go up a grade. Sometimes I feel a little worried that I'm gonna fail.

—*Darrion, African American, charter school, low income*

NWEA is where we get on the computer and take tests and see where we at and what we need to learn more about. It's only benchmark and NWEA. MAP tests, they're really frustrating because they giving us the test to see what we gonna be in life. They practice. They give us work like it. Until we get there, they training, we practicing, the way we go, we train, they giving us papers so we can get better. And we take them in April.

—*Darnell, African American, charter school, low income*

In the beginning of the year we have a whole lot of them. I hate them. I just don't like the feeling of having a test which I don't know about, I don't know anything about 'em, and I just hate doing them. I don't feel good about them. Because I like taking my time better than rushing and having to get all these bubbles done in like an hour—and it just sucks.

—Lucy, white, Catholic school, middle income

They're frightening and they're weird 'cause you have like two books and then you have to, like, look in them. Like sometimes I mess up 'cause there's G, H, and then I go, like, the row down.

—Sean, white, Catholic school, middle income

Some are hard an' you are timed for it, so it's a little rushed. They feel stressing, like you're stressed.

—Alyssa, white, Catholic school, middle income

METROPOLITAN

MAP tests are kinda hard. Like I'm feelin' like I'm gonna faint or something, 'cause there's a lot of questions, I'm like, I don't get it. If you don't finish 'til lunch you gotta do it tomorrow.

—Bernardo, English language learner (Spanish), public school, low income

They wanna try to trick you in communication arts like, say an answer that makes no sense and like three other ones that are kind of hard. And they're gonna try to throw you off by like making one like, like it was on decimals they're gonna make you, they're gonna try to trick you.

And so why do you take those tests, do you think?

To see if you're listening in class and to see if you're not just like daydreaming. 'Cause you really have to know what you're doing when you're taking those 'cause yeah. 'Cause [*sigh*] they wanna try to trick you a lot. Like on the MAP test. It was fun because I got to—it was kind of fun but I didn't have trouble on a lot of questions but some they just threw me off sometimes. Mostly the math 'cause communication arts was kind of good for me. I liked communication arts. 'Cause that's the most trickiest one but sometimes the trickier stuff is easy for me and the easy stuff is hard for me. 'Cause it's not like it's challenging, that's just what people said it was. 'Cause that's what they are—that's what it is to *them* but it can be different for other people. Easy can be—it can be opposites. Easy can be hard and hard can be easy.

—Brianna, white, public school, fragile middle income

I don't like it. Because it's a little booklet and then we have to sit there quietly, and you have to finish it in a certain amount of time. And then I don't catch up as fast, so I get kind of a lower grade. All I know is it's in April. We prepare because our teacher tells us what we do and what we don't have to know for the MAP test. So she said there's not gonna be a buncha algebra, because we don't have to know it in fourth grade and it's not gonna be on the MAP test.

—Chynna, African American, public school, middle income

Chynna has been taught that there are things she does and does not have to know. Because algebra is not going to be on the test, higher achievement in math is ruled out in her fourth-grade curriculum. Judging by performance outcomes as well as the perceptions of students like Chynna, limiting academic achievement for low-income students of color is exactly what high-stake testing practice is designed to do. Targeting and meeting benchmarks does not constitute teaching for maximal growth and development.

INNER-RING SUBURB

We take standardized tests so teachers and other schools and colleges know how smart you are and how—what you're good at and what needs work on.

—Logan, white, Catholic school, middle income

OUTER-RING SUBURB

Right now we have a practice packet that we're gonna go over tomorrow during PALS time. We practice that, yeah. Sometimes I get nervous because like they're long and I don't know if I'm gonna get it right or not. Our teachers tell us to get a lot of sleep.

—Janelle, public school, middle income

We take the MAP test to see at the end of the year how you're gonna be in fifth grade, or, what kind of grades you can get, how good you are. Like, I had special classes, next year I'm not gonna have to have them, because I passed, I got six-six-six-five-six-six-six. And the max score you can get is six. And I only got a five on writing. I got a six on reading for English Second Language, the ESL.

—Artur, Polish American, public school, middle income

I thought it was kinda hard, because last year I went with Ms. S. to practice—Yeah, cuz, it's, like, getting harder and harder each grade. The MAP is to help you, so that your teacher next year can see what you know. I feel kinda nervous, like I'm like, is this right or is it wrong or what am I gonna get on this question.

—Mallory, Jewish, public school, middle income

A special note about Mallory's remarks. On the MAP test, answers are either right or wrong. Because the state cannot possibly grade hundreds of thousands of tests in a timely fashion, there has to be only one right answer. In schools that embed robust formative and summative assessments, facing right-or-wrong questions from time to time is perfectly fine. But good teaching is unlikely to happen in places where the annual test is *the* test, one which carries a great load of economic and social significance and exclusively asks questions that have only one correct answer. Moreover, a high-stakes testing environment conditions students to the idea that learning in school is about coming up with answers to other people's questions.

It can really be boring 'cause you have to take a long time to do it. Your hands get tired. And a lot of people don't like the timed ones. But their favorite part is when we get extra recess 'cause we get extra recess 'cause of the MAP and snacks.

—*Madelyn, white, public school, fragile middle income*

The ITBS? It was a first this year. And yes I got really nervous about that and sometimes when I didn't have time to study, ah, I worry about it a lot and I turn out to get 100 percent [*laughs*].

—*Anne, white, Catholic school, middle income*

SMALL CITY

Andrew and Toby show how discriminating and reasonable kids can be. While they are highly critical of the frequency and redundancy of the testing they are subjected to, they submit to the MAP as a necessary instrument for measuring all kids at one fell swoop: "You have to take that," Toby says, and his friend agrees. What these boys want is a test "that just gets everything." Kind of like a dragnet. But of course these are children; adults should know that there is no such thing as a test "that just gets everything." I suspect that the perspectives of Andrew and Toby are influenced by their parents, who are university faculty.

Who do you think decides what children need to learn?

TOBY: School board, and I hate the school board.

Why do you hate the school board?

TOBY: 'Cause they make us do all these tests just to put some numbers in the computer and I don't think that's fair. It's just, we're doing SO MANY TESTS!

ANDREW: Yeah, at the end of the year . . .

TOBY: I mean I think we've had so many tests I think they know how good we're doing—

ANDREW: Yah, like we've taken this test where it recaps over everything we've done this whole year, we've taken it like three times.

TOBY: It's not the same one but there's the DRA, too.

Are you talking about the MAP test?

ANDREW: No—

TOBY: You have to take that—

ANDREW: Yeah, you hafta take that, but we took this one in math where it was over everything we learned—

TOBY: I know—

ANDREW: We took it like three times but it was different because we did like one different thing in math then we took it again and another one and we took it again and I don't—

TOBY: Why can't we just do that at the end?

ANDREW: I don't get why they don't just make us take it at the end because then it just gets everything.

—*Andrew and Toby, white, public school, middle income*

RURAL

With regard to the purpose and feeling of testing, Oliver, Frannie, and Cleo are in the "it's not so bad" and "it's for my own good" zone of understanding. Oliver's mom is a teacher and his father is securely employed; Frannie's family farms. Blaze doesn't mind the MAP because filling in bubbles, to him, doesn't feel like thinking.

Oh, we haven't been doing science because we have been doing a lot of things like MAP testing. We just got finished with testing. We also have to do a DRA test. We read to the teacher and see how we go through and if we do good we stay with the teacher, if we need help, we go with Mrs. G. On the MAP test, I think I'm confident about myself and it's really great because they need to

know what you're learning and to see what you need help on or to
see if you're gonna pass.

—*Frannie, white, public school, low income*

I think I take, we take MAP tests to see how well we're doing
with the things, because one teacher that comes in to help, Ms.
W. always says, like, she's a reading helper, and she helps the kids
that need a little more help on reading, and, but when we were
practicing for a MAP test, we were all together practicing for it,
she said, "None of this is over your grade-level work, it's all fourth-
grade work." And, the MAP test, basically, sees how well, sees how
well you remember what you've learned over the year, and how
well you can do with it. I sometimes am a little nervous at the very
beginning because, like, I'm nervous I'm not gonna do as well, but,
usually, after a while, I don't become so nervous, and it just seems a
lot easier after you get used to it.

—*Oliver, white, public school, middle income*

Well, like last year I was really nervous 'cause it was my first test but
now I'm used to it. I'm not so scared of it and we've been practicing
so, I know what's gonna be on it and how hard it's gonna be and all
that so it's pretty easy.

—*Cleo, white, public school, low income*

The MAP test's kinda easy because all you have to do is fill in a
bubble when you're done instead of thinking of the answer. They're
to see how well kids can do in the subject. They kinda show you,
like, every now and then if you're at Proficient or Advanced or
something.

—*Blaze, white, public school, low income*

We take the MAP test so that we can go over like everything that
we've learned over the year, and they can see how well we've done.
    Who is "they"?
    Well, the people that have the MAP test. Well [*sigh*], I don't

know. Like the Missouri people in charge. I dunno [*laughs*]. Like some type of really, really smart Missouri people [*laughs*], I dunno.

—*Rosie, white, public school, low income*

I don't really like it. It's really long an' hard.

—*Brody, white, public school, low income*

We have an enormous problem. Our hidden curriculum is teaching too many kids that their high-stakes performances correlate with fixed, intrinsic, and individual aptitude, ability, content mastery, and achievement. Interpreted statistically, any test is only deemed reliable if the same student would earn the exact same score every single time she or he took the test. For young children especially, this is not the case; their scores are particularly unreliable. With respect to self-assessment and identity, some children are downright confused by what standardized tests make of them. For such kids, the tests contradict ideas, even false ideas, they have formed of themselves either in school or at home. Spend five minutes with Ruth, for example. An intellectually energetic kid in a rural community, she is verbally gifted and keenly observant. Ruth can always think of counterexamples and contradictions. She responds to nearly every question with the phrase "it depends." Toward the end of our interview, she even calls attention to her tendency to say "it depends" and explains, laughingly, why she can't come out with a simple answer. Ruth's sophisticated way of thinking about stories is not especially useful to her as a language arts student in school. Because she is an intelligent person, however, and math mastery is more clear-cut, Ruth does do well in math. And so she has come to think of herself as "way better at math than com arts."

> Things on the MAP test, she told us this, that there's gonna be things that we don't know, cuz MAP test wants to see what you know, so sometimes she doesn't teach us the stuff, but she gives [the test] to us, anyways. So that way, we, she can know if, what we're capable of. She told us this, because, to compare us to other kids, to know what we're learning. They don't give us any grade. They

just give us this and say, "Well, hopefully you did a good job." This year, Mr. P. [the principal] looked at our grades from last year, like, just a couple weeks ago. Cuz you don't get the grades til the whole next year. And if we get, like, Proficient on math and reading and stuff, then down in the gym, there's this party, and it's watching a movie. OK, so there's this Proficient, and there's com arts, and there's math, and yeah, I figured I would get Proficient in math and not com arts, but I got it in com arts and not math, surprisingly. And like, I'm way better at math than com arts, but I got Proficient in com arts and not math.

That's interesting, why do you think that is?

I don't know. The questions were a little more confusing in math, because, like, I had no clue, because, last year's, like, "what's a prime and composite number," and we didn't learn that until this year.

So, what you're saying is you feel like in school, you do better in math than com arts, but on the MAP test, you got Proficient in com arts and you didn't get Proficient in math?

Exactly! Because I usually get As and Bs in math, and, like As, B, A-minuses, B-plusses, and sometimes even a C in com arts, and then on the MAP test, I don't even get Proficient on math, I get Proficient on com arts. I was very surprised when I saw that. I think that they kind of, since math is a easier subject than com arts, I think they wanna give us a little more challenging questions, because, like, math is just a little bit easier than com arts, so I think that they're giving us questions that we don't know. I think that's why.

—*Ruth, white, rural, public school, low income*

Ruth does her best to explain the inconsistency across her assessments. Math is easier than communication arts, she reasons, so naturally "they" will want to push her further, to see what she can do that's beyond what comes easy. What's going on here is complicated. Does the MAP measure what kids already know, or does it—as some kids, including Ruth, suspect—try to assess what kids *might* know or be able to figure out even if school has not covered the material, or covers it in a misguided way? An hour of conversation convinced me that it is the school's language arts curriculum and perhaps her teacher's limited pedagogical and/or content knowledge that has given Ruth the idea that she has less aptitude for language arts than for math. What Ruth needs is a more insightful teacher who can create lessons that are more responsive to Ruth's abilities.

So how, exactly, has the MAP's focus on Ruth as an individual made her teacher and school more accountable in the context of her academic performance history? It would take a great deal of time and money to puzzle through these questions for each individual child. But only through doing so would we even begin to make appropriate use of the MAP outcomes. In the field of assessment, summative tests are called instruments. Extending the figure of speech, I would say that, as an instrument, the MAP test is like a pair of calipers that has fallen into the open wound of a patient lying on the table. It's an instrument in the way.

HIGH-STAKES TESTS AS COMMUNITY EVALUATIONS

In this group are the kids who understand that the MAP and other high-stakes tests not only attempt to capture their own personal academic accomplishments but also affect their teacher, their school, and their community. In the last few years, education policy makers eager to quantify a teacher's effect on students have turned to statistical methods that rely on hierarchical linear modeling. These methods, called Value-Added Assessment or Value-Added Measurement (VAM), are being used to hinge salary, promotion, retention, and tenure on the tracked and measurable changes in the test scores of an individual teacher's students. In order to show how we might evaluate teachers, the Bill and Melinda Gates Foundation recently spent $45 million—a thousand times more than I spent researching and writing this book—on a 2013 study involving a team of researchers who reported on thousands of teachers in six cities. Their data included student surveys, teacher observations, and the individual teachers' students' test scores. As documented by the National Education Policy Center (nepc.colorado. edu), the Measure of Effective Teaching Project ran into problems with their randomized sample and with the nonparticipation of some of the teachers and students. Upon analysis of the data they did collect, the team "found correlations so weak that no common attribute or characteristic of teacher-quality could be found," the NEPC reports. In other words, you can't measure teachers at scale and by formula. Nevertheless, the federal Race to the Top program requires states to include standardized test scores as a significant factor in teacher evaluation. Given the complex and dynamic historical, emotional, temperamental, intellectual, physical, cultural, and environmental factors that go into any student's performance on these tests on any given day—factors that extend far outside of the classroom—this model strikes many people in education as scientifically unreliable, invalid, and even Orwellian. Like other developments in public education, however, enough people with the right combination of money, power, and authority are making it happen. And the kids have been paying attention. They get the picture: if they screw up on the tests, their teacher and school will suffer. Of the many terrible ways high-stakes testing plays out in real life, making young children feel responsible for their teachers' livelihoods is among the most dastardly. Think Fagin in *Oliver Twist*.

METROPOLITAN

Why are you learning what you're learning in school?
To take the MAP test.
And why do you take the MAP test?
To see how well teachers teach.

—Maria, Mexican American, English language learner
(Spanish), public school, low income

INNER-RING SUBURB

We take standardized tests to judge students in Missouri like how smart they are and like, well, I heard this story in Atlanta. Right before this really big test the teacher told them, they said the lesson right before the test and—and then they all got it right. And then it was really bad. Like, they cheated.

—Evan, white, Catholic school, middle income

RURAL

Well, I know that the MAP test is a big part of a grade in school which, it really helps your school. Like my parents have told me that if you do good on the MAP test it helps your school quite a bit. I think we do MAP testing to monitor how kids are doing in school and like, how much education has changed between the 1970s and present. You know there's always, that one bad test taker in class or that one person that gets nervous easily. I don't think I'm that person. 'Cause there's quite a few kids in my class who, they'll get nervous, you know. I get nervous from when I am studying for it, but I usually do all right. I think the last time I saw my results . . . I know I got Advanced class last year. And then the last time I got my results was in second grade I got 99 percent, I think. So I think that was the last time I actually saw my grade.

—Hunter, white, public school, low income

MAP test, I took it last year and I got a really good score so it's not really [*long pause*] I don't know how to say it but it it, it's not hard for me. It's fer, to see what you've learned throughout the year, and see how good you done, and the schools compete fer who has the best scores of what they've learned throughout the year. It just shows you who's got the most scores throughout the schools. You get to walk in the parade, if . . . it's a town parade that we have and you walk behind a banner that says *Proficient* or *Advanced MAP Test Scores*, you walk behind it, you get to walk in the parade. Last year I did. It's just to see who's got the best scores in the school.

—Noah, white, public school, fragile middle income

You get pretty nervous. But once you're doing it, to me, it's kinda fun 'cause you don't have to do anything else, but, and there's complicated ones. You kinda struggle, but, you'll get over it. Yeah. I do pretty good, I think I got, I dunno the highest one. I know they're not used on whether you're passing fourth grade or not. I think they're just telling 'em, how much you've learned through the whole school year, an' they're judging all the teachers, of how good they've taught you. And like people, teachers *can* get fired for

like, if you get, if your class does bad on that test, you can get fired
for that.

—Casey, white, public school, low income

Well, I think they're pretty challenging, because, but some of
the questions are pretty easy, and some of them are challenging,
because we don't even get a chance to learn 'em. And there's a
whole bunch of questions and sometimes it's not like a regular
paper [in school], like your teacher knows what you're meaning to
say. There's actually real people in college and stuff grading it, so
you have to say exactly what you mean, and yeah. And the thing
about it is you can't, like, if you color it, if it's multiple choice
questions, you color it in, and you, like, get one little tiny dot on a
different question, it'll count the whole thing wrong.

Well, I feel pretty relaxed, because usually my mom makes me
a really good breakfast, especially on the MAP week, and there's
these signs, like, all around the building that they did in art and
stuff, that says, "Be Relaxed" and stuff, and "Do Good on the Test."

—Nathan, white, public school, middle income

I felt that some problems were pretty challenging like some like
if you had to flip 'em around I found them really easy. Like some
questions, they say what would this shape, what would this thing
look like, would it look the same if it was flipped around. And some
wouldn't and, there would always be one that would. It was multiple
choice. Well, MAP doesn't count as a grade. They take it to see
how good the school's doing, and if the school doesn't do that good
for multiple years in a row the school can get shut down. I think
the people [who would shut down the school] are either in Jefferson
City or New York, I don't really know.

—Blaze, white, public school, low income

I think we take MAP tests to get like more money for our school
for, like I don't know, to buy some more equipment for recess and
all that.

—Carolyn, white, public school, middle income

Do you guys take the MAP test starting in a couple weeks?

DAKOTA: In seventeen day—

KAYLA: In eighteen days.

DAKOTA: We're counting down in our classroom.

Why?

KAYLA: Because Ms. S. wants to prepare us because lots of times we get mad and we get stressed out and we don't wanna take the MAP test and we get really mad and we talk and we don't do the MAP test.

And why do you take MAP tests?

KAYLA: Because the MAP, 'cause you learn each stuff and you take a regular test that adds up for your grade for that quarter, but when you take the MAP test it clears out everything that you know, but it doesn't only just go for you, it goes for Ms. S. because it teaches whoever that Ms. S. is a good teacher and shows that she teaches us well.

In general, what I heard among children in rural communities was acceptance and, for the most part, compliance. Kayla talks about resistance and kids getting mad, but she also conjures up an image of the MAP as an agent of spring cleaning—*it clears out everything that you know.* The teacher puts knowledge in, and the MAP vacuums knowledge right out. Kids take the test because that's what's expected, and what's expected is a reasonable thing to ask of people who want to support their schools, their teachers, and their community. Remember that this is the same population of children for whom A.R. quizzes drive the reading curriculum.

STANDARDIZED TESTS AS A REASONABLE PART OF INSTITUTIONAL SELF-ASSESSMENT

Kids in the comfortable, more secure middle class and other communities of relative privilege do not suffer the day-to-day testing pressures

as do children from either underresourced communities or communities where the scores will make or break a district's autonomy or get
a teacher fired. I am setting aside the highly disordered high-stakes
testing of preschool or college-bound children in places where parents
frantically spend a lot of time and money preparing their children to
compete for spots in highly selective schools. This is really bad, too,
but in the context of what's going on in the country as a whole, especially in poor rural and urban communities where children, families,
and teachers are dealing with test prep as curriculum, we can't talk
about such tribulations in the same breath.

Kids of higher social status may or may not like taking standardized tests, but generally accept them as part of the baggage of formal
schooling, as they are taught to do by teachers and school administrators. As Marley reveals below, these kids tend to see standardized tests
less as a menace, and more as a way for the teachers to help themselves
improve. Another way of understanding the less pressured experiences
is to hear that the students realize that the information they are pro-
ducing on the tests is for local use, for their own teachers and schools
to incorporate in instructional design. Jennifer says it outright: the
tests help the teachers learn "what they need to help us do better on."
Teachers use the data from tests to shape future instructional practice.
Among kids like Jennifer there is no talk of alien "smart people"—test
writers and test graders—who live far away in Jefferson City (the state
capital) or New York.

URBAN

So we have stuff called ERBs, and we actually just had those, and
they're like the big test like everyone has a sheet and it's really big
and so those I think like those are kind of hard but they're not as
fun. They're a little bit boring compared to the other tests we have
'cause I think the teachers are creative in how they like state it.

Why do you think you take ERBs?

I think it's mainly for the teachers to see how we're doing and
also so everyone, so teachers can see how the school is working and
if we got this one problem right they can look at our scratch paper

and see how we did it to see how, why, and what methods are good and work and then if we got one wrong and they look at the paper, then they can say, "Hmm, we need to change that, 'cause I don't think this student understands that."

—*Marley, white, private school, high income*

The ERB wasn't really that hard for me. I did really good. I believed in myself and I tried my best.

—*Barack, African American, private school, middle income*

Well, when we had the standardized tests I got kind of bored. Cuz I always finished, like, and there was still twenty minutes left for the test and she can't stop it. It's like, we do a bunch of different ones. Like, for social studies, math, all that kind of stuff.

—*Margaret, white, Catholic school, middle income*

David, below, had an exceptionally accurate and sophisticated understanding of the aggregative power of standardized testing. He understands that the purpose and function of these testing processes is to compare and contrast groups of children with respect to standards normed to a mainstream population.

I think we take ERBs, we usually do this to, well, I think the tests are standard because we don't want to use a completely different system, so it's easy to compare and contrast.

—*David, Jewish, bilingual (Italian/English), private school,*
high income

INNER-RING SUBURB

We just finished doing those like a month or two ago. And we were all like stressed out and we're just like *ahh* but we got to eat candy so—but I don't do candy so I had mints. We take them for the teachers to figure out what level we're at, if we're like behind, ahead,

or like just where we should be. Sometimes I feel a little stressed.
Other times I'm just like, I know what I'm doing, it's not a big deal.

—Louise, white, Catholic school, high income

We do ERBs. Those I think are pretty fun but we, I mean now we're
doing 'em where she reads the questions to us out loud, and then we
fill in the best answer and we have these little things so people can
[gestures to protect/guard her work] . . .

—Shelby, African American, private school, high income

OUTER-RING SUBURB

I feel kinda nervous. But I feel good about the MAP testing 'cause
it's not part of your grade.

—Nuri, Syrian American, Islamic school, high income

I'm not scared at all. I think it's in two weeks. I think we take the
MAP test so it helps our knowledge and so, the teachers can see
like how we're doing on what they need to help us do better on.

—Jennifer, public school, middle income

MAP tests we take at the end of the year to see, that's when they
see what we've been learning.
    And who's the "they"?
    Our teachers.
    And, how do you feel about those tests?
    I don't really care, I just go through 'em.
    Do you have any trouble answering any of those questions?
    No.

—Joey, white, Protestant school, middle income

Well, I know we take the MAP test so we can get challenged
classes in middle school and the next year our teachers know how

well we know so they can place us in challenge groups or a lower grade or an average group.

—Neelish, South Asian–Ugandan, public school, middle income

GETTING ASSESSMENT RIGHT AND FAIR

As Neelish suggests, it should be the classroom teacher's responsibility to figure out what her students know. However, as massive amounts of research have shown, gutting the core of a teacher's professional responsibility is one of the worst outcomes of the high-stakes landscape. Mechanistic, binary, right/wrong forms of student assessment are incapable of measuring the most important qualities of teaching. Canadian scholar Charmaine Brooks writes:

> The critical balance between public accountability and professional responsibility needs to be regained. An education system fixated on ensuring accountability through data collection feeds a discourse of problems and solutions, failing and passing, us and them. Education, not unlike other professions including medicine and the law, lives in the realm of the uncertain, and requires professionals who are empowered to conduct themselves from the core of their knowledge and skills. Accountability policies must reflect the nuances of teaching and learning, and the professional autonomy of teachers, if public education is to serve the needs of society in an increasingly complex world.[*]

But alas, nothing going on in the real world has been able to loosen the attachment federal policy makers and federal and state lawmakers have to high-stakes testing. If crash tests are good enough for a BMW, well then, they're good enough for a child. This attachment results in the inequitable, viselike imposition of the worst kind of testing on

---

[*]Charmaine Brooks, "Teaching in Full View: GLA as a Mechanism of Power," *Policy Futures in Education* 7, vol. 3 (2009), 318.

children in low-income communities. Looking at the lay of the land today and recalling the children's perceptions I have shared, we can all see what I have seen:

- Widespread cheating, and a demoralizing awareness of cheating, on the part of teachers, principals, and children.
- The inequitable application of the testing machinery on children from different social worlds, with poor children in rural and urban settings as well as children in our fragile middle class suffering the most pinched and pinching testing policies.
- The misery of yearlong test preparation in the classroom for teachers and children alike, including the stripping away of time for recess, art, music, social studies, physical education, science, and other nontested content areas.
- The increasing awareness among parents that this whole standards-to-test system is predicated on theories and practices lifted from business and grafted onto growing people, that benchmarks are in fact management tools that are meant to help set industry bests.
- Studies conducted by reputable scholars and experienced teachers that challenge the validity and reliability of high-stakes test results.

In defiance of reality, those who wield power and make policy continue to mine teachers and kids for data. There are political reasons for this practice, but one thing is certain: collecting data is profitable. Indeed, as I described in the chapter on reading programs in schools, the highest stakes of all, even higher than those set up by the high-stakes tests, are the stakes played for by the gigantic, complexly structured transnational corporations who produce, sell, and score the tests, create the materials for the tests, and otherwise keep people in schools buying their test-related stuff to the tune of hundreds of millions of dollars a year. The people playing for *those* high stakes have a lot to do with why Darnell, whose words entitle this chapter, feels that standardized tests are there "to see what we gonna be in life."

Right now, Darnell is correct. The testing apparatus is making sure that Darnell grows up to be the kind of person whose performances are always tested and evaluated by other people. For Darnell and other kids in this position, the national conversation must turn *away* from how best to test and *toward* putting into standard practice enlightened forms of accountability in education.

Which brings us, finally, to accountability. I'm a taxpayer. And even though I'm a New Yorker, I'm also from Missouri, the Show-Me State. I want to know what's happening with my education dollars. If we rid ourselves of the high-stakes tests, how will I know what's happening behind the classroom door? How will I know I'm getting my money's worth, or that the kids are learning what they're supposed to learn?

Assessment of teaching and learning is an important and interesting field of study. Indeed, a healthy learning cycle (or spiral) is only realized when lesson design, instruction, and assessment are all sound and mutually influential. Academic researchers and classroom-based researchers therefore examine both processes and products of assessment. While an in-depth exploration of assessment lies beyond the scope of this book, I will mention a few rich veins. Performance-based assessments, for example, draw upon carefully made and documented observations of culminating unit projects. Traveling portfolios help teachers track progress and growth over time. Instructional interventions can be designed and implemented by teachers working alongside instructional coaches, administrators, and university faculty. Teachers themselves can conduct inquiry into assessment that serves students, improves practice, and builds knowledge. Collaborative initiatives around assessment can cross boundaries of content area and grade level. Technological advances allow us to integrate quantitative and qualitative analysis in new and meaningful ways.

Wonderful things are happening in schools, in universities, and in new hybrid spaces that bring together university faculty and school-based practitioners in both formal and informal teaching and learning settings. Professional journals, faculty lounges, and authentic professional learning communities are full of best and developing practices for conducting both formative and summative assessments. There are people in every educational domain who can figure out how to assemble both quantitative and qualitative data for interpretation at the local, state, and national level. How about we redirect those hundreds of millions of dollars we currently spend on standardized, high-stakes testing into the best practices that really do help us beneficently account for status quo—not everything's broken!—and promote warranted change? Nobody wants lousy teachers working with children, but the people who would most love to see lousy teachers leave the profession are the millions of decent, good, and great teachers who sincerely want to keep getting better at what they do so that their students will learn more.

And while we're at it, how about we start to finally take into account the serious work of reputable, established, realistic scholars, educators, and leaders, including Nell Noddings, Deborah Meier, Diane Ravitch, Alfie Kohn, and others? Getting education right for everyone means that we should be paying closer attention to the kids, as well as to people like Lee-Anne Perry, a school principal and Erica McWilliam, a university-based educator: "In a complex, expert system such as teaching, it is not possible to make all practices transparent, auditable and accountable. The language of trust, so critical to the teaching profession, exists in a discursive world that is outside the language of accountability . . . narrowly-based, quantifiable performance indicators can be not only self-defeating but at times quite absurd."*

Fourth-grader Lisa guessed on that question about the number of feet in twenty-five miles. She happened to get the answer right. But we are not fourth graders and we do not have to either guess about what's going on in schools or slice and dice kids' learning from on high.

---

*Lee-Anne Perry and Erica McWilliam, "Accountability, Responsibility and School Leadership," *Journal of Educations Enquiry* 7, vol. 1 (2007), 38.

6

ON BEING WITH OTHER KIDS ALL DAY

"If I Was Alone, What Would I Do?"

The one thing everybody knows about schools is that they are characterized by the presence of bunches of kids in one place. Teacher-student ratios may vary, but a place that calls itself school will generally have more kids than adults in it. Maaz, whose rhetorical question opens this chapter, views other children as essential to time spent in school. For some parents who homeschool, that's the problem with school: other people's kids can hold their own children back, or demand too much of the teacher's attention, or set an example their own child can't keep up with, or be mean, or not pray the way they do, or come to school with lice, and so on.

On the other hand, for many people who send their kids to school, that's what's great about school: for better and for worse, their children will have other children to learn and play with. Scholars who study children's overall well-being look at the relationships children do and don't sustain in order to assess degrees of well-being. Viewing friendship as essential to life and learning, researchers examine the way children construct relationships and consider well-maintained friendships as social capital. One recent study of roughly 4,500 secondary school students in the United Kingdom surveyed their experiences around family, neighborhood adults, friends they were on good terms with, friends they were on bad terms with, and people who bullied them, or treated them unfairly. The researcher, Haridhan Goswami, found that family, positive relationships with friends, and being bullied had the highest effect on children's subjective well-being. Two of those three factors—positive relationships with friends and being bullied—are shaped by life at school.

Children sharing classrooms and recess yards today will be sharing offices, working spaces, and civic lives tomorrow. Learning how to get along with each other is probably the most important thing they are up to all day long. Their relationships with each other affect how they feel. Their feelings affect how they act. How they act affects how teachers treat them. How teachers treat them affects how they learn. Therefore, getting to the root of what, how, and why kids are learning requires that we carefully consider their social lives. And like everything having to do with human beings, what's going on socially is complex and dynamic; careful consideration does not mean keeping a lid on drama so that the children are pliable and quiet, or think of each other as potential threats to classroom order. It means making an effort to understand what's going on among children without allowing social matters to boil like lava over everything else going on. The ingredients of childhood friendship—companionship, intimacy, and affection—can be nurtured. As Judy Dunn has written, "Friends matter to children. The pleasures, but also the betrayals, the jealousies and tangled intrigues, make friendships key to the quality of children's lives."*

When speaking with children, I heard more higher-level critical thinking on the subject of social matters than I did about anything else. So what *do* they say when they get to talking about other kids?

Well, they have a lot to say. Unlike topics where the ideas tended to fall into rather large thematic clumps, the talk about friends and friendship disclosed many different themes. Children expressed a range of critical thought and subtle reasoning as they spoke about themselves and their experiences at school in the context of other children. Ideas about friends and friendship touched on intersecting and overlapping subjects:

Cheering each other on and giving academic, social, or emotional support

---

*Judy Dunn, *Children's Friendships: The Beginnings of Intimacy* (Malden, MA: Blackwell Publishing, 2004), 3.

Playing together

Negotiating shifting friendships and conflicts: one-on-one, small inter-group (cliques); and intra-group dynamics

Matters of leadership; distributions of authority and power among peers

Dealing with adult interaction around social matters; suffering or working things out below the radar of adult attention

Handling distractions caused by other children

Being bullied; having been a bully

Talking things out; communicating with each other in general

Being confused about what others kids mean

Ethics of right and wrong social behaviors

Being "loners" in the context of school

Experiences across grades with children of different ages

Affirmations of identity in social interaction, both positive (as a caring helper of others) and negative (being a victim)

How family members (typically parents, often siblings) help them handle challenging social situations with sayings, advice, or some other form of support

Since a granular analysis of each one of these ideas might easily turn into an *Oxford English Dictionary* of childhood social life, I have collapsed the talk into three main categories: cheering and support; conflicts, confusions, leadership, and treachery; bullies, meanness, and being something of a loner.

The most important thing to realize is that dynamic, profound, and complex qualities of life in school come straight to the surface when children understand that we are genuinely interested in their social experiences.

CHEERING AND SUPPORT

Not having to "go it alone" is important to children in all types of schools. Some need a playmate in order to escape boredom; some depend upon an academic or social role model; others need a shoulder to lean on when times are tough.

URBAN

I had a friend, she knowed me for four years. And we always give each other stuff, like one time, she gave me a puppy dog's foot and it's like different colors and it glows at night. And it was a necklace and she gave me that one. And she gave me another necklace, that's like a cherry, a pink cherry. She has three of them. One of them she gave, it was like a "Best Friends Forever," and I had "Friends" and she had "Forever" and this other girl had "Best." She had a sister but her sister didn't want it. So she gave me one, and her one, and a cousin one.

—*Maida, Bosnian American, English language learner, public school, low income*

It feels nice to be with friends 'cause when you down, you'll have somebody to talk to.

—*Kashena, African American, charter school, low income*

If I was the only one in the class then I would be super bored all the time and I wouldn't get—I wouldn't get to do anything at recess.

—*Vince, white, Catholic school, middle income*

When somebody's sad, we just try to cheer them up. Because if everybody's sad, then they just turn sad with them. But if everybody's happy, then they become happy, too.

—*Daisy, white, Catholic school, middle income*

I feel like one time in music I was having trouble with a song on a recorder and my friends were there to encourage me and say "Come on, you can do it," so I think they help and when they're in the environment they help you like, they're always there for you and also sometimes when I'm taking a hard test, I look around and I say, "If my friends can do this, then I can do it, too," so it gives me like that encouragement that I need.

—*Marley, white, private school, high income*

Friends cheer me up, they help me if I have a problem. And they will support me. And if we have a project . . . I've had partners for a project and they'll come to my house and we'll work on it.

—*Barack, African American, private school, middle income*

METROPOLITAN

They make it more fun and sometimes they make it just a funner day and they make me happy when I'm sad so they kinda cheer me up when I'm at school sometimes if I'm not liking it really. Mostly everyone's mostly kind to each other.

—*Brianna, white, public school, middle income*

They make me feel good like when I'm sad. And they make me feel happy. So that makes me happy the rest of the day. 'Cause my dog and my grandma died this year.

—*Madeleine, white, public school, fragile middle income*

They are helpful, they always help me in everything and we always play together. We used to do groups, reading groups. Now we just do them independently. Now we can buddy-read, like we read with a friend.

—*Jamil, Yemeni, English language learner, public school, low income*

INNER-RING SUBURB

I have a lot of friends. So like they're really nice to me. Like if you get a like bad grade or if you feel sad they'll always be there.

—*Martha, white, Catholic school, high income*

I'm usually happy, and I feel like I have a lot of fun in school every day. I think it's because all my friends are here and it's fun to learn with them and play with them. I think they make it more fun than it was already because we can do lots of stuff with them there.

—*Miranda, white, private school, high income*

OUTER-RING SUBURB

Friends make me feel good. My friend, he helps me, well, he helped me before, and it made me feel better cuz I was frustrated on a question.

—*Douglas, African American, public school, middle income*

We can probably learn better with our friends. I think it's harder to learn with like strangers, people you don't really know. Because your friends, they can like help you out, and you're used to talking to them, and they know how you speak to them, but other people they don't really know how you talk, you know. Like some people have different ways to talk and say things. Like me and my friend Rachel, we made a secret language without using our mouths, like we don't talk, we just come up with the words that we would normally use in a sentence.

—*Jennifer, white, public school, middle income*

They really make it, like, a really nice time, cuz if we didn't have any friends here, then . . . cuz friends here, they just really make school all that much better.

—*Gracie, white, Protestant school, middle income*

I heard on one commercial that kids could do school online. My mom said that was an option. I was like, "No way, you don't have any friends." Another thing about that computer thing is you'd lose the . . . you wouldn't get as much, I'm not sure how to say this, socialization, I think. Like being twenty-four other people in there.

I look at the whole class and I'm like, "How do I know all these people's names?"

—Greta, white, Protestant school, middle income

Well, when I first came [this year] I was always welcomed and at my other school they were just like, "Hi, how's it going?" and stuff, but at this school, they actually talk to you about interesting things and they're really nice to you, and they tell you secrets, and they won't, and I could tell them secrets and they won't break them.

—Justine, mixed ethnicity (Cherokee/white), Protestant school,
middle income

I'm happy that I get to spend time with my friends, and I like doing schoolwork and stuff, so . . . that's pretty much it. Yeah. If my friend's having a bad day, it makes me in kind of a bad mood. If we have trouble, like, me and a group of friends when we have paper, we just go over, like in vocabulary, we have the list with their meanings up on the board, so me and my friends just normally sit down and do the vocabulary on the floor, and then, we help each other with that.

—Helen, white, Protestant school, middle income

They really make it nice 'cause every time I get back home, I'm like, good thing I have friends at school 'cause then the next day has something that I could do. 'Cause basically the thing that makes you happy to be at school are friends.

—Nuri, Syrian American, Islamic school, high income

SMALL CITY

ANDREW: Friends make school a lot funner because—

TOBY: —'cause you're around people—

ANDREW: Yeah, you're around people that you like.

—Andrew and Toby, white, public school, middle income

RURAL

My life is a lot more fun when I'm at school, cuz I actually have friends to play with. And when I don't really understand the question when Ms. F. tried to tell it to me, and, like, it didn't really make any sense to me, when she told me, and she didn't know how to explain it another way, one of my friends would help me with it.

—Ruth, white, public school, low income

Friends make it fun, because like when you're at home you don't really get to see your friends much, 'cause like sometimes like your parents have stuff to do and you can't invite them over so like at recess you have things, you get, you have friends to play with at recess and everything.

—Harold, mixed ethnicity (white/African American), public school, low income

My friends help me a lot with my school. If I have trouble on something, lots of times, like, something that I wasn't there for that day, if I was sick that day, if I wasn't there to know what they were talking about that day, I can ask friends, ask 'em about if they know how to do it, or something.

—Oliver, white, public school, middle income

I'm just so tempted to talk to 'em in class, and sometimes they're pretty good, because, like, if you're having a bad day or something, they're always there.

—Nathan, white, public school, middle income

When children got on the subject of enjoying each other's company at recess, I was always on the lookout for signs of imaginative social play—pretend role playing as opposed to rule-following games or sports. I did not hear much. On the whole, kids in rural communities were more likely to engage in pretend play of the kind described by Tori and Meredith:

Usually my friends Mary and Danielle and I will go on the swings, and Mary made up this club, well, kind of a made-up person called Shims, and we'll like play that, and we have baby walnuts and stuff, and hers is named David. Mine is Fluffy.

—Tori, white, public school, homeschooled through third grade, middle income

Me and my friends play this game like we're werewolves and vampires, but yeah, or my friend Elizabeth and Kayla is a werewolf and me and my friend Elizabeth and other girls are vampires, yeah.

—Meredith, white, public school, low income

Girls like Frannie and Chelsea, below, love their friends so much it's palpable. As Maida described when discussing the divvying up of the "Best Friends Forever" necklace parts, these sorts of best friends are essentially co-living their lives in the past, present, and future: Frannie and Rosie are planning on opening a veterinary clinic together.

School's great because of my friend. Rosie, she's really nice, we do mostly everything together. Friends make it easy because I think about them when I'm doing homework or something. Sometimes I think, like, "Rosie would do this so . . . I could probably do it." And it's probably not hard so if Rosie would do it it's probably not hard so I would probably do it and it's not hard and I just got another thing done. I try to make friends with everybody, like, girls. I try to cheer people on. Like with their work, I try to help people, like the little preschoolers. Sometimes we gotta go over there and help them, like last week we got ta help them pick up trash ta help the environment. I say I don't wanna go to school but I have to. And then when I get at school I'm happy to see my friends here, have a good time, do work and then get the weekend and sleep during the weekends and hopefully, we, in the summer, I'm going to summer school, that means there're going to be a lot of activities. And . . . Rosie, Megan, Amanda, me, all going to summer school so it'll be really fun and we're gonna sometimes play I think, so I think it'll be a really fun activity.

—Frannie, white, public school, low income

My friends make my life really good, like they're always there for me and they support me and all of that. I just feel like they're sisters to me, kind of like, they feel like sisters 'cause they're so close to me and like if I have a problem or anything I can just text 'em or call 'em or something and I can tell 'em or I can tell 'em at school. I think they're good kids. Most of 'em, they're just good kids.

—Chelsea, white, public school, fragile middle income

CONFLICTS, CONFUSIONS, LEADERSHIP, AND TREACHERY

This is one of those subtopics that warrants a whole separate book. Children reveal depth of thinking, specificity of observation, and sheer wordiness in storytelling and explanatory effort. Compared to charged social complexities, math facts and A.R. quizzes are an incidental cognitive sideshow. The most vexing and painful social negotiations happen during recess and lunch—when children have precious minutes to themselves. Thorny group dynamics unfold during classtime, too; some are illicit and, if caught by a teacher, disruptive. Perhaps echoing what adults say, the kids call a lot of this stuff "social drama."

URBAN

In many public schools, the children of recent immigrants and refugees work out their friendships across cultural and ethnic differences. This is Azra, a second-generation Bosian American, speaking of her friends Nasrin and Bahar, both of whom were born in Iraq. Azra and Nasrin dress secularly in the school uniform. Bahar wears a head scarf.

Girls have drama. Sometimes I get into fight with my friend, her name's Nasrin and one time we got into a fight over her shirt when it was Friday. It was Friday so we can wear whatever we want. Tweety Bird was on the shirt except it was only a face, and she's like, "Tweety Bird's a girl." And I was like, "No, it's a boy," and she's like, "No, it's a girl." And we got into a fight over something stupid.

So then what happened?

Our school counselor, she usually just figures out the problem. Whenever this, not my really good friend, her name's Bahar, she sometimes get in the way of our friendship, like Bahar wants to hang out more with Nasrin. I don't know why but Nasrin doesn't want to hang out with Bahar. So the counselor said, OK this is us friendship and this is her. She's by herself. She's new, not really new, she moved here last year. She's like getting in the between us and then we're gone. That's what the counselor said.

—*Azra, Bosnian American, public school, low income*

Girls can spend a lot of time being confused about why other girls suddenly shut down or run away.

My bad days are when everybody's fighting and one girl or one of my friends is sad. And then for some reason they're mad at me and I don't know why. And I try to walk over to talk to 'em, but then they don't really talk to me. They just run away. That happens with one of my friends, and she'll like run away and then the thing that gets her mad is when everybody's trying to chase her, to get her to talk to me or someone else. To try to make them, like, be friends again. She'll just start running off. And then she'll say, "If you keep on chasing me, I'll tell the teacher." That's where, kinda, the drama is, too. And sometimes I tell her, "If you keep on running away you're never going to fix the problem." And she says, "I know," and she'll run off. And then sit by the dumpsters all sad, like this [*assumes a hunched and sad posture*], and then people'll start walking over by her that wasn't chasing her and she'll say, like, "Joanna got me mad," or someone got me mad. She never really tells me the problem. I think it's something little, like if she's talking to me and I didn't hear her, like I was talking with my other friends, and I didn't hear her, she'll get mad. Once that happened. She said, "You didn't talk to me, you were just ignoring me," and I said, "Well, I couldn't *hear* you, I was talking to some *other* people."

—*Joanna, white, Catholic school, middle income*

And there's a lot of sorting and shuffling of individuals, figuring out who belongs among whom.

> Mostly everyone treats each other pretty good, but there are a couple of people who have like . . . levels of coolness or popularity which I don't like but they're like [*indicating the levels with her hand*], OK, these people are up here, these people are here, these people are here, and these people are here, and there are a couple of people who are really competitive, like if we're playing soccer knockout they're like, "Yeah, I got you out," or, "Yeah, I scored a goal," you know, and I think it's fine to be like happy and cheer but don't like rub it in our face. But mostly over all, I think people treat each other pretty nice.

—Marley, *white, private school, high income*

> There's like this group of people that only play soccer during recess. And that's all the boys. Then—but some boys do like this other thing. They don't play soccer, they just talk. And then there's the girls that just play hide and go seek with me. And then there's these other groups that just jump rope. And that's pretty much it. And that's actually pretty much who we hang out with. But there is this one boy that doesn't like sports or anything. He's my friend. His name is Henry. He's in the other class. He really doesn't have any guy friends. He has only girl friends.

—Cassidy, *white, Catholic school, middle income*

METROPOLITAN

> These group of girls would be talking about you, and you'd be talking and they, and this little girl, she'd be eavesdropping and turn around what you said and she'd go back to her little group and say you said this, and you didn't say it. We try to talk, but then it leads to an argument, and then we avoid each other. And then soon the people just turn around what I said and go tell the teacher, and then I end up getting in trouble.

—Chynna, *African American, public school, middle income*

SUBURBAN

My friends, last year they came up to me one day, I was in their class, and they said, "Get away, you're annoying us, you're stalking us [laughs]," and I'm like, what? So sometimes they treat each other badly, and sometimes there's lots of fights. For the girls. But I'm not in those fights. I'm the solver, so sometimes it's a lot of fights and I get left out of stuff a lot.

—*Rosemary, white, Catholic school, middle income*

OUTER-RING SUBURBAN

School's full of your friends, and people that want to be your friends, and then there's people that want to be your friend but they don't act like they want to be your friend. People are thinking they're so cool that they are better than everyone or something so they're mean to them, and they take friends and they start a group and they don't let friends come into the group, so, yeah . . .

—*Eleanor, white, public school, middle income*

I have a friend, I'm not gonna say names, but—she is kind of on and off, and sometimes she's really happy and nice, but then sometimes she, she shows me her dark side and I don't like that. And I have a friend, again I'm not gonna have names, but this is from my old school, she would talk, we would be talking about something and then all of a sudden she would walk away, an' just, like, go away because she was unhappy about what we were talking about or something. And she always wanted everything to be perfect for her and, like, all that. And I really did not like that.

—*Susan, Jewish, public school, middle income*

I stay with one particular group. Sit with them at lunch everyday, and then two of our friends that used to be in that little group just left. Used to be a group of five but I think it's a group of four now. It used to be six. And then Shawn's gonna leave and it's gonna be three. That is a crisis. At recess, I've seen a couple of the boys go, "I wasn't out." Mostly at the teachers but then sometimes at the kids who threw the ball at them. I just sit out at dodgeball and watch other kids go, "I wasn't out," "yes, you were," "no, I wasn't," "yes, you were," "no, I wasn't." And then in the classroom mostly like passing notes and stuff. Not—not many passing notes because then Mrs. P. gets the notes and that is very embarrassing. I relearned that lesson like nine times.

Greta, white, Protestant school, middle income

Sometimes some of them are a little bossy, but they're nice most of the time. And sometimes in our lifetimes we all have friend problems. I've been having them this year. My friend Hope, this year I'm kind of figuring out she's kind of bossy. The last time me and Hope had a friend problem she went to the counselor. And it kind of took time out of both of our school days. And she's going this year. And our bonds are kinda snapping and we're just growing farther and farther apart. She's either moving to another state or moving to Korea. She moved here in second grade. She moves every three years. Her dad's in the military. He's an eye doctor, and they travel with him. I'm pretty sure my group of friends are all gonna be affected. And she's always there, talking. Yeah. She's always there. I can't remember the last time she's been absent from school.

—Marian, white, public school, fragile middle income

Marian's gravity as she recounted her history with her friend Hope and the "snapping" of their bonds was quite moving. Hunter, below, relishes the complex relationship he has with a kid he can talk things over with.

RURAL

We're kind of frienemies. Well, we can be mad at each other or we can be good friends at times. When he comes over to my house we'll kinda discuss things, talk about things like in-class assignments. Something that we think was ridiculous that some[one in] class did, like, you know, fall out of a chair for no reason.

—Hunter, white, public school, low income

In addition to the confusions and complexities, ideas about leadership only come into focus in social situations as children come to understand who's getting who to do what, or setting examples for others to follow. Many children were perfectly frank about not being leaders among their friends. Others had very specific ideas about what it means to be a leader. Children understand that they can be leaderly in one context, like school, and not so leaderly in another, like home. And vice versa.

URBAN

The leader is usually like the scariest person. Like if you don't do this thing then, I'm gonna get you in trouble or something. I don't know about last year. Because in some ways I coulda been that with those girls, like, "If you don't do this I'm gonna tell on you," but sometimes I think we just had fun. We're one of the big cliques, kind of. Like there are three cliques. There's a boy clique, and there's us girls, which are like five people, and then the rest of the girls and boys that don't really have that much friends, they kinda just join into the leftovers. Not—I am not trying to be mean like *leftovers*—but the people that don't really have a clique.

—*Brigit, white, Catholic school, middle income*

Brigit was the only student who introduced the idea of the leader as the scariest person, the person to be feared on account of their power to get you in trouble, and also the idea of the misfit, the kid who has to take social refuge among those whom she calls leftovers, so many slices of gristly roast beef on the playground. It seems rather a harsh land-scape, and a sobering reminder of why adults should never romanticize the daily life of children.

OUTER-RING SUBURB

I used to be the leader of our group and I would be walking the track and then these other girls would be walking the track and then we'd all just start joining together with them. A leader is like someone who . . . it's kinda hard because you have to point where everyone's gonna go, like, "You go over here, you go over here, you go over there," and they're like, "What, where do I go? Where do we go, where?" You have to keep repeating things.

So leaders have to repeat themselves?

Yes, a lot. Like Mrs. M. [the teacher] has to repeat herself a lot. Especially to me because I don't like to listen. I'm not a direction listener. I'm a direction follower but I'm not a direction listener so oftentimes I don't know what I'm doing.

—*Greta, white, Protestant school, middle income*

RURAL

With my friends, I'm not really a leader. There's no one that everybody's playing with, we all play with each other equally. There's not like the two groups that have like *one main person* that everybody wants to play with. That's usually the person that gets 'em into fights, but it's easier if you don't have a main person.

Does your group have a main person?

We're all equal, the three of us. It's usually better with equal people, like four people. If two are mad, they can't, just two people go against one person.

How many are in your group?

Three, but we all get along, besides Lydia, well, my friend, plays with us sometimes and she's nice, we never get in fights.

How would you describe what a leader does?

A leader makes decisions for everybody, like sometimes a leader'll tell you what to do like, the president makes decisions for the country, he makes sure everybody's safe. He like, makes *important* decisions.

—*Kaytie, white, public school, low income*

In the passage below, listen for Julian's awareness of how his identity as a leader shifts depending on where he is, who he is with, and what social role he is playing. Just like adults, children pull identities together in a social context.

I [consider myself] a leader because I'm the oldest out of four. And my little brother, he has a little bit of a speech problem because, I don't really know why, so, like whenever he says a new word that he hasn't been able to say, I get all like a mother does whenever they find out their baby just said their first word. I treat him really good, and my sister has anger problems, so whenever she gets really mad and wants to hit something, I stand where she is and she just hits me. But when it gets to where I need to do something, like when she turns around to do something, my mom doesn't really care, because I was defending myself. Not very hard, I just get her in the back of the leg and knock her down and tell her she needs to calm down. And that's usually all I do. I would describe a leader as a really nice, generous person, who doesn't care very much about himself, but cares more about his team than he does himself. At school I'm not really a leader because other kids who are a lot smarter than me, and a little more generous, like there's people who when they get stuff taken away from 'em, they don't cry, they don't throw a fit or anything, they just let the other person play with 'em, play with it for a little bit, then they ask him for it back, and whenever I get something taken away, I get a little mad and do something about it.

—*Julian, white, public school, low income*

I found a positive correlation between high reading ability and having a nuanced grasp of social patterns. Lorraine, below, happens to be a voracious independent reader, one of the few I interviewed. Like Marian, she understands the politics and social and emotional complexity of what's going on among friends. She begins by distinguishing intragroup fights from intergroup fights. The density of Lorraine's perceptions, the detail with which she describes how people are treating each other, and the general conclusions she draws about attitudes toward change strike me as downright Tolstoyan.

OUTER-RING SUBURB

At our school, the girls are never usually any problems, like if there's *this* group of friends and *this* group of friends, those two groups don't usually fight but kids get in fights with their own friends. But it's not like, usually, a huge fight. And the boys, they're a little bit more mean to each other, just like, cruel kind of, and they tease other boys. And it's kind of sad to watch them do that because they're just mean to certain people, like if this certain person does something, they'll be mean to him and if another person does it, they're not mean to him because they like that person. I guess it's just because they just don't like him because this certain boy, his name's James, he's never really had any friends because he just doesn't really get his work done and stuff, and he doesn't really have very good social skills so he doesn't know how to approach someone an' become friends with them, and so he's never really had a really good friend to lean on, so it just started, he's always been the person they could pick on because he doesn't have really anyone to support him.

A lot of people, their friends that they've been friends with throughout the whole school time, they change friends because they want to be, I guess you could say, they just wanna be with those. Like, there's this girl, Elyse, she's always been friends with these certain group of girls, and I guess she just, I mean she still likes them but I guess she just wants to be friends more with us, because a lot of people, like I guess you could say they like our people, I mean, they like everyone else, but, I guess you could say we're popular? I don't really want to say that [laughs] but . . . so she started sitting by us at lunch, she always starts talking to us now and she's changed a lot because she just wants to be friends with us so much and she used to not even care what we did, and that's just how she is now.

So is your group letting her come in? Or is she going to shift friend groups?

I don't really know, because the other girls, I'd be fine with her coming, like, I love having new friends and stuff, but they just always want these certain group of girls to sit at our table and I actually like when other people sit at our table, like, Hallie and James and Sophie. I like when other people come sit at our table because it's something different, not always the same girls.

But you're not sure if that's going to actually happen.

I don't know, because they just don't really like to change and I don't mind change.

—*Lorraine, white, Catholic school, middle income*

Reading books helps children notice and understand social complexities in their own lives. In the absence of good fiction, a child who thinks through complex social arrangements tends to have support from either friends or family. Kaytie, whom I quoted above on leadership, has a social action plan laced with if-then contingencies that result from the other person's behavior and friendship status. She concludes with the hypothetical conditions for retaliation she has co-constructed with her father: she can only defend herself if the person has said something mean to her in front of others—not in private—and if nobody else is defending her.

RURAL

If you fight with someone and they're not your friend, just don't play with 'em, go find somebody else. Like if someone's mean to you or they just all of a sudden stop playing with you and say I'm not your friend anymore . . . like there's one girl in my class, she plays with one of the girls in the big groups and the girl always does that, like, "I'm not your friend anymore" and always gets her into fights with other people.

So what's your advice for someone like that?

Everybody needs ta just stop playin' with the person that does that and they'll learn their lesson. Like my dad says, if they don't have any friends, they'll learn to be nice and they'll want friends 'cause if someone's mean to you, you can try to be nice to them but if they're not nice to you still then just ignore 'em, but just don't be to mean to 'em unless they say sumpin to you mean in front of everybody and there's no one defending you, just defend yourself but don't be mean to 'em.

—*Kaytie, white, public school, low income*

Kaytie's actions are shaped by a rule based on a precedent. She cites an adult authority to back up her stance. In her thinking and her words, there is both conceptual clarity and subtlety.

Here is Chelsea's story. It's not a bully story, or even a story of someone being mean. It's just a very weird upsetting incident, after which Chelsea goes straight to her mom, who helps her work through the postincident reconciliation.

This little girl, and her name, I'm not gonna tell her name. She saw this wrapping paper and she goes, "Oh, that wrapping paper's pretty," and then she told the color that it was and she said "gray" and I thought it was silver, so I said, "I think that's silver," and she just kinda looked at me for a minute and then slapped me across the face and I don't think I'll ever forget that. I don't know if she got mad because my opinion was that was silver, but I don't know. . . . And, school was almost over so I went down to my mom [who works in the building] and told her, and the little girl stays after school in Ms. J.'s classroom, so me and my mom went up to her and my mom talked to her and was like, "Please, don't slap my kid ever again," and then I was afraid to tell my teacher, 'cause like, I just didn't wanna get in trouble and 'cause she might have thought I was lying or something so me and my mom went to school the next day and we talked to my teacher and me and that girl went to the principal and I just had to tell the story and then I was let go and I didn't get in trouble or anything like, I just got to go back to class but the little girl, I don't know if she got a spankin' or what but . . . she got, I think she got a note home to her parents about that. She apologized and stuff and I accepted her apology and yeah sometimes we play together but not, not a bunch like, I just play with her a day at recess and then I'll wait like, two weeks and then, I mean I don't really play with her that much. I go with my friends that care about me because I feel more safe with them because I don't want her to do that again.

—*Chelsea, white, public school, fragile middle income*

What I find most interesting about the ending of this story is that Chelsea does play with this other girl every so often, just not enough to risk getting close to her again. Chelsea has figured out how to maintain a deliberate and mature distance in her play.

MEANNESS, BULLIES, AND LONERS

Going to school means facing people who can be mean to you. There is well-warranted attention on bullying right now, but it's always important to remember how insensitive even average kids can be. Learning about emotional boundaries—what can and cannot be said without hurting the feelings of someone else, what forms of expression you can and cannot tolerate from others—is an important lesson. Sensitivity is acquired through experience.

URBAN

Kids push each other and when they talk to each other, it's not what you should say to a friend. Sometimes, even if you're playin' they say, like, "You so ugly," and that's a mean personality.

—*Kiara, African American, public school, middle income*

Kids keep yellin' at me. They keep callin' me a mouse.

—*Malik, African American, public school, low income*

When someone's kinda mean or leaves me out—but it doesn't happen very often—it usually kind of sets me in a bad mood for the rest of the day. But I wanna be mean to other people because of it, it just sets me in that kind of crabby mood.

—*Faye, white, private school, high income*

OUTER-RING SUBURB

I just don't want to be around kids that are annoying. Like they're always asking me to do something like, let's say that I am just sitting around doing nothing and then a kid comes up and he goes, "Would you like to have a tea party with me? Would you like to have a tea party?" and I'm like, "No, I don't really like tea parties." And then he keeps asking me, asking asking asking and

I'd say, "Please stop." Some of 'em are really friendly, some of 'em not too nice.

—John, white, Protestant school, middle income

Where meanness and insensitivity shift into something we can call bullying is subjective. I can imagine that taunting John into a tea party, for example, might be considered an act of bullying. Other cases are absolutely clear-cut. In such cases, the life of an isolated bullied child is so hard, it seems a miracle that anyone has the strength to endure day to day.

Julian, who spoke at length about being as excited as a mother when his little brother says new words, is morbidly overweight. He wears glasses. He lives in poverty. His mother works an overnight shift. Every so often, if his mom wakes up before he leaves for school, he can give her a hug before facing the day. His biological father was physically abusive. About a child in Julian's position words are insufficient; there are only actions adults must take to protect him and nurture his power to withstand and overcome the social position he is in.

When I am outside, I don't have very many friends, and so, that time goes by a little slower.

Some days are just bad?

Yeah, like in the morning, when I don't have my clothes picked out, because I usually pick 'em out before bed, and when my [step]dad, he's a neat freak so whenever we don't clean our rooms, we get yelled at. And just pretty much when I've been yelled at the entire day.

By who?

Pretty much everyone. Pretty much anyone that doesn't like me and that's pretty much everyone. I guess the first time I met 'em I made a bad impression.

And then what makes an especially good day?

Not getting picked on on the bus, and that kind of stuff. And just completely ignoring anyone that tries to make fun of me and that's it. That's usually it. I go on the swings. I don't really like to play sports, but, if they're really mean to me, and really rude, when they're playing football and have a ball behind their back, I run behind them and knock 'em out of their hands. Only if they're mean to me. If they're nice to me, I just avoid 'em. As soon as I knock it out of their hands, I start running.

—*Julian, white, public school, low income*

There are different ways to go your own way. Being something of a loner on purpose is different, of course, from being socially isolated. In general, the boys I interviewed at the highly structured, silenced, and regulated charter schools tried to keep to themselves, mostly to keep out of trouble. Other kids had other kinds of individual boundaries. Casey was very clear about what drove her, at times, not to talk to other people; Casey was plainspoken about how people get along; her identity as a member of student council and her understanding of herself as a person who likes to help people persists alongside her acceptance of not having to get along with everyone.

RURAL

I have friends, and I have enemies like everybody. Not all the people in your life you're gonna like. I like to joke around a lot and sometimes they're really serious and they take it in the wrong way. I don't mean it like that at all, but that's just how they are, so I don't really talk to 'em. They get mad at me, so . . . [*laughs*] I'm in student council. It's really fun. You get to help out a lot. In my opinion, I like to help people! If you say it's boring you're really lazy. Like, I like to walk around and run and do stuff with people. I may not seem like it, but I do.

Do you consider yourself a leader?

Sometimes. Sometimes I, I can be really rowdy. I mean, most of the time I am, but if I take the stuff really serious, I can be, I could be a good leader, but most people think I'm probably not because of the way I act at school. A leader is somebody who will take up for you, and if you get bullied or something, somebody who's nice, somebody who . . . not necessarily gets good grades, but works, like, they actually work for their grades, and they try.

—*Casey, white, public school, low income*

In contrast to Casey, Jane's solitude in school is a consequence of a more serious passivity and lack of personal autonomy.

> A bad day is when people don't want to play with me and like maybe like I don't wanna do something but then they make me do it.
>
> —*Jane, white, public school, low income*

GENERAL IMPRESSIONS OF SOCIAL LIFE IN SCHOOL

In general, kids in school long for opportunities to talk to each other. How schools manage this longing sets kids up for learning how to manage conflict and develop compassionate friendships. The negative experiences of in-school student-to-student talk—being "distracted" by classmates, getting in trouble for talking, being bullied during recess—tended to happen in the schools most highly regulated, the schools where talking was least free. In addition to designing curriculum and instruction that make the most of the social energy upper elementary kids bring to school—small-group learning, paired discussions, collaborative projects—we ought to be paying much closer attention to developing the care and compassion children can and do exercise when we're not around watching and listening.

7

THE GOOD STUDENT

"They Get All As, Never Get Sent Out of the Classroom, Have Shirt Tucked In, Wear Appropriate School Clothes, and Be on Time"

W hat makes a good student?

A. Critical thinking
B. Compliance
C. A little of B, but mostly A
D. It depends who you are, where you're from, and what adults expect you to be when you grow up

Trick question! The answer should be C, but right now the answer is D. We tell ourselves that we want all students to be critical thinkers—innovative, good-in-a-fix, collaborative, competitive, high-achieving, problem-solving members of a global knowledge economy. We want all students to be able to pose the right questions. In a manner of speaking, we want kids to be intellectually unruly and, in a Common Core phrase, "college or career ready" by the age of eighteen.

Research since the 1920s has indicated that knowledge and understanding are constructed by the interested, engaged learner alongside more expert peers or adult guides, and we know that making room for individual and multiple voices engaging in dialogue—explaining and discussing—is necessary for learning. We know that the most important lessons are learned through failure and getting the answers wrong before we get them right. We know that a positively energetic classroom can generate fruitful collaborative learning as long as there is also room for quiet reflection, for thinking about one's own thinking. Classrooms designed for citizens of the middle and late twenty-first century should take these research-based facts into account. As I have shown, classrooms designed for the children of the social elite already do.

But the preponderance of fourth graders most often agree with Kashena, an urban charter school student quoted in this chapter's epigraph, that good students are the kind of people who are quiet, get straight As, pay attention, do all their homework, raise their hand, never shout out, have neat handwriting, set a good example, and are calm. In other words, the kind of person who never causes any adult any trouble at all, is easily managed, and does not resist the highly regulated processes of school. We should be troubled when we hear a nine-year-old today describe a good student in terms exactly like those my grandfather would have used to describe a model student in 1914. Attending to individual student identity and development means attending more openly to context. In this chapter, therefore, I will take considerably more time to connect children's words and worlds.

Christopher is a small, pale, school-loving boy in a poor rural town. Generally happy and obedient, Christopher says that one day he would like to be "a preacher or a NASCAR guy." Christopher is considered a good student. I know this because he likes being in school, takes an interest in what he is learning, and feels that what he is learning matters. Hundreds of miles from an ocean where whales swim, many thousands of miles from the nearest wild zebra, Christopher is—as I showed in chapter 4—nevertheless hooked by the idea of these creatures. And so he happily makes it his business to learn about them. Meaningful learning does not happen without student engagement.

Christopher is also called a good student in his world because he causes no trouble. He is an easily managed person. Fond as Christopher is of school, as proud of his own accomplishments and abilities as he seems—"I feel like I like I know a lot of things, and I feel like I can take a test and know everything"—Christopher positions himself on the receiving end of decisions made by his teacher. When we slow down and really listen to Christopher's words, it becomes obvious that he is a person who is always "getting to" do this or that. Christopher has come to understand that a good student is one who relishes the permission given him to engage in the process of learning, and to wind up assimilating an already-known bunch of facts: "We were supposed to realize," he said, implying his teacher's power to determine what he, Christopher, needed to realize. He also said this (emphasis added):

> Sometimes *they'll let us* find our own partners.
> Sometimes she'll write on the Smartboard, like *what we're supposed to do* today.
> *Ms. W. will tell us what we need.*
> *She just tells us to* line up.
> *If she says you can't you can't, but sometimes she lets us.*
> *She'll let us* do the math facts on the Smartboard.
> *We get to* read books.
> *You'll get to* raise yer hand for what you want to read, and *then she'll put you* into groups.

Like many of the students I interviewed, Christopher seems to be thriving; he feels that he is a successful student. In his context, he is. That said, his success—his good-studentness—is grounded in a temperamental and intellectual alignment with a climate of compliance his teacher expects and he takes for granted.

Since the dawn of compulsory schooling on a national scale, being a good student has meant being obedient, orderly, disciplined, and, above all, quiet. How else, back in the nineteenth century, could school officials, policy makers, and teachers have controlled the masses of non-English-speaking children shuttling between school and increasingly populous and ghettoized urban communities characterized by poverty, concentrations of crime, and what education reformers of that time considered the amoral anarchy of the brothels, dance halls, saloons, and streets? How else, out on the frontier, where kids only attended school when their families could spare them from farm duties, could an itinerant schoolmaster or lady teacher control a roomful of mixed-aged students of mixed abilities and extremely mixed attitudes toward book learning and figuring? The common school movement emerged out of ideas about national identity and assimilation, in practices that calmed kids down so that they could be drilled row by row to read and compute in an age of assembly-line efficiency. The early versions of today's public schools were charity schools and reformatories, places where adults tamed and managed the unruliness bred in the urban and rural spaces children occupied.

Even if we allow that there was once a time and a place for masses of children to be schooled in this way, and even if, taken singly, some of the qualities kids mentioned above are desirable at appropriate moments, the problem is with these qualities taken as a whole for everybody today. The problem is that the person who embodies all of these qualities all the time—the docile, compliant, dutiful, obedient, rule-following answer generator—is not the person celebrated in the twenty-first century as an ideal student. Moreoever, when schools continue to celebrate *exclusively* this kind of a person, and children absorb that only this kind of a person is a good student, then too many children will self-identify as "bad students," if by "bad" people continue to mean disruptive, active, loud, challenging, disobedient, and noncompliant.

Alienated and noncompliant in the system we've set up for them, children who understand themselves to be "bad students" will conform to that identity. And then what? What meaningful activities are available to a person—especially a person who is poor—whose need for engagement and history of noncompliance has rendered him unfit for school at the age of fourteen or fifteen? His gifts, capacities, and aptitudes will be applied somewhere else. Consider the fact that Robert DeNiro, Rosa Parks, Peter Jennings, Richard Pryor, and the Wright brothers never completed high school. Why are so many schools *trying* to create and sustain the conditions that a significant number of people will find insufferable?* There are times for compliance, and times

---

*A 2003 Bureau of Justice Statistics report found that the number of people who have dropped out of high school is twice as high in federal and state prison as in the general population. When surveyed, incarcerated people say the number-one reason they left school was "behavior, academic problems, or lost interest."

for resistance and questioning. Willy Loman and Walter Mitty resist in their dreams, but only in their dreams. The figures of the past we admire—and expect children to admire most—actually *were* noncompliant resisters who questioned authority: Copernicus, Galileo, Jesus, John Adams, Jane Addams, Mother Jones, Martin Luther King Jr., and on and on.

So how do we nurture just the right balance of compliance and critical thinking? And whose kids are getting praise for being what kinds of people? This is an extremely complicated pair of questions, because income level, geographic region, environment, parent education level, degree of meaningful exposure to people outside their own worlds, school culture, religious orientation, individual temperament, family engagement, and bodily health all contribute to the development of critical thinking abilities. That's a lot of factors. Which means that to begin with, we need to look for signs of critical thinking in multiple places—not only when children are at their desks writing "constructed responses" to standardized prompts. We need to pay attention to the ways kids think, speak, and act in a variety of settings, because everything they say and do reveals where they seem to be on the compliant/critical continuum at any given moment. As developing intellects, as participants in the institution of school, as social actors among peers and family, and as citizens of a larger community, kids have multiple domains for exercising personal agency and critical thought. What we say to children, what we do with children, and how we do what we do *with* them and *to* them positions them as individuals with various degrees of agency. Some schools—mostly secular private and well-resourced public—create a great deal of room for genuine critical thinking; other schools create spaces that are far more constraining physically, emotionally, and intellectually. The counterintuitive fact is that kids can be passive and compliant where you least expect it, and full of resistance and pushback where you don't.

With these ideas in mind, and with the goal of updating our ideas about what it means to be a good student, we need to listen to how kids assume an energetically critical stance or active perspective in any way, shape, or form. How does student agency play out in schools, families, social groups, and communities? I heard four main themes expressed in student talk: the sound of compliance, the sound of self, the sound of critical thinking, and the sound of collaborative critical talk.

THE SOUND OF COMPLIANCE

Wherever kids go to school, adults tell them what to do and expect them to do it. That's the rule of the schooling game. Policies can be fair or unfair, enlightened or constrained, democratic or tyrannical. In any environment, some children will comply, some kids will resist, and some kids will respond in one way or another depending on different factors. In this section I will describe the obeyers. In general, the obeyers attend schools dominated by ideas of control and human management. In addition to sharing the sound of compliance, however, I hope to illuminate indications of openings—room for critical thinking—where the seeds of student agency are audible in student talk. Given how difficult it is to transform entrenched school cultures, I believe it is crucial to see opportunities for nurturing student self-efficacy and critical thinking no matter how a school is run.

METROPOLITAN

Maria is a straight-A bilingual student. Her parents are from Mexico. They are employed in low-wage jobs. They are monolingual Spanish speakers and very involved in school. They bring a district-paid translator to all teachers' conferences in order to get a clear picture of Maria's progress. Maria's family lives in a small, tidy bungalow decorated with doilies, figurines, and other ornaments. Maria carries with her the whole family's hopes; she is, for them, a source of pride. Like Christopher out in the rural southwest, Maria is considered a good student. And what makes a good student? Maria says, "A person who doesn't get in trouble and is respectful-responsible-safe-kind-and-cooperative." She strings the adjectives together so quickly, has committed them so permanently to autospeak, that I have trouble understanding at first even though I ought to know them by heart, too; these words are printed on colorful, commercially produced placards and posted in school hallways all over Missouri.

I would agree with Maria, who agrees with the state, that good students are those things, but I am suggesting that good students *as we now say we want them to be* are also more than that, or not only that, or also break from those qualities at times. Here is Maria talking about how things generally work at school:

> At our school there's the gifted program. Yeah, they pull us out on different days. We have to do different stuff in there. Ms. O., she has centers, and if the whole class, like the majority of the class is doing it wrong she pulls us out individually.
>
> Our math tests are just all the questions, Ms. O. cuts them out and then puts what she wants us to do. We get jobs. Ms. O. made a list of all jobs and she picks sticks and we getta choose what we want.

If you listen closely to the action, you can hear that it's the adults in Maria's world who are doing most of the deciding and doing. When Maria does get to choose a classroom job, this only comes after her teacher has made the list and picked the sticks. School insiders will recognize Maria's particular use of the verb "pull." Gifted and special-education programs are spoken of as "pull-out" or "push-in" depending on whether the specialist is overseeing the student outside or inside the mainstream classroom. Of course, teachers are in charge of designing the learning environment; all good schools are good by design. But good design positions students as active learners. By contrast, kids who hear teachers routinely speaking of all this pushing in and pulling out come to think of themselves as passive objects of an educational system's management rather than active constructors of their own learning.

Listen again to how Maria replied to the questions that typically, from other students, elicited longer pauses, longer responses, or even hesitant, doubtful responses. There is an airless, catechistic rhythm to our exchange.

> *Why are you learning what you're learning in school?*
> To take the MAP test.
> *And why do you take the MAP test?*
> To see how well the teachers teach.
> *And why do children go to school?*
> To get smarter and get a job and a scholarship.
> *Who decides what you learn in school?*
> The district.
> *And who are those people?*
> The board members, I don't know them all.

As I have mentioned, I was never trying to get at what is true and what is not; I was always trying to understand what children *think* they are supposed to be like, what is happening to them from their perspective, and the connections between these ideas. If we want to transform schools, we have to begin with what students already know and believe. What Maria has picked up is exactly what the adults in her world—to whom she is keenly attuned—are telling her to pick up. To a person like Maria, the system appears doubt-free. Therefore she is doubt-free.

Hear how clearly and effectively Maria has absorbed a specific social and cultural message, as well as the proper way of responding to questions posed by adults—simply and efficiently. Maria is learning what she is learning in school in order to do well on a single, high-stakes test administered in April. The test sees how well teachers teach. What she needs to learn is decided not by her parents, not by her teacher, not even by her principal. Lots of kids named all of these people, as well as themselves, and even the president of the United States, when explaining who decides what kids need to learn. Maria knows that there are specific people called "board members" who make the decisions about what she is learning in school.

I view Maria's clarity about the location of the decision-making power in her school a hopeful sign and not uncommon among bright kids from communities of relatively low social status. It struck me that her parents, who were taking advantage of every service provided by the school, were probably playing an important role in shaping Maria's understanding of the district's decision-making power. Compliance does not necessarily entail ignorance of structure. The smart model prisoner with any intention of one day changing the rules needs to know whose rules he's following for the time being; think of all those convicts who read law.

URBAN CHARTER

Kashena's family is African American. She attends a city charter school. Although rigidly structured, the charter is run by an idealistic "turn-around principal," a Teach for America veteran. The guy runs a tight ship. The three students I interviewed at his school sat with me one by one in his office under his friendly but watchful eye. I was never invited into a classroom. Kashena said she likes school, does well in school, and was a little sad that the year was drawing to a close. I asked why she believes she is learning what she's learning in school.

So when we go to college or something we have to know the steps when we take a test.

And how does school experience compare with life outside of school?

Not that much because most of the times, you don't get to do what you wanna do. When you're in school, you have to follow instructions.

And how would you describe a good student?

They get all As, never get sent out of classroom, have shirt tucked in, wear appropriate school clothes, and be on time.

And the principal?

To keep you under control, like, because, some have accidents and stuff, and they have to have a conversation with the principal to get back on track.

Like Christopher and Maria, Kashena is also playing by the rules. Her school is a more rigid environment, however, with clear-cut roles for everyone, a place where kids are kept under control—in uniforms, on time, and on track. Kashena associates school with being *under control.* School is for knowing steps and following directions. With regard to curriculum, school is for learning how to take tests, so that when she gets to college she will know how to take tests there, too. In Kashena's mind, a good student complies with the steps she has to take in order to take tests, and test taking is what school is for.

However, as we saw in an earlier chapter, Kashena reads and writes for fun; she keeps a diary of her feelings. She has a clear sense of a future profession driven by an altruistic desire to help others. She learned about this possibility not in school, but from watching TV:

> Yes, I write about how I feel. I read fashion magazines, kids, pop stars . . . I see myself being a lawyer. I really want to be a lawyer to help people. It was this movie on Lifetime, it was a true story, and she needed help and so the lawyer volunteered without any pay. She helped her get through it so they can win and so she could be free.

A teacher interested in developing Kashena's ideas about being a lawyer—forming arguments, making a case grounded in precedent and evidence—has plenty to work with. On her own, through reading and writing and active engagement with a cultural product—a Lifetime movie—Kashena has already laid the groundwork.

Jonah, also African American, attends a different charter school. He has been retained in school, is eleven years old in the middle of fourth grade.

> *When you move around the building from place to place, how do you go?*
> Stayin' in line. She'll tell us to stop at a door, and that's it.
> *At school what are grown-ups like?*
> Teaching me. And taking me to specials. And programs. And assemblies. Cuz I have problems with reading. I don't know what the words mean. I don't know big words. Cuz every time I read, everything goes blurry. I can't . . . can't see it.
> *And what are adults at home like?*
> If you want to go on the weekend over somebody house, you can ask and they might take you over there. And grandparents give you stuff.

Tell me some things you know about the world that's outside school and outside family.

I don't know.

Like anything you know that goes on outside school.

Um. People get in cars. I don't know.

Jonah's putty-like compliance with all that adults do with him, for him, and to him, was the most obvious and depressing feature of his talk. Throughout the interview, Jonah positioned himself over and over again as the passive object of other people's actions. He gets taught things. He gets taken places. He gets given things. The most frequent declarative sentence beginning with "I" he formulates is "I don't know." Jonah could hardly respond to a question about what he knows or has noticed about the world. By his demeanor and language, I could tell that he had difficulty reading and that he is constrained and on guard in the unfamiliar situation I had put him in. Jonah seemed to me the most oppressed student I spoke with. Where, in what language, might there be a ray of hope? I went back to the transcript of our interview to look for any signs of agency, for any "I" talk that might mitigate my impression of his atrophied selfhood.

Things always get more interesting when we slow down and question what at first seems obvious. It turns out that Jonah did sometimes act with willful purpose, although not in matters of academic curriculum:

I don't have anybody to play with. Sometimes I be bored. Sometimes, in the basketball game, they be knocking you down. In football, they tackle you and the teacher said no tackling so I just stop playing. That's when I play with other people in other classes . . . I write letters to my, I got people on my dad's side that are in Decatur . . . I watch TV or play with my friend across the street. Sometimes I cook things. At my granny house, I make pancakes and bacon and eggs. And I play with my dog. And puppies . . . I want to be a soldier so I can save the community. From people that are doin', came to attack our community. People that soldiers fight.

Who are those people?

I don't know.

In recess, unwilling to continue to be knocked down and tackled, Jonah chooses to play with different kids when his classmates are breaking the rules and start tackling. When talking about home, the verbs turn positively active: he writes letters to family in Illinois. He cooks and plays. And he has a professional aspiration to be a soldier. Even though Jonah's experience in school is not doing anything to foster initiative or critical thinking, Jonah's agency and personal drive have not been entirely extinguished. We just have to look elsewhere in his life. A good teacher would be building on what Jonah is already doing—making pancakes, playing with his dogs, writing letters to his out-of-town family, expressing community loyalty—to develop his skills and abilities as a reader, a writer, a thinker. That's how to make Jonah a great student. Right now, school is doing everything possible to make Jonah no kind of student, no kind of human being at all.

OUTER-RING SUBURBAN PUBLIC

Bethany is a white, quiet, small, thin child who attends public school in a middle-income outer-ring suburb. She described an evangelical home life, telling me at one point that "some people think that we were made from monkeys." She also expressed her family's economic struggles: "I do nothing 'cause we can't afford anything . . . When I was three I did horseback riding, swimming lessons, and ballet. I couldn't do it anymore . . . I forgot how to swim so I have to take swimming lessons this year and my grandma's paying for it, 'cause we can't pay for it."

Like Jonah, Bethany spoke about her problem with recess. Unlike nearly every single child I spoke with, Bethany hates that time of day: "I don't care if we miss recess. All my friends want to do is sit on the bench and talk. I don't really wanna hurt their feelings. I just get a little afraid that they're not gonna like me anymore." Bethany's language and demeanor suggest that she feels relatively powerless in the context of her social life in school and her economic security outside of school. She is frustrated by the limitations on her experiences that result from economic hardship that is beyond her control to ameliorate. Like Jane in the previous chapter, she hasn't the nerve to risk antagonizing her friends.

On the other hand, Bethany can and does write. She writes on her own and it's her favorite subject in school. Writing gives her the opportunity to make up stories. After an oral interview, I gave Bethany a paper copy of my interview questions and said she could pick out which extra questions she wanted to reply to in writing. Bethany wrote:

> What makes me unique because my name means Warrior Princess. Stories of people who do weird things make me laugh. Some people don't believe in God, so nobody talks about him in school. I don't think there is an adult in this building that understands me. My friends affect me in school by talking to me and I don't say anything, but only I get in trouble. Some people keep being mean to others like somebody keeps saying "stop bringing blah blah blah's apple juice" because I brought it in my lunch and so did somebody else, and the guy saw it. Sometimes kids talk back to the teachers. I write in my diary my personal feelings. I also email my cousin Caroline in Boston. I play on the computer game called Kerpoof. I only get to see my two cousins one week every summer over here, because they're from Boston. I think nobody should quit school unless you need food and a job, because they [if they quit school] couldn't be smart.

In this passage we can hear Bethany's social isolation and lack of agency: no adult understands her, and she gets blamed even if it's other kids who are doing the talking. On the other hand, we can also hear a strong critical mind at work. Using the evidence of the apple juice story, she warrants her claim that some people are mean. She laughs at stories of people doing weird things. She wishes she could spend more time with the people she loves, her cousins in Boston. And she records her personal feelings. Thanks to a curriculum that makes room for writing, an independent life of the mind, and perhaps even a religious orientation that sets her up to be critical of the secular norm in school, there are opportunities for developing Bethany's well-established critical capacities.

INNER-RING SUBURBAN PRIVATE

While compliance and obedience as markers of "good student" identity are most salient among children in low- and lower-middle-income communities, I spoke with students from more solidly middle-income and well-off families who understood the meaning of "good" in similar ways. In parochial, independent, and public schools in wealthier districts, many children comply with very traditional notions of what the good student is supposed to be like. Jordan, for example, is an athletic boy who goes to private school in a leafy suburb favored by the social elite:

> I just do what I'm supposed to do and just check it over, I don't rent a tutor.
> *Do you consider yourself a leader?*
> Yes.
> *What makes a leader?*
> A leader is someone that always does the directions and they always listen and they say, "It's not time to goof around. Be quiet."

I like the idea of leaders listening, and I also like the idea of leaders telling people, at times, to knock it off and be quiet. But I am not so sure that we want kids to think that leaders always follow directions. Sometimes they do, but often they do not—at least the leaders I know and respect. The best leaders understand that if rules are wrong and directions are bad, the right thing to do is not to follow them.

Compliance takes on yet another meaning when students are complying with policies and practices that allow them to be active learners and fully realized individuals. This is the little bit of compliance, or trust, necessary for learning in less locked-down, scripted settings. The good student in a progressive school tends not to have to object to what's going on because the school has designed student agency and critical thinking into its curriculum and instruction.

URBAN PRIVATE

Marley attends an urban private school favored by the professional elite. Considered a good student, one who complies with everything

school asks of her and enjoys nearly all aspects of school, Marley nevertheless positioned herself as an evaluator, a person with enough critical
confidence to not merely describe her school experience, but to let me
know whether she thought "they" were doing a good or bad job.

> I think Grant School does a really good job mentally and
> physically because I mean the teachers, they're not really
> really strict, but they're not all "woo-hoo" [*indicating a free-
> for-all*]. I mean they stay with their plans and, one thing I
> really like is the PE program. I think it keeps us fit and it's
> also really fun. It's really one of my favorite parts of the day.
> I also like, I think they do the plays really well, 'cause I just
> had my play, my big play on yesterday, yeah, and I think it
> teaches kids to act and be in plays, not have stage fright,
> but it also teaches them to be a good audience and listen,
> so I think they do that really good.

I shared Marley's thoughts on reading in school earlier. Here they
are again in the context of agency.

> Fourth grade, they don't make you, they don't say, "All
> right, the whole class is reading this book and you have to
> finish it by this day," they let you, I mean we have to read
> for thirty minutes but that's not a problem because they
> have such good books that everyone is excited to read and
> so I feel like I have a lot of freedom when we have reading
> because I can read any book I want! I could read this book
> *and* this book and I really like that.

Marley is absolutely confident that her school is doing things just
right. Her compliance is unspoken and total. Moreover, I do not have
to search, probe, and revisit, as I did with Jonah and Bethany, to find
the germs of self-efficacy. Marley is bursting with self-efficacy, so much
so that she feels entitled to tell me, an adult, what the adults in her
school are doing well. For kids like Marley who attend schools where
teacher professionalism is valued and students are granted autonomy

within reasonable structures and systems, compliance with the ways of school is all right, at least up to a point. Marley's experience seems to be missing the exposure to other kinds of people that would nurture more compassion and humility with respect to schooling. I would argue that right now, there is a Candide-like, "best of all possible worlds" quality to her perspective. A few of her classmates and students at other private schools confirmed this hunch: the children of privilege who attend "the best" private schools would be well served by interacting with people who live in worlds beyond the enlightened classroom.

THE SOUND OF SELF

In contrast to obedience and compliance, what does a child's critical itch and personal agency sound like? The very first thing we need to listen for is the "I." The first-person pronoun tells us that there is an active self and what that self makes of itself. What is the "I" up to?

Bernardo, for example, has a powerful sense of self. Born in Mexico, he is a cheerful boy, the son of parents who immigrated for factory jobs. He attends a diverse metropolitan public school and has an imaginative, talented, energetic classroom teacher. Although he is bullied by other kids for being small and suffers the routine rounds of skill building, skill drilling, and high-stakes testing, his outlook is sunny. His intelligence, keen-eyed energy, and confidence filled the conference room where we met. Sitting down and getting his bearings, Bernardo said he had been expecting a dark studio and a bright overhead light like the interviews he has seen on TV. He was a little disappointed to find only a woman with a spiral notebook, a felt-tip pen, and an iPad. Right at the start, Bernardo tells me that his parents named him for his grandfather: "They like to name me that cuz I'm naughty like my grandpa. He yells. I yell, too. When somebody does wrong things, at my house I yell, and [smiling] he does the same." Bernardo said:

> I'm a good teacher that speaks Spanish cuz my mom needed help. Actually, I know how to teach people who speak Spanish, and my mom needed help to speak English

so I helped her. Like she didn't know how to say this food that was on there, but she saw the picture, and she say it was so delicious, and it was like this cake, it was cheesecake. I'm the one that know more in the family. That's why they always ask me the questions.

In the morning I dress, then I come to school, eat breakfast, then we go to the gym, sometimes I don't go to the gym 'cause when I finish breakfast the bell rings, then I hurry up to class, if we don't you get a tardy slip, so I hurry up, sometimes I'm always the first one. And then you put up your book bag, you get out your planner and your homework. On Friday you gotta get out your reading log, to make sure that you read.

Social studies we're learning . . . like, these papers, news, we're learning news, like stuff that happens, *Time for Kids*. It's news and you get to see what happens all around the world, and I went on that. And there's a lot of things going on around the world. Like wars, earthquakes, tornados, and where there's a lot of grass, they're called paries [prairies], and there's prairie fires. . . . There's like a billion stars out there.

Mexico, I can tell the people are a lot there, but if they're drunk, the police always go over there and look for them. And they put 'em to jail. Yeah, 'cause they usually get guns out of the pockets and start shooting people. Like in Mexico there's this guy that always wears bandanas and he gets guns and he never been caught. So that's why they have a lot of polices around, the polices are nice to me, 'cause they know me. They know me, all the polices know me. They know me 'cause I been friendly to them.

At school you get in trouble for talking. They'll like call your mom, or just write you a note, she [teacher] writes everything you say, she keeps it there [in a notebook], and when conferences are here, she shows it. I only have one right now. Most of my friends have thirty. Some say cusswords, so they get referrals, and when they push in line, and hurt somebody, they get referrals also.

A good student be respectable, responsible, safe, kind, and cooperative, and like just talk a little bit when the teacher says, and say and do all what the teacher says to do. Some people don't do it. Today we have substitute, and one of my friends just flicked that substitute. She wasn't watching but the friend told me so I went to tell, so the substitute wrote something, then when Mrs. O. comes back she's gonna read the note.

All through this excerpt, we can hear a personality, a real voice, a voice comfortable using lots of words. We can also hear how important Bernardo's English-Spanish bilinguality is to his sense of identity, autonomy, and accomplishment; he is a useful, competent member of his family. Bernardo understands good students do not talk so much—*just a little bit*—and nearly verbatim declares his school's posted adjectives (*respectable* is actually *respectful*), but he also served as whistle-blower when a classmate gave the finger to the substitute and told him about it. Like his grandpa, Bernardo speaks up to challenge what he perceives as wrong. It seems to me that children lacking the urge to resist, those who view silence as the most important mark of student quality, are telling us what *we* are suggesting to *them*: good students are quiet.

In contrast to Maria, Kashena, Jonah, Bethany, and others, students like Bernardo seem far more able and likely to identify, name, analyze, and attempt to think through problems in order to reach solutions. And since this is the process we are talking about when we talk about critical thinking, it's important to listen very closely to what these kids say and how they say it. Someone with a strong sense of self is more likely to be able to think and speak critically about a textbook, a classroom practice, a disciplinary measure, or any other real-world circumstance. Bernardo is already primed to be the kind of student we say we want to develop. It is up to his teachers, administrators, and district leaders to implement the instructional approach that will build on what he and his family have already got going.

THE SOUND OF CRITICAL THINKING

It's not always easy to listen to people who notice things. It's especially difficult when those exercising their critical capacities aim at us, at the way we do things. And it can be hardest of all, or at least most challenging, when the noticer and namer occupies a position with less power and authority than we have. But who else is exposed to our seamy underside? And another problem: we say we want critical-thinking kids, but we keep telling teachers to raise test scores. These missions are at cross-purposes. This is too bad, because teachers with time and support to elicit deep critical thinking about real-world matters would hear more from kids. The students in this section have everything they need to develop into "good students" in our twenty-first-century sense of the word.

RURAL

Hunter lives in a low-income region of the state and says he can fix just about any problem relating to computers. He reads and draws for pleasure. Hunter, who is white, spoke at length and thoughtfully about justice in school.

> A troublemaker in my class, you know he does a lot, bad. But sometimes, I'll sit there and kind of think that's not fair, he wasn't doing much bad. You know, he was just messin' with his pencil or something. That I feel sometimes, they're unfair to him, because, I don't think that some of the consequences the school issues is right. Like, he was messin' with his pencil and you know kind of tossin' it back and forth and you know he was kind of *puh-puh-puh* [*mimicking a gun-firing sound*] you know at the wall and he got ISS [in-school suspension] for that. Like with this penny he's kind of, kind of sword fightin', and like his fingers and things. And he got ISS for that which I think, you know a lunch detention is understandable, because you know, it's not very appropriate. But ISS, I think that's too far. I think it shoulda been lunch detention at the most. Five minutes of recess at the least. I

told him that I thought the consequences were kinda ridiculous. He agreed. He said he didn't a lot of times he doesn't, he says to the teacher he doesn't understand, and Mrs. P.'ll say that's an excuse. Well, [in] my head it's like we can't understand, we're in fourth grade. We can't understand everything that we do, you know? We're in elementary school. Which he talks back, too. Like, we were messing around and then, she told us to stop. Okay, I stopped. Then he talked back. So he had to go to the focus seat, which is like time-out. And then, sumpin he did. He went to the office.

Hunter grounds his ideas for policy change in moral discourse, in his own sense of right and wrong; he feels and thinks that the way things are now is not fair. Hunter manifests a critical perspective on school as a social and historical place, an institutional world where people make decisions that should not go without comment. That's what I would call critical thinking.

Less overtly critical, Nathan is a soft-spoken boy who, like Hunter, is white and attends a rural public school. Nathan drifted onto the subject of discipline and behavior management.

Since starting a couple weeks ago, if you're talking in class, you don't follow what the teacher's directions, and you really just ignore 'em or stuff, you have to go in to their room, and they get to decide what you do. They can either decide to put your head down, make you clean the classroom, make you do worksheets, or somethin' like that. Yeah, I do feel like it's fair, except for one thing, that she gets to decide if you can clean. You can clean, or you have to copy the dictionary down or something, and it's kinda harsh, a little bit. You did waste their time, so they can waste yours, but we didn't waste their time, like, *that* bad.

I think teachers gotta remember one important thing, that they're not perfect, either, and, like, every time they make mistake, they usually just say "oops" and then every time we make a mistake, we get kinda, you know, *punished* for it. I guess it's kind of the right thing to do, to punish us, because, you know, if we make a mistake, when you grow up, you know not to do whatever you did a couple years ago when ya made a mistake, so you know not to do all of that stuff.

Nathan concludes with a kind of shrug in his tone, an acceptance of the harsh justice at work in his school, teachers' absolute authority when it comes to issuing punishments, and unequal treatment under the rule of law at school. Nathan accepted this jurisprudential landscape, but I got the distinct impression that he doesn't entirely approve of it. (Recall how in chapter 2, he spoke of cameras aimed at the playground.) Most of the children I spoke with have no problem at all being corrected for their misbehaviors. If anything, they don't trust adults who will let misbehavior go. The problems they identify have most often to do with consequences being fair.

OUTER-RING SUBURBAN PUBLIC

Students who move beyond simply noticing and naming injustice or wrongdoing but also act upon what they notice are taking critical aptitude to a next level. Like Bernardo, Jennifer, who is white, feels moved to act on her perceptions:

> I am not really a bystander, like some kids like acting out in class. I just try to say "would you do that if the teacher was here." Leaders kind of respect other kids in good ways, and if someone is not respecting another kid, then they stand up for the other kid that's being bullied, I guess you could say. And they aren't really afraid and they treat teachers kindly and other kids kindly.

Teachers who want to develop the good students we are talking about now need to cultivate ideas like Jennifer's. Kind and unafraid, students show respect for peers and teachers; they step in to right wrongs. These are some of the difficult things good students do.

OUTER-RING SUBURBAN PRIVATE

Helen goes to a Protestant school about a half hour's drive from an urban center. Although she says she has "a lot more money than the people in our class," she also reports a recent fall in economic status, having to "get rid of a" maid, for example, when her parents divorced. Although she earns As, she is not a goody-goody. Like Bernardo, she is sometimes noncompliant.

> I'm kind of a troublemaker [*smiles*], but I normally don't get time on the line.
>
> I sometimes talk in class. I'm one of the more popular kids and they normally get in trouble a lot [*laughs*]. And I hang out with the people who always get in trouble, so she [the teacher] always thinks I help do it, too, but . . . like I sometimes stay in for recess. We have a couple of the good students, never get in trouble, they just sit there, raise their hand, like we have a kid in our class that raises his hand way too much, like, even if she doesn't ask a questions an' Mrs. P. gets kinda mad 'cause they always have their hand up. They have it up more than they have it down.
>
> A lot of people pass notes if they aren't good [*laughs*] 'cause they tell us to be quiet, we're being quiet if we're passing a note. She can't read our notes because we write them backwards. We write our notes backwards, and then we put 'em up against a light, you can see it shining through the other side. You just figure out how to spell it and then you write it backwards, and then you turn it and then you shine it up through the light, a lotta kids in our class figured that out. Yup. The teacher didn't figure it out yet [*laughs*].

Like many children who figure out clever adjustments to rules they want to break, Helen and her friends are technically abiding by the expectation to be quiet. Passing notes is quiet and allows for sociable communication among friends. In addition to her classmates, Helen has formed meaningful attachments to family and friends outside of school. Listen to the schedule of a child whose parents both work and do not live together. Helen is confident and secure within the web of family support she and her brother receive. My hunch is that her empathy for others and her sense of personal responsibility for helping those who need help are well nourished by her family's practices.

My parents are divorced, so when I'm at my dad's I'll have him check over my science and my math and when I'm at my mom's, I'll have her check over reading and science. My best friend's a boy. And we're always doing stuff together, we're always texting and stuff. His parents are divorced, too, so we both know what each other are goin' through. They got divorced when I was five, but I still, it still makes me sad, because my mom's getting engaged, my mom's engaged, so we switch off every week.

I spend a lot of time with my grandparents. Since my mom works till six every night, and she has to go to work at eight, so she drops me off at seven, me and my brother, with my grandparents and then they take me to school and then they pick us up and then my grandma on my dad's side drops me off, goes over to our house, and then they pick us up from school.

Some kids in our class, we have a kid with a hearing aid and no one treats him the same as the rest of us. Like, people just leave him out of stuff and so me and some of my friends try to sit by him, and let him sit by us and stuff. I don't get bullied, but some people do in our class. A lot of people do what I do. A leader is someone that people look up to and a lot of people, whatever I do, they'll do. They'll sit by me, they'll ask me what to do if they have a problem.

[In church I learn that] you aren't supposed to be mean to people, you're supposed to help 'em and if they're not feeling good, you're supposed to help 'em feel better, and if someone hurts them, you're supposed to help them get back to their full strength.

What makes Helen the kind of person I am calling a good student? She is compassionate. She is moral. She is playful. She knows what it feels like to suffer, but not too much. She is developing self-reliance out of school as she copes with newly emerging family patterns. She is resourceful and ingenious, albeit in slipping notes to friends. She leads others. She has learned in church that she is supposed to help people. In all of these settings Helen is acquiring the habits of a good student.

Like Helen, Greta attends an outer-ring Protestant school. Greta had a lot to say about her schedule.

> Break time is usually five minutes long and that's not enough time to get a drink and get your books and go to the bathroom and everything. Break time should be ten minutes. And that's not nearly as much time to get your books or, you know, go to the bathroom and get a drink and talk with your friends. Five minutes is not enough time to do all that. If that takes one minute for all of them you'd have one minute left when you get back in the class-room so, you know, change that to ten minutes. Like if you forget your books you should just be allowed to go get them. In your locker, if you forget your reading book when you're supposed to bring your reading book in, and then the teacher comes in and closes the door and says okay, ev-eryone has their reading books and I don't have my reading book I have to get two minutes on the line at recess and then go out and get my books.

It's easy to get lost in the minutiae of these various infractions, but the sequence was crystal clear to Greta, and indicates how grounded in concrete detail her critical thinking is.

Faten is the middle child in a family originally from Jordan. She attends an independent Islamic school, having transferred from pub-lic school the year before. Faten is very concerned about her school achievement; she worries she is going to be "held back" to repeat fourth grade. She worries about finals. She worries about her grades. She thinks she is not such a good student. And yet Faten is observant and verbal—she is bilingual Arabic/English. As we learned in chapter 4, she spends weekends working in her father's beauty supply shop, where he relies on her to work the cash register. At home she is expected to serve food and drinks to his friends when they come over to socialize. Faten was speaking of teachers accidentally using *bad words*, which led her to share her personal impression of some of her father's customers.

> Because in the shop, there's, you know, bad people . . . and they come in and say cusswords, and, you know, and they just grab stuff and they're rude. But my dad, he tries to tell me to control my anger, because, you know, they really haven't been taught. They yell at their kids in bad words, I mean, I was looking at 'em like, "Just give her a piece of gum!" A little girl was asking for a quarter, and then the mom's like "No," and then she started crying, and then I just gave her a quarter to go get a piece of gum, and then the mom's like, "Where'd you get that quarter?" She thought she took it from someone, but then I told the mom, "No, I got it!"

Faten is an intensely focused participant in an occupational setting. From behind the cash register she watches the goings-on in the world and responds in highly critical ways. With the gift of a natural story-teller, Faten describes what she sees, what she hears, what she thinks about what she sees and hears, and how she believes what she sees—the behavior she is observing—ought to be different. Her detailed recapitulation of this telling case, her moral stance when slipping a quarter to the customer's child, is a coordination of Faten's feelings, thoughts, and actions; all aspects of her personality are recruited when she enacts critical and moral agency in her world. Setting aside the content of her real-world story, where Faten may be misperceiving, misrepresenting, and misjudging her observations about the people in the shop, we still have to take seriously Faten's representation of her experience because such narratives indicate a lively, energetic, highly developed capacity for critical thinking and real-world agency. In the context of school, Faten's not an exemplary student; at work and in life, Faten's a good student.

METROPOLITAN

Chynna is African American. Her classmates are white, African American, Asian, and include about a half-dozen Spanish-speaking English-language learners. She's not a consistently high-achieving student academically but spoke honestly about curricular materials she found personally offensive.

> We actually get to do projects and we don't have to sit and read out of the textbook. Because a lot of the textbook is, we don't read it because it's most of the time stereotyping and lies. Yeah, so we don't have to read it. Like, in the social studies textbook, there was a page about slaves, and it said "black people," and they listed all the things that black people eat, and then on it, it had yams, chicken—I don't eat yams at all, I don't like 'em—and they have sweet potatoes and all this stuff that black people eat. We don't read it.
>
> [Another case of a stereotype in our textbook] is that all Mexican people eat tacos, nachos. My Mexican friend Rosa, she hates nachos. Tacos, nachos, chimichangas. Sterotyping is basically putting people into groups and stating facts about them. And they're not really true—about, they say *all* black people eat this, *all* Mexican people eat this. It's not true at all.

Something is going right in a classroom when a student can openly push back against a textbook on the grounds of it being untrue. Chynna's teacher has made room for Chynna and others to exercise critical thinking upon classroom materials; kids are people with the power to inform the teacher's decision whether or not to read a given text: *we don't have to read it.* In defense of her position, Chynna can cite evidence from the text itself, various statements in the book that are normative and stereotyping. This is hopeful instructional practice.

RURAL PUBLIC

Like Chynna, Ruth objects to a specific matter of curriculum and instruction. In Ruth's case, the problem is with pacing and individual progress.

> I got in trouble once because I was working ahead. I think it's really weird that we get in trouble for working ahead, though. It really doesn't make sense, cuz, if you know it, then you should just get to work it, because, like, OK, so one time, we were in the groups, like three here, one here, three here, one here, and all my group over here worked ahead, and they all had to move their clip [*a rule-infraction consequence*], and we all owed ten minutes. It was terrible.

Ruth openly critiques a practice that links progress with punishment. She does not understand why a self-identified good student should feel that being good—getting her work done steadily and moving on—is actually bad and merits punishment. But this whole topic of infractions and consequences raises even larger questions in the context of the identity of "the good student." We want children to be able to think through possibilities and alternatives to the status quo. In their world, the status quo involves a lot of rules and regulations. But kids know they are kids, and that they will make mistakes just like grown-ups do. If we want to develop higher-order thinking and critical capacity, we need to invite kids into the process of rule making. In schools where character education is most organically integrated into the whole community, teachers run democratic class meetings at the beginning of the year and all throughout the year to establish rules that seem fair to everyone. When teachers facilitate open conversation about consequences and infractions, kids show more respect for the rules. When the rules are imposed from above and seem immutable, kids can only complain or act out.

Teachers are under so much pressure to keep kids in a group, to keep the group on task, and to cover curriculum, there is simply not enough time in the day to listen to the lengthy and logical complaints of every single kid with a gripe, or to elicit the gripes of everyone so that people can exercise their critical capacities in real-world situations. On the other hand, making and taking the time for class meetings throughout the year can go a long way toward establishing and promoting a democratic culture of critical thinking and problem solving.

But even without class meetings, family members, coaches, and other adults can help children work through some of what they perceive about school from a critical stance. So much of critical thinking is a matter of exposure to the real world, where responsible adults can help guide the development of this faculty. It is possible to design opportunities—times and places—when and where productive critical talk can take place.

THE SOUND OF COLLABORATIVE CRITICAL TALK

Andrew and Toby, introduced in previous chapters, are neighbors and friends; they attend the same public school. They live in a university town in the middle of the state. They are both white; their mothers are Jewish, their fathers not. I interviewed them together, in the backyard, late on a warm spring afternoon. These two boys often finished each other's sentences, at times speaking directly to each other and leaving me entirely out of the conversation. In the role of researcher I tried to keep my responses neutral; had I been playing the role of a teacher facilitating critical thinking, however, I might have challenged the boys to think through what they were saying, to go deeper, to imagine and entertain possibilities for change.

Andrew was temperamentally reserved, Toby more animated. Where they perceived unfairness, they named it. Where they felt boredom, they described it. They described activities they liked with sincere affection. Sometimes at school they got in trouble for talking at the wrong time. They were often kept in for recess. They watched the news and knew—whether from family talk or exposure to media—about devastating despair and catastrophes around the world. They knew about housing and banking unfairness, about foreclosures, about the presidential election. Because Toby's mother works part of the year researching abroad, Toby could situate his life and privilege into a global context. Both he and

Andrew expressed empathy for one of their classmates, a boy who was just learning to read that year:

> TOBY: See he never learned to read 'cause he would go to school, and when it's reading time, he would just goof off, go to the office, and no one would have to know that he couldn't read. And so this year he's improved a lot. And he's not, he's still reading picture books but he's reading! And, I mean things at home aren't easy for him, and that's part of the reason, I think if he didn't, if he had an easier life he would do way better.

In this comment we can hear an important outcome of academic heterogeneity within a classroom. When kids bring different experiences to school, everyone learns something new. Listening closely, I suspect that his phrase "things aren't easy for him" may be borrowed from an adult. Perhaps Toby bounced his concern for this nonreading classmate to a teacher or parent, who helped Toby learn to look up and out of his immediate world when trying to understand problems. I will even venture a guess that Toby has learned to see beyond a deficit framework on account of sharing space with a student from a different background. Two times in this brief example Toby began a sentence with a negative idea about his classmate. First, he intended to say that this kid was not reading. Then he catches himself, and revises the thought to a positive statement of what this other kid can do: "he's still reading picture books, but he's reading!" Second, he begins to evaluate the quality of his classmate's home life—"I think if he didn't . . ."—and, again, catches himself mid-sentence in order to frame the experience without casting negative judgment upon the classmate's family—"if he had an easier life he would do way better."

A good student is someone who is always open to accept an alternative way of doing things, or see a better explanation or practice. This is a stance of inquiry that should, in the best of all possible worlds, apply to math problems, science experiments, story interpretations, basketball plays, and all other nonacademic settings. Andrew and Toby never took what they experienced in school as nonnegotiable. Andrew's description of their line formation drew a critique from his friend:

ANDREW: He [the teacher] tries to make it [girl-boy] but sometimes it's like girl-girl-boy-boy . . .

TOBY: I think that's kind of sexist. Kind of. Well, I mean, they're always like, "So you're not gonna talk so we'll put you by a girl." It doesn't mean you're not gonna talk to a girl. Girls are just the same.

ANDREW: Yeah. I mean, I talk to girls all the time.

Toby objects to the logic of his teacher's tactics. If the goal is to have a quiet line, then putting the kids in girl-boy order is sexist: why would the teacher believe that boys and girls would not have anything to say to one another? It is also illogical since Andrew, for one, talks to girls all the time. Although Toby and Andrew also object to the fact that the line has to be quiet, and will explain exactly how talking on line will cause you to "owe the whole recess," which will, in turn, make Toby "really fidgety in school," they have the ability to see, name, and analyze exactly how the policy sets them up to get in trouble.

An explanation of bathroom policy elicited a similarly granular critique:

ANDREW: In my class, after lunch the whole class has bathroom break, if they want it. Otherwise, you get one break before 11:20 and otherwise you owe five minutes of recess if it's after lunch.

So if you've gone after lunch but you have to go again later in the afternoon you have to have five minutes off recess.

ANDREW: You owe five minutes off recess.

And what do you think about that?

ANDREW: It sucks—

TOBY: —I know that seems crazy—

ANDREW: —it sucks because then I have to go two hours without going to the bathroom. Well, no, two hours and thirty minutes without going to the bathroom.

Like all kids I spoke with, all kids I have ever known, including the kid I was myself, Andrew and Toby were exquisitely sensitive to fairness:

TOBY: Like there's this teacher who I hate 'cause she's sexist.

ANDREW [TO TOBY]: Who?

TOBY [TO ANDREW]: Mrs. S.

ANDREW: Yeah, she is.

What do you mean?

ANDREW: She like—

TOBY: She's like, OK, let's get team captains [*mocks the teacher's false "thinking" voice*]. Hmm, it's like three girls and then boys always last.

ANDREW: Yeah.

TOBY: I just, ugh, she's unfair, too.

ANDREW: Or it's like a competition, like you have to get, you watch a video and then you have to remember the instruments that they were playing and it's always boys versus girls—

TOBY: I know. It's never, they never—

ANDREW: They never let you like—

TOBY: Some of the teachers, not all of them, they're old, like you know, back nineteen fif—no, not fifties, like sixties, seventies, like it was like girls on one side of the room, boys on one side of the room.

This kind of frustration with the power that adults have to make unfair-seeming arrangements is a part of growing up. Or, I would argue, needs to be a part of growing up. Tapping that frustration and helping kids work with it, channel it into envisioning alternatives, is something adults who work with kids in and out of school should be doing. The world is filled with people who make unfair rules and set unfair policies. Andrew and Toby seem to have just the right exposure to lousy rules and intelligent, empowered adults who have helped them voice their perceptions. With respect to their socialization, the relationship between compliance and critical thinking seems just about right. Of course, the cost of this exposure is rather high. Unlike their peers at the highly re-sourced private schools who don't have much to complain about, school-wise, Andrew and Toby don't like going to school all that much:

How do you feel when you're in school?

TOBY: Not another day, oh no.

ANDREW: Yeah, I'm like—

TOBY: And then I encourage myself, [*claps*] only one more week.

So you actually think "not another day, oh no" when you go to school in the morning—

TOBY: Yeah, I don't really like school, I mean there are things that I like in school, like my favorite subject's social studies, but—

ANDREW: Usually in school I would just count, the number of minutes until next hour, and the number of hours until the next recess, and then the number of days 'til the weekend, and then the number of months 'til school is over.

See the problem? These kids are amazing. They buckle down and work when they are interested in a subject. They read independently. They are compassionate. They respect teachers who know what they're doing. With an intellectually rich and stimulating home life, academic aptitude, and healthily developing critical powers, they are the stu-dents we want and need to remain in our public schools. But school's not so great for them. Toby alluded somewhat ruefully to his possible migration into private school for middle school and high school. It came up a second time when I posed a blanket question:

What would you guys say is the most important thing you have ever learned in or out of school?

TOBY: Hard to say, I mean . . . like not everything's gonna go my way, like you have to learn about the outside world, you can't just pretend like, if you live in North America, you're well fed, sleep good, get enough sleep, you know, have a good family, and then there are these people, in Africa let's say, and they're not getting enough food, and like in—where's that place? Where Kony is?

Oh, Central Africa, Uganda—

TOBY: —Uganda, where people are suffering from Kony and it's like, girls are being taken as sex slaves and you can't just pretend just 'cause you're not in it, you just can't pretend that there's nothing going on. Like public schools, you go to a public school for a while so you, there are maybe unwealthy people there, and then go to a private school just 'cause there are wealthy people there, like there's a poem by someone I forgot and it's like, it's "one dies, thousands cry, thousands die, none cries." Like in America, Trayvon Martin, that's a big deal, like in Africa, people aren't getting fed, that's thousands die! And barely anyone's paying attention and . . . yeah.

As with Faten's account of her father's beauty supply shop, my aim is not to unpack Toby's conflated jumble of ideas—an Ugandan warlord, public/private schools, wealthy people, and the connection between the unjust shooting of Trayvon Martin and the global response to mass starvation in Africa. It would take considerable teaching to help him sort this out soundly. The point is that Andrew and Toby regard and interpret the world with moral confidence. They know that they see things they don't approve of and they feel free to talk about those things. Boys and girls shouldn't be positioned as inimical. Controlling toilet use is barbarous. Kids with hard lives at home can have trouble reading at school. School can be boring. Andrew and Toby see injustice in the world and understand inequity. They understand that the way their school is organized is just one of many different ways kids can spend their time.

MAKING EVERYONE A GOOD STUDENT

I have focused on individual children talking about individual experiences, but never forget that no two children are the same, and we are talking about a lot of kids going to elementary and secondary school in the United States—in 2013, there were 55 million kids in a country of about 316 million people. Seventeen percent of our national community. Fifty million kids in public and charter schools. Private schools enroll 1.5 percent of the total, about 5.5 million kids. Saying we want them all to be good students is one thing; meaning it and making it happen is something else.

Bernardo, Hunter, Jennifer, Chynna, Faten, Helen, and Nathan may be less accomplished than Andrew and Toby in school, or accomplished in different ways, but they are all good students. They are the kind of students we say we want more of. So what can we observe about all of them? They are distinct individuals, but what do they have in common?

All of these kids talk a lot. They speak in active, declarative sentences. They begin sentences with the word "I." They notice things in detail; they don't pretend they do not see things. They have a sense of humor and laugh freely. They tell stories. They draw upon strong family and community support to help them make sense of what's happening in school and outside of school. They resist rules now and then, and sometimes get in trouble for it. And they can do real things, meaningful things, in the world outside of school. Toby said he was really into ornithology and can hack computers. Andrew is gifted in math and accomplished in sports. Faten knows shopkeeping. Bernardo is a competent translator for his family. At their best, and to different degrees, they show compassion for those who are different than they are. They think, speak, and act on moral and ethical matters.

Given these observations, what might we do so that all students will develop a social conscience, individual agency, and critical faculties? In the next chapter I outline specific classroom practices for teachers eager to nurture these qualities. Regardless of what kind of school our kids attend, or what kind of school we work in, what can we do to nurture good students in the twenty-first century?

Most urgently, schools need to complicate ideas about the good student. Children will come to an understanding of "good" only if adults with power change their expectations. "Good" can no longer mean only quiet, docile, submissive, compliant, obedient, and unquestioning.

Good students ask good questions, and not all questions are good questions. Teachers and administrators need to find age-appropriate ways to encourage questioning, resistance, autonomy, and critique. What "getting in trouble" means needs to be seriously assessed and reconceived. The behaviorist, carrot-and-stick incentives and disincentives must be shed from school practice. Students need to see teachers initiating inquiry. In other words, teachers need to be observed asking far more questions they don't already know the answers to.

I've been arguing for policies and practices that view students as one of a kind because that's what student-centered pedagogy is all about. But I will close this chapter with quasi-universals, because that's what human-centered education is all about. A few years ago, just for fun, I started a list of what nearly all 7.2 billion of us have in common. I knew the list would be short: all human beings raised among other human beings will acquire a mother tongue, perceive the world through her senses, see patterns in what she perceives, interpret the meaning of those patterns, and be impelled to act upon the world in some way. This is what's going on in our first years of life, and school should be one of many places where humans can continue to develop. The real thing we need to be talking about is expanding the identities and aptitudes of young people in the present—the student as flower—so that they will become problem-solving adults. If by "good" we mean innovative, self-motivated, compassionate, and collaborative, good students can come from everywhere.

8

BALANCE AND GROWTH IN SCHOOLS

"Everybody in the World Wants to Know Something"

Paolo's words in the epigraph above neatly express everything anyone needs to know about education. Everybody in the world *does* want to know something. Everybody also already knows some things already. Many things, actually. Before trying to teach anybody anything new, the most important thing teachers do is figure out what people already know and what they want to know next. The same process holds true for meaningful reform of a complex social and political system: before trying to change anything, it's a good idea to really understand what it is you are trying to change and why.

In this book I have not talked about the subjects thrown overboard in communities lacking resources—art, music, PE, computer science, foreign language, and so on—even though these activities are essential to balanced education, high academic achievement, and meaningful personal development. I have limited my topics to the purpose of school; the role of teachers; the state of curricula in our core subjects; high-stakes testing; friendship; and student identity. In each chapter, I have presented what we say we are aiming for alongside what kids express about these matters. In a way, I have tried to reconcile our educational targets with our educational outcomes as they are experienced by students today. To briefly summarize these findings:

Why do kids go to school? Collectively, adults believe that the aim of schooling is some combination of these goals: to produce people who know what we know and will be able to pass it along; to produce people to do the work that will need doing when they grow up; to develop fully realized people who can live and act in the world with meaningful purpose; and to develop people who will care enough and know enough to transform the world into a better place.

The four main reasons why most children think they go to school is to fill up their brains with knowledge; to progress to the next grade level, one after another, and on into college; to take annual achievement tests; and to be prepared for getting a job. At scale, what children believe school is for is not aligned with progressive assumptions about the purpose of schooling.

What makes a good teacher? Ideally, teachers design environments where students can construct understanding in social, active, personally meaningful ways. Teachers can help students build on the knowledge, values, customs, and language they bring to school from home and community. Intellectuals themselves, exemplary teachers create just, trusting, caring, ethical, collaborative, democratic, interactive classroom environments. Exemplary teachers model self-efficacy, intellectual and critical agency, problem solving, compassion, courage, flexibility, grit, persistence, resilience, and all the other traits we hope to cultivate in our children.

Children say that good teachers are nice, fair, and playful. Children say good teachers know what they're teaching and can explain it; and children describe teachers as disciplinarians and behavior regulators. Most students in well-resourced schools express high regard for their teachers' professional abilities. At scale, children have both intuitive and experiential appreciation for teachers' competence. The generally high regard children have for their teachers aligns with attitudes in countries like Finland, where educator preparation and ongoing professional development increases, rather than decreases, teachers's professional identities. The generally high regard children have for their teachers does not align with ideologies that have taken hold in the United States over the last fifteen years or more. With the intrusion of commercially produced curricula and testing instruments in an increasingly anti-union, pro-privatization, pro-charter-school climate, the American way has been to strip teacher identity down to that of a robotic, script-following cog in a school-as-business operation—teacher as behavior manager and curriculum transmitter.

What is reading? Literacies are social practices and ideas about reading and writing. We *do* literacy. Books are one kind of inscribed-text storage system where print appears on paper. Electronic gadgets and computers are another, where texts appear in multiple forms—tweets, posts, blogs, audiovisual collages, and so on. Graphic symbol systems express ideas in multiple genres—poetry, mathematical formulas, lab reports, social science, novels, sermons, drama, information texts, and so on. Meaningful literacy learning entails reading, writing, speaking, listening, and thinking. Education researchers and scholars of learning understand literacy in ever more expansive ways.

Children say that in school they are mostly clicking through reading levels by means of a commodified virtual program and premade quizzes. Free-reading oases are offered by teachers at times. Kids in some religious communities are reading texts in English, Arabic, and Hebrew. Some children read for personal enlightenment on subjects that interest them. A dwindling number of children read books for personal pleasure. These five ways of reading correlate with particular socioeconomic characteristics of schools and students. It is safe to claim that online, commodified reading programs predominate in public schools in less wealthy communities. Reading for enlightenment is practiced more often in more wealthy communities and independent schools, although there are exceptions in public school settings where parents are highly educated. At scale across the state, schools are misaligned with current research and knowledge about literacy.

What's math and science learning like right now? Ideally, mathematics and the natural sciences offer modes and methods of inquiry and explanation about how the world works. The best teachers engage students in learning both scientific processes and science content. Curiosity leads to questions, questions lead to evidence gathering, data analysis, and knowledge building. Knowledge leads to new questions, revised knowledge, and better explanations. All of this takes time. Numeracy and science-related understandings exist in an empirical world whose qualities can be observed and measured. Science, technology, engineering, and math are areas of practice that will help us adapt to a climatically unpredictable planet where our currently favored energy source is running out and expensive.

Children say that math is mostly for counting money and getting and doing jobs. Most children are not saying too much about science at all. Other children are thinking about animals and habitats, or reading about what other people have learned through scientific inquiry. Kids with teachers who make room for science are engaging in exploration and inquiry. Kids whose parents are scientists or whose families relish deep ties to the natural world—through hunting or farming—are accustomed to observation and inquiry as human activities. At scale, schools are misaligned with current knowledge about the purpose and processes of science and math.

What counts as assessment of learning? What writing assessment scholar Brian Huot calls an "unwarranted faith in the technology of testing" means that high-stakes testing remains a blight on the development of teachers as professionals and children as students. If I had to name one feature of schooling today that is most obstructing the improvement of educational experiences and achievement outcomes in communities of relatively less privilege, it would be high-stakes tests. The pressure of high-stakes testing ruins curriculum, morals, and morale. Test results are often used to harm communities, compromise student and teacher identity, and damage human relationships.

Many children subjected to these tests view them as essential reflections of their very selves; others understand the tests as systems that either punish or celebrate their teachers, schools, and communities. Children in communities of higher status understand the tests as institutional self-assessment, nothing too traumatic or dramatic. At scale, we have created and continue to sustain a dystopic, unjust, and shameful means of accounting for what happens in schools.

How do friends shape schooling? Children need friends. They need the support, intimacy, affection, and companionship of other people their own age. Learning how to get along with other people is one of the most important things happening at school—learning how to resolve conflicts fairly, learning how to celebrate differences among us. Teachers who spend time facilitating care, compassion, and respect in a classroom are contributing to a child's long-term well-being. In many ways, schools today are what sociologist Erving Goffman described as total institutions. Many elementary school children arrive before 7 A.M. for breakfast, and leave when they are picked up by working parents at 6 P.M. or later. Goffman wrote of the unauthorized tactics people in all-encompassing institutions develop in order to get around seemingly nonnegotiable assumptions about what they are permitted to do. He called these adjustments "the underlife" of the institution. Kris Gutiérrez adapted the concept to classrooms, calling for teachers to pay attention to both individual development as well as the collective scripted and "counterscriptual" experience of the group. At school, recess is one of the few moments in the day when many children have unscripted time together. Stripping minutes of recess from children is stripping away opportunities children have to figure out their relationships with others. Especially where high degrees of quiet, order, and control are imposed in the classroom, the blank canvas of recess offers a setting for relationships to get interesting, if troublesome.

The children who told me that other kids were primarily a source of distraction and "getting them into trouble"—people to be avoided—tended to be from low-income communities, where recess was curtailed most drastically. By contrast, children in high-income communities had complex social relationships that were taken up during recess and through group work during classtime. At scale, children figure out how to connect with each other, whether through bracketed and highly regulated time and space like recess, during formal class time, or in the underlife of the classroom. At scale, the hard, messy work of building a trusting, beneficently social community among peers is at odds with test-driven curricula and instructional design.

What makes a good student? Good students are people of any age who learn. People in the process of learning are in the process of transforming from one kind of person to another kind of person. Transforming happens through activities designed by teachers that build upon students' authentic interests, identities, and abilities and require students to be active in the construction of new knowledge and new abilities. People who are learning tend to fail along the way. Developmental psychologists tell us that children need to feel a sense of autonomy, belonging, and competence and suggest that schools should nurture a climate that will nourish these feelings. Drawing connections between home and school, scholars of learning ecologies provide evidence over and over again that, when tapped with integrity and purpose, family and community practices can bolster student achievement. No respected scholar or practitioner says that good students are always quiet, obedient, compliant rule followers and straight-A-getters who never fail.

Most children described good students as quiet, obedient, and compliant rule followers and straight-A-getters who never fail. Some good students do get straight As; many people who get straight As are not good students; many people who do not get straight As are very good students. At scale, we have to change how we think and talk about being good.

SALVAGING SCHOOLING

Scholar Michael Cole has described formal school in ancient Assyria. Dating from about 2000 B.C.E., it was a place where an adult man taught middle-class boys arranged in rows of desks how to etch cuneiform into wet clay. Novice inscribers in formal schools today scratch graphite marks on floppy white sheets made from trees. Many also tap bare fingertips on keyboards or screens. Many things have changed, but an institution that is recognizable after four thousand years is awesomely serviceable. There's a great deal that kids, families, and teachers really love about school exactly the way it is. So what do we keep, what do we scrap, and what do we transform?

John Dewey's words at the beginning of this book remain as true today as they were a century ago: parents and teachers design environments. Adults provide the conditions that stimulate thinking. Adults take a sympathetic attitude toward the activities of the learner. Adults enter into a common experience: they do things, too. A Deweyan approach to schooling aims for student growth in understanding, sensibility, and character. Dewey-inspired educators try to create a diversity of learning opportunities in order to expand the purposes, possibilities, and responses available to individual students living in association with others. For an educator who thinks this way, the essential school subject is, as Dewey suggests, life itself.

For the last thirty years, scholars have extended Dewey's ideas in order to talk about schools as communities of practice, about learning as acquiring repertoires of practice, about schools as concrete, material spaces where development happens over time and also across a social group and within individual people. Anthropologist and educator Shirley Brice Heath has said that all children deserve health, peace, empathy, imagination, and competence in a meaningful activity. An ideal school will enable children to access these qualities of life in a social setting. So how can it be that so many children still suffer school with a sigh because they believe, as Lindsay says, that all the work we make them do will one day "pay off"? The plasticity of mind, abundance of curiosity, and phenomenal energy of young humans deserve better than what we have got going on at scale—the generally held idea that even though school can be fun, it is mostly a drag that will ultimately "pay off."

I began this book with ideas about heterogeneity of temperament and community, so it should not surprise us that Robert's experience of school is completely and totally different from, say, Gabriel's or Farid's. Or that Jennifer and Yasmin are getting more out of school than Julian or Bethany. What we cannot do is pretend that we cannot do a better job at providing a formal education for people who do not have much money. As Jonathan Kozol has observed, people who sneer at bleeding-heart attempts to throw money at tough educational problems are often the very same people who are paying $430,000 to send a single child to private school from kindergarten through grade twelve. And this number—nearly half a million dollars—does not account for after-school music lessons, sports, travel, language, and other enriching life experiences a typical private-school family will provide for each one of its children.

Assuming that more equitable distributions of human and material resources across our national community are not imminent, are indeed being fought *against* here in Missouri as I write in winter 2013, there is a lower-cost way to improve the day-to-day learning experiences of most children and the teaching experiences of most teachers. Drawing upon everything I saw and heard over the year I spent interviewing children, I pulled these eight ideas directly from my data. In all communities, what the most socially, emotionally, intellectually, and critically grounded kids had in common was the fact that someone in their lives was allowing this stuff to happen.

Foster talk. Using words naturally—orally and in writing—expresses identity. Find a way to incorporate authentic talk and writing into everyday practice. Quiet talk, loud talk, monologue, dialogue, group talk. There will be times for working in silence and reflection, but there needs to be much more time where children can speak and document their ideas freely and know that what they say is valued by a sympathetic listener and reader. Make room for students and teachers to speak freely together in informal ways, student to student and student to teacher. This will allow vocabulary and content to rise in meaning and value. Much has been written about classroom meetings. Hold class meetings and take them seriously as forums for talking about civil social engagement. A civil society is one that talks and listens to itself with patience and an open mind.

Encourage storytelling, adults and children alike. Narrative performance—oral and inscribed—can happen every single day. There is nothing wrong with show-and-tell, as long as everyone's ways with words are accepted and valued. Topic-associative or topic-centered stories are just fine. Prompts and open-ended questions allow children to construct and share narratives about their lives, about what they're learning, about anything they want. Encourage peers and teachers to respond to the story with genuine interest, asking for details or more information. As school and classroom culture makes room for storytelling, the "I" will return. Listen for the active voice, the declarative forms of the verbs. Shaping life experience into narrative helps kids defog the mirror in which they see who they are.

Focus on sensory perception, close observation, and detailed description. Allow observations and thought to feed curiosity and the formation of questions. This is a transdisciplinary exercise and comes with the territory in arts and science education. Whether in science, math, language arts, social studies, or any other subject, students need to pay attention to what they notice. Center all learning in the senses of the students, and nurture their ability to see, hear, feel, taste, and smell for themselves. Help them translate curiosity into empirical observations, observations into words and images, words into questions, questions into interpretive hunches. Hunches solidify into claims, explanations, or theories that can be tested and checked against the claims of others through research or trial and error. Lo and behold, new knowledge gets made.

See the value of humor and nurture all varieties except for sarcasm and the practical joke. Humor can relax people. Humor can release tension. Humor unfixes or destabilizes power. A sense of humor is a sign of intelligence. Look for incongruities, reversals, surprises. Find out what strikes kids as funny and play with them.

Treat elementary school recess as sacrosanct. The scholarship is clear: children need unregulated, unstructured play. A half hour a day in the morning, twenty minutes after lunch. Let's stop taking recess minutes away as a consequence for disobedience, late work, anything. Kids need the freedom and free time to develop friendships. Working through social complications, confusions, and conflicts *is* curriculum.

Recruit and value the competence students have outside of school. Kids do things! Babysitting, dog walking, translating, lawn mowing, computer fixing, caring for older family members, helping parents at work. Encourage students to talk about what it is they do well that they do not or cannot do in school. Locate books, articles, and science materials that address in some way what these activities are. Build curricula out of a child's competence and prior knowledge.

Use books, magazines, maps, speakers, field trips, and the Internet to expose students to the world beyond their classroom and local community. Walls down, windows open: schools should celebrate students in community. Children need to know about geography, the environment, and human affairs across the state, national, and global landscape. Viewing themselves in relation to people from dissimilar backgrounds brings the big picture into focus and develops critical thinking. This feature is especially important for the most and least economically privileged students, who otherwise can remain sheltered from the challenges and experiences others face day to day. Meaningful exposure to wholly different worlds—in person or via human mediators or curricula—is good for people. Looking out the classroom window generates questions that can inspire and energize problem-based learning. Empathy and civic engagement may not be possible without an informed critical perspective.

Draw upon family and community. I have seen how important family members and other trusted adults can be with respect to nurturing strong, critically minded children, even those who attend repressive, mechanistic, or highly militaristic schools. Family members who are themselves highly schooled can set an example for children as active, critical minds. This is the case with Andrew and Toby. Especially in rural and inner-city communities characterized by low levels of wealth and formal education, recruiting the authority of educated adults who are familiar with cutting-edge intellectual achievement would benefit kids.

While teachers can try any of these things in classrooms and be well on the road to Deweyan transformations, education is more than school. Education includes all that we learn from families, television, video games, books, movies, music, the Internet, toys, communities, faith organizations, friends, museums, science centers, libraries, our own mistakes, and every other social or cultural expression and institution. The child who has been optimally educated will be optimally prepared to participate in our shared world, and will find life more satisfying and meaningful.

In order to create systems, policies, programs, institutions, and cultures of education that meet the needs of real people, we have to ask ourselves far better questions and attempt to answer them far more honestly. Why are we doing what we're doing? What's it for? What's the purpose of this or that instructional practice and what's its real effect? Because teaching and learning are interactional, to teach students better we have to know them better. This project was my attempt to figure out ways we might know fourth graders better for the purpose of aligning the forms, functions, and effects of schooling at the roots, which is where students and their teachers live each day.

Missouri mirrors the national stage, so I remain curious about places that do not. I would expect to find regional educational quirks in Arizona, Alaska, South Dakota, or Vermont, for example. What sorts of perceptions do kids have elsewhere that don't show up in Missouri? I hope someone will be inspired to go find out what these patterns might be. Only through deeper familiarity—hunkering in the local and continually trying to figure out what's going on and why—will we will be able to transform schools into places that respect the dignity of growing people who have so much to learn and do in the big wide world.

ACKNOWLEDGMENTS

To the 166 students who were fourth graders when we met and are sixth graders now, I thank every single one of you for gracing me with conversations that may have seemed odd or silly. This book would not exist without you; this book is you! To all your family members, teachers, and principles: thank you all for trusting me.

I thank Amelia Schoenbeck and Ellyn Horan for helping during my pilot interviews. Thanks also to Dominick Lawton, who helped Amelia assemble demographic data and school contact information.

For tremendous help with interview transcription, I thank Christy Callahan, Devon Camp, Chip Houser, MaryJo Maliekel, Roxanne Marina, Amanda Mincher, Liz Peter, Lindsay Shadwell, Ryan Smith, Kent Walker, and Amanda Wynn.

To those I have learned from, especially Mrs. Brogman, Mrs. Rabie, Mr. Calhoun, Mrs. Robb, Mme. Bleu, Mme. Leonard, Mr. Gatch, Mr. Alexander, Mr. Terban, Mr. Galinor, Prof. Griffiths, Prof. Pritchard, Prof. Gewertz, Susan Talve, Martha Stegmaier, Dan Riles, Marty Hoessle, Wendy Saul, Wolfgang Althof, Rebecca Rogers, Irving Seidman, Jane Zeni, Doug Lowney, and dozens and dozens of other teachers and friends: thank you.

To anyone who has ever learned anything from me, in or out of school—especially Aikeen Webb—thank you!

To the dedicated people of Normandy School District: although I wish I could mention everyone, I acknowledge and thank those who made room for me in one important way or another right from the start even if you didn't realize it: Terry Artis, Alice Bell, Amy Blackwell, Phillip Boyd, Kevin Crutchfield, Kristin Guile, T-Herbert Jeffrey, Tyler Jones, Carrie Launius, Joan Lee, Ty McNichols, Andrew Miller, Derrick Mitchell, De'ja Penn, Sherrill Rayford, Willie Robinson, Arlandis Sutherland, and Aleshia Vaughn. Very special ecological thanks to Terry Hurley.

I heartily thank Laura Dail for championing the animal books that paved the way for this one about human beings. To Eli Lieber: thank you for creating Dedoose and being so accessible to this happy user.

The background material in chapter 3 first appeared in a column published in the *St. Louis Beacon*, my hometown's online daily. I thank my *Beacon* editor Donna Korando for welcoming my words about education since spring 2011.

I thank Susan Salesky Rudin for teaching me the alphabet; Eve Schaenen for playing school, store, car window secretary, and vacuum cleaner with me; and my nieces, nephews, extended family and friends for freely sharing impressions of school that are always ripe food for thought.

To Michael Dee: thank you for lifelong love. To dearest Nathan Dee, Pepper Dee, and Stella Dee: you inspire me always.

I extend deep gratitude and respect to Diane Wachtell, Tara Grove, Jed Bickman, and Maury Botton at The New Press for their gracious encouragement and collective expertise. Here also I honor the career of the late André Schiffrin, who passed away the weekend I wrote these words.

Finally, I really wish Studs Terkel were around so I could thank him in person for making books that, for me, hit home.

APPENDIX A

Social and Historical Context of Missouri and Research Procedures

Situated at the confluence of the Missouri and Mississippi Rivers, the state of Missouri is in the middle of the middle of the United States. From St. Louis, it takes about five hours by car to get to the farthest reaches of the state. Of our state population of 6 million, about 4.4 million live in metropolitan St. Louis and Kansas City, situated like ears on the eastern and western edges of the state, respectively. The rest, about 1.6 million people, live in three or four smaller cities, our small towns, and our rural communities. Some of our farms sprawl in pastoral splendor over rolling hills and lush valleys. Some are vast and corporate. Some are forty acres or less and tended by farmers who have second or third jobs as mail carriers or mechanics, and require the help of extended family (including their fourth-grade children) to keep the farm productive and lucrative. Many rural Missourians are struggling. A drive through certain parts of the state, particularly in the southeast and southwest, takes you past houses in need of major repair and trailers surrounded by rusting appliances. Some of these homes fly the Confederate flag. During the Civil War, Missouri was a divided state; our rural communities, and individual families, were torn in two.

Colonized in the eighteenth century by French trappers who traded with the Osage and delivered fur out of the Ozarks into boats along the Mississippi, Missouri has absorbed waves of immigrants from its earliest days: French, English, Scots-Irish, Germans, Creoles, Italians,

Irish, Jews from central and eastern Europe, and of course formerly enslaved people of African heritage from the deeper South. Over the last several decades, Cambodians, Bosnians, Hmong, Bhutanese, Chicanos and other Latinos have come to make Missouri their home. We have prototypical suburbs, exurbs, and rural hinterlands. We are a state divided in fairly clear ways by demographic variables: cultural and ethnic background, income, religion, political affiliation, and education level and quality. Schools, neighborhoods, churches, country clubs, entertainment venues and other sites—particularly in St. Louis—tend to be associated with individual and somewhat stable social groups. Lines are drawn in Missouri, especially along perceived racial boundaries; tensions between those who maintain and those who challenge the racial lines have resulted in far-reaching consequences with respect to schooling, housing, income level, and access to social goods overall.

One of the more disturbing trends here is the relationship between state spending on higher education and spending on corrections. Between 1997 and 2012, the percentage of our revenue spent on higher education has gone down 2.6 percentage points to 9.7 percent. Allocations for corrections have gone up during those same fifteen years by 2.3 percentage points to 7.5 percent of our revenues. We are on track to be spending more on prisons than colleges in a matter of a few years. As in the country as a whole, this trend will accelerate an increasingly uneven distribution of well-being. A 2012 Robert Woods Johnson Foundation study found that higher education correlates with both health and life span, measured by deaths before the age of seventy-five. With regard to health and economic well-being, things are already not so good: data show about 22.6 percent of the state's children living in poverty. In rural parts of the state, that number is more than 25 percent. In the most impoverished rural county, 45 percent of the children under eighteen are living in poverty. Furthermore, a third of Missouri's low-income children between the ages of two and five are overweight or obese. Thirty percent of our adult population is overweight or obese.

Although we raise soy, corn, cattle, hogs, and turkeys, agriculture and mining constitute less than 2 percent of our business. Financials, education, health services, and government jobs account for most of our employment here. We still make a lot of cars, trucks, minivans, and aircraft equipment, but manufacturing has been hit hard by a decade of recession. At the other extreme, some very large profitable corporations—ten among the Fortune 500 list for 2012—are headquartered in Missouri, including Express Scripts, Emerson Electric, Peabody Energy, and Monsanto, among others. Although Anheuser-Busch remains a symbol of St. Louis and many Busch scions continue to live, learn, and work here, the business was sold a few years back to a Dutch company with international holdings. The wealthy communities of St. Louis and Kansas City are wealthy and healthy by any measure: our business leaders, doctors, lawyers, and other professionals live in luxury, belong to posh country clubs, travel the world, own multiple homes, and are generally quite philanthropic, supporting the arts, academic enrichment, social services, cultural institutions, and a host of nonprofits. Gala attendees appear in the glitterati pages of our newspapers and magazines.

Other features of our state are less sparkling. We have a thriving methamphetamine market; in 2011 alone, there were more than two thousand raids on meth labs. Although a lucrative enterprise in times of widespread economic hardship, meth addiction takes a toll. Houses used as meth labs can blow up and contaminate the environment. A dentist I know near Potosi, for example, routinely contends with patients who manifest the blackened, rotting tooth condition known as "meth mouth."

Missouri is the only state without a prescription drug–monitoring program, which makes us a hospitable environment for physicians who run freestanding pain clinics, the so-called pill mills. These are places that dispense muscle relaxers, psychotropics, stimulants, and other pharmaceuticals until law enforcement catches on and shuts them down. "If they [the addicted folks] overdose and kill themselves," the *St. Louis Post-Dispatch* reported a Missouri state senator as saying in July 2012, "it just removes them from the gene pool." This representative also happens to be a physician. People do not come to Missouri to be mollycoddled.

Before the Civil War, before the formation of tax-financed schools and compulsory schooling, Missouri made do with a hodgepodge of makeshift forms of education. Poor rural children had practically no opportunities for formal education; they worked in the salt and lead mines in the counties of the southeast. Children from families of means were sent to Canada and France, or learned from private tutors. Some teachers opened "private" schools; others teachers served as itinerant educators who lived with a family and taught on subscription a small group of students whose parents paid them in things like calves or wild honey. There were Catholic schools, dame schools, and Baptist schools for free African Americans. When state law prohibited black citizens from being instructed, Rev. John Berry Meachum, who had been born a slave in Virginia before earning enough money to buy his freedom, ferried students out to a riverboat where his work as a teacher of African Americans was protected under federal law. In 1865, teachers who had been Confederate sympathizers were barred from public schools and consequently taught off-license.

Today, high poverty in our rural areas continues to affect schooling, particularly in public schools. One principal serving in a poor rural district says the number of students in his building is steadily dropping and most of his colleagues in similar demographic regions would tell the same story. "People can't afford the gas to drive up every day to [the large town twenty-five miles away] to work minimum-wage jobs," he says. "And there's not enough low-cost housing to keep them here. They're better off saving the gas money and spending it on an apartment near where they work." One consequence of this migration is the expansion of school populations around the rims of the state's smaller cities and towns.

Missourians are rather overwhelmingly—82 percent—Christian. Thirty-nine percent of our 2008 electorate was white and Evangelical. Within the Christian community as a whole, about 45 percent are Evangelical, with the rest evenly divided between mainline Protestants and Catholics. The numbers of parochial elementary schools across the state attest to these percentages. Driving into the rural heart of the state from St. Louis, my radio tuned to NPR, there always comes the moment when my connection to public radio thins to nothing and all I can find, zipping along Interstate 70 at seventy miles per hour, are Christian broadcasts: "Only God has the strength to lift the pressure within you," a voice tells me. I zoom past a billboard that pictures the black iron gates of heaven framing a question: "**Did you defend the un-**

born?" Waking up the next morning in a large rural town, population nine thousand, I might choose among fifteen different churches, including three Baptist, one Mormon, an Evangelical, two Episcopalian, a Catholic, a Presbyterian, a Methodist, a Lutheran, a Jehovah's Witnesses, and a couple more with theologies I could not interpret from their names alone. Up in the rural northwest, Oliver told me that the most important thing he had ever learned in or out of school was "probably something to do with church." Oliver loves the stories of the Bible, and I asked him what lesson, specifically, meant the most to him, one that he felt he would carry throughout his life. "I guess," said Oliver, "John three, sixteen," citing chapter and verse, and quickly adding at a tempo so quick I could hardly follow, "For God so loved the world that he gave his one and only Son, that whoever believes in him shall not perish but have eternal life." The theologic fibers of Oliver's experience are essential to the fabric of his life of learning.

Missouri is what some political analysts call a purple state, mostly red in the country and wealthier suburbs, and mostly blue in St. Louis and Kansas City. Missouri lawmakers have trouble figuring out the politics of public school funding across wealthy and poor districts—particularly around St. Louis City and St. Louis County—in the wake of what had been a mandatory desegregation program, and is now a voluntary desegregation program. In the summer of 2013, the Missouri Supreme Court ruled that students in unaccredited districts would be allowed to enroll in other districts, and that the sending district would have to pay the tuition as well as the transportation cost to at least one of the receiving districts. As I write, the unfolding ramifications of this decision are front-page news, with the governor pledging to find and deliver the $600 million that would fully finance our state's funding formula. Educational equity is a highly vexed, politically charged, and ongoing problem in state governance.

Hunting is less vexed: with 800,000 hunters, and what the conservationists call a "positive hunter replacement ratio," namely a strong and steady supply of up-and-coming hunters, Missouri protects the rights of gun owners, who in turn conduct training and apprentice programs in what is considered a world-class hunting environment that relies upon a legally protected, well-endowed, regulated, public-supported trust. For more than a generation, a fraction of our sales tax has gone straight to the Missouri Department of Conservation. With a source of reliable funding untouchable by politicians and a million and a half acres of protected national forest, Missouri is a national leader with regard to environmental restoration and conservation.

In many ways, the distribution of rights and liberties here in Missouri is particular to Missouri. With the lowest cigarette tax in the nation, we are friendly with respect to smokers' rights. On the other hand, Missouri's political leaders do not favor any expansion of reproductive rights for women. Nor do Missourians favor regulation or oversight of places that care for very young children and very old adults. Spanking, or "paddling," is still officially legal and practiced in our public schools as long as parents consent; more than one of my participants mentioned paddling as part of a principal's job. We rank forty-eighth out of fifty states with respect to legislated support of foster care. We rank twelfth in obesity. Only 63 percent of rural Missourians have access to broadband. And in 2012 our lawmakers introduced a bill to deport undocumented immigrants and crack down on the enforcement of immigration policy.

In general, and with the exception of the hunting-enabling policies noted above, Missourians do not welcome an activist, regulating, overseeing government. Basically, Missourians do not like other people, especially people who seem like they are from someplace else, to nose into what they are up to. This temperamental aversion to the nosing-around outsider challenged my ability as a researcher to connect with school people. Luckily for this project, I know how to persist.

In addition to marking the ten-year anniversary of the 9/11 jihadist attacks, 2011 also marked the year nearly all of my participants turned ten years old. A few of the older fourth graders turned ten before the start of the school year. Those who had birthdays between August and October I asked specifically: "Does your family have any stories they tell you about your having been born right around nine-eleven?"

Another feature of interviewing in the fall of 2011 was the fact that the St. Louis Cardinals had progressed to the World Series, as they did again in 2013. Many of my late fall interviews, even those in rural communities far from St. Louis, were affected by postseason baseball. Whether students were tired from staying up watching games late into the night, or anxious because parents, watching games, were less available to help with homework, or angry because one of the celebrated players failed to visit their school as expected, or simply keyed up because their teachers were fans—baseball spiced the spirit of this study during late October.

RESEARCH PROCEDURES

I am including a description of my procedures in case anyone is interested in giving this kind of research a whirl in a different setting.

First, I turned to online data sources (dese.mo.gov; privateschool review.com; schooltree.org) to create a spreadsheet of approximately 1,700 schools with fourth grades across the state. I noted community type, geographic region, and school type (whether the school was public, independent, parochial, or charter). I then estimated the percentages of participants across these variables that would expose me to what I deemed a trustworthy nonprobability sample of the total population of our state's approximately 16,000 fourth graders. At this point, following Irving Seidman's theorizing with respect to external validity in interview studies, I relied on a combination of quota sampling, snowball sampling, and purposeful sampling to locate participants, who finally numbered 166 students, 73 boys and 93 girls, attending 35 different schools. I contacted 13 participants through my personal or professional network. The rest of the sample was derived from the sampling strategies above. Once I sought and made contact with a school on account of its region or school type and initiated the consent process, I had no control over whose parents would permit me to interview their children. For each participant I obtained signed consent from a guardian or adult family member. The semistructured interviews ran about forty-five minutes. After a year, even allowing for the individuality of children, I was no longer hearing any new themes introduced in the data.

Ethnic identity. (Figure 2) shows the relationship between the identities of the children in this study and state demographics. With the exception of the representation of the African American community, these numbers do not precisely correlate with the state's statistics over all. In order to make greater room for heterogeneous perspectives, my sample had a higher proportion of students who came from non-mainstream families with respect to cultural and ethnic identity, including students whose mother tongue was not English.

	White	African American	Other Including Latino, Asian, Jewish, Muslim, Native American, Hawaiian
State-wide	83%	11%	8.1%
Fourth Grade Subset n=166	67%	13%	19%

Figure 2

Region. Overall, half of the participants lived in places I have designated as metropolitan. This is a far lower percentage of the population than that which resides in metropolitan areas over all, and reflects a decision on my part to deliberately seek people in communities which are less frequently studied, particularly our far-flung suburbs—what some call exurbia or outer-ring suburbs—and rural towns. With this in mind, 25 percent of the 166 students I spoke with (n=41) lived in rural communities. And a small percentage, just 3 percent, lived in smaller cities or towns.

	Metropolitan	Smaller Town/Rural	Totals
State population	4.4 million (73%)	1.6 million (27%)	6 million
Fourth Grade Subset n=166	83 (50%)	82 (50%), including: Central: 21 Northeast: 9 Southeast: 30 Southwest: 17 Northwest: 5	166

Figure 3

School type. There is homogeneity across the public school system in this state. This is why I made relatively more room for the wider range of perspectives I might hear from students attending nonpublic schools, particularly the secular and charter school students. The relatively high number of participants from Islamic schools simply reflects a high degree of participation in response to my outreach.

	Public	Catholic	Protestant	Secular Independent	Charter	Jewish	Islamic
Missouri Schools with fourth Grades	67%	14%	14%	4%	1.3%	<.01%	<.01%
Fourth Grade Subset n=166	52%	16%	12%	8%	7%	<.01%	4%

Figure 4

INTERVIEWING, RECORDING, ANALYSIS

I tested my original set of questions with three students who had just completed fourth grade in the summer of 2011. Research interns sat in on these first tries, taking notes and debriefing with me afterward. I tinkered with the wording and sequence of questions, deleting some, adding others as necessary. The final version of the questions is shown in Appendix B. Gaining access to the schools, obtaining signed parental consent, and arranging the interviews took a great deal of time and persistence. Ninety percent of the interviews were conducted in schools, sometimes with a parent present—on the floor, in conference rooms, nurse's offices, hallways, windowless storage areas, empty classrooms, and libraries. The remainder took place in students' own homes with a parent nearby. Most of the interviews, 85 percent, were conducted one-on-one. For logistical reasons, the rest were group interviews. In nearly all of these I turned to students one by one and focused on the questions I felt would be most interesting. In one case, when interviewing a pair of good friends in one of their backyards, responses seemed to flow more naturally. The boys took turns, finished or supplemented each other's thoughts, and so on.

I recorded every interview with TagPad, an interview application designed for the iPad. I also took notes on a yellow legal pad. As backup, I also ran a small digital voice recorder. At the end of every interview I took a picture of the child, which I retained in order to keep faces and voices linked. As a gesture of gratitude, I always donated copies of the middle-grade novels I've written and offered to come back and talk and teach about writing if the teacher was interested. I also offered to leave or e-mail the interview questions if the teacher or principal was interested in putting this process to use. Finally, I handwrote and mailed individual thank-you notes to each child, trying to refer to an interesting insight I had gained thanks to their participation. In every way I could think of, I tried to make sure the children understood that I viewed them as consultants without whom I could not have written this book. For each student I have maintained a file containing signed consent forms, a photograph, handwritten field notes, other notes I made during analysis, any piece of writing the student happened to give me or mail me subsequently, and pages of transcribed interviews. All digital data are stored on password-protected hard drives.

I personally transcribed sixty-eight of the interviews. Reaching a point where continuing on my own in a timely fashion was no longer feasible, I developed a detailed and consistent transcribing procedure and reached out to university colleagues to build a team of transcribers to assist me with the rest. I checked each transcript against the audio version of the interview for accuracy and made corrections on the texts as needed. Drawing upon my field notes, the photographs, analytic memos, and general impressions of the interview, I composed brief descriptive paragraphs at the beginning of each transcript.

Once the transcripts were complete, I began an iterative process of content analysis and coding. To facilitate my analysis, I worked with Dedoose, an Internet-based application designed for qualitative, quantitative, and mixed-methods research. This powerful tool enabled me to drill deeply into my tremendous dataset. I was able to integrate demographic data with the concepts that emerged out of my reading and listening. In order to sharpen the focus for this book, Diane Wachtell and Tara Grove, my editors at The New Press, suggested that I identify key topics and distill student talk into a manageable format within which I might weave my interpretations. Once I had figured out my topics, I could concentrate on seeing patterns in the context of our broader national conversation about education.

APPENDIX B
Interview Questions

NOTE TO RESEARCHERS OR TEACHERS: *This semistructured process is not about eliciting and capturing empirical facts. This is about trying with an open heart and open mind to understand what children believe is going on when they come to school. In other words, there should be no probing for "right" answers. You can always say "hmm" or "got it" and move on, or follow through on a thought with "why." Try not to even say "cool" or "that's interesting" because then you are evaluating, and the encounter can shift to one where the child is trying to please you by answering in an adult-pleasing way.*

INTERVIEW INTRODUCTION

The more I know about you, the better teacher I can be for you. Your responses to these questions will help me know more about you—that's the whole idea! Please be as truthful as you can possibly be, but there is no pressure to answer anything. If you would rather not respond, or you need more time to think about an idea or question, or you need me to put the question in different words, please just say so.

OPENING QUESTION

Do you have any questions for me as we get started?

PERSONAL

Tell me about your name. Is there a story behind it? Does anyone call you anything else?

When is your birth date—month, date, year? Is there a birthday you especially remember?

What grade did you begin coming to this school? [If there is memory of a previous experience, what was that like?]

SCHOOL AND ATTITUDES

What's it like here?

Have you had a favorite subject until now?

What are your favorite subjects? What do you like about them?

What do you not like about your not favorite subjects?

How would you describe your feelings about time throughout the day: relaxed, tightly scheduled, rushed?

What kind of free time do you have at school? What do you do then?

In general, how much freedom do you feel you have in school to make decisions about what you are doing?

Do you ever feel bored at school? When?

Do you feel the work you do is mostly challenging, mostly just right, or mostly too easy?

How do you think I will figure out how well you are learning what I am teaching?

Why do you think you take standardized tests?

How do you feel about tests in general?

What are your most and least favorite times of day in school? Why?

What is your most and least favorite time of year in school? Why?

How do you feel when you are in school, most of the time? Why do you think that is?

What makes an especially bad/good day?

FOOD, PLAY, BEHAVIOR, ROLES

Tell me about what you like to eat and what you do eat for breakfast, lunch, dinner, and snacks.

What games do you play during recess?

Do you feel like the recess you get is connected to how kids behave in class? How do you feel about that?

Kids and grownups all make mistakes, and sometimes kids get in trouble at one time or another. Have you ever gotten in trouble? What happened? Did you think the consequences were fair? Have you ever been in trouble for a reason that did not feel fair?

Do you ever have ideas for consequences that you don't see in school?

How would you describe a good student? Teacher?

How would you describe a principal's job?

What do you think adults in schools need to especially remember about people who are around nine or ten years old?

HOMEWORK

How much time do you spend on homework every night, more or less?

When do you do it?

Where do you do it?

Do you get help if you need it? If so, who helps you?

Why do you think teachers assign homework?

ABSTRACT IDEAS

Why do you think you are learning what you are learning in school?

How does your school experience compare with your life outside of school?

Why do you think kids go to school?

Who do you think decides what children need to learn?

Do you think there might be other ways for kids to learn what they need to learn? What might those ways be like?

SOCIAL LIFE

Do you consider yourself a social person?

How do your friends and classmates affect your experience of school?

Can you tell me or show me the different groups you belong to—in or out of school—that mean the most to you?

Do you do things with students in other grades? Tell me . . .

How do kids treat each other here?

How do adults treat each other here?

How do adults treat kids here?

How do kids treat adults here?

Is there any bullying at school? If so, what happens?

Do you consider yourself a leader? What is a leader?

Are your in-school friends the same as your out-of-school friends?

Is there an adult at school you feel most understands you?

Is there another kid your age who does, do you feel?

Are your teachers like the adults you know at home or in your community outside of school? How? How not?

What kinds of things do you read and write outside of school—diary, e-mails, texts, tweets?

What video games, if any, do you play?

Tell me some things you know about the world outside of school and family.

[Optional: Tell me about any traveling you have done.]

LEARNING

What is your favorite place to learn new things?

Where do you learn most and best?

Do you think everyone should go to school?

What is the most important thing you have ever learned, in school or out of school?

Tell me about something that happened one day in school that you think you will never forget.

SPIRIT

What makes you feel unique (different from other people)?

What kinds of things make you laugh?

How would you describe the spirit in our classroom?

Your school?

How would you describe your spirit while in school?

[If parochial] How does the idea of God fit in with your experience of school?

ROUTINES

How do you feel on most school mornings when you first wake up?

Where do you eat breakfast? What do you usually have?

How do you get to school?

What time do you arrive in the morning?

Do you go right home? If not, what do you do?

How do you get there?

Do you participate in any organized activities outside of school?

If so, what? How often?

What, if any, chores are you expected to do?

What do you like to do in your free time?

How do you feel at the end of your school day?

How do you get ready for bed at the end of the day?

How do you feel when you go to sleep at night on school days?

What is your bedtime on school nights? What time do you wake up?

How do you get up (alarm, awakened)?

BACKGROUND

How would you describe the place where you live?

Where are you in the birth order of your family?

Who do you live with?

Do you have any pets? Tell me about them.

What is your neighborhood community like?

What do you see yourself doing when you grow up?

Who is your personal hero? It can be real or pretend.

MISCELLANEOUS

What else can you tell me so that I really understand your thoughts and feelings about school or anything else?

VERY IMPORTANT

Now that we are at the end of our interview, do you have any questions you would like to ask me?

APPENDIX C
Participant Index

All 166 students who participated in this project have informed my interpretations—everyone's words mattered. That said, this index represents only the students I've quoted by name—137 out of 166 total participants. With the understanding that I might have made different decisions with regard to representation, my three main reasons were these: first, I was mindful of space constraints; second, I tried to illustrate common perceptions without imposing on my reader too many students expressing different versions of the same thing; and third, I wanted to make room for some of the more compelling voices to be heard on multiple topics.

PUBLISHING IN THE
PUBLIC INTEREST

Thank you for reading this book published by The New Press. The New Press is a nonprofit, public interest publisher. New Press books and authors play a crucial role in sparking conversations about the key political and social issues of our day.

We hope you enjoyed this book and that you will stay in touch with The New Press. Here are a few ways to stay up to date with our books, events, and the issues we cover:

- Sign up at www.thenewpress.com/subscribe to receive updates on New Press authors and issues and to be notified about local events
- Like us on Facebook: www.facebook.com/newpressbooks
- Follow us on Twitter: www.twitter.com/thenewpress

Please consider buying New Press books for yourself; for friends and family; or to donate to schools, libraries, community centers, prison libraries, and other organizations involved with the issues our authors write about.

The New Press is a 501(c)(3) nonprofit organization. You can also support our work with a tax-deductible gift by visiting www.thenew press.com/donate.